# NO FEAR
## SHAKESPEARE™

# NO FEAR SHAKESPEARE

SHAKESPEARE SIDE-BY-SIDE PLAIN ENGLISH

# NO FEAR
## SHAKESPEARE™

# Othello

**DELUXE STUDENT EDITION**

*sparknotes

There's matter in these sighs, these
profound heaves. You must translate.
'Tis fit we understand them.

(*Hamlet, 5.1.*)

# FEAR NOT.

Have you ever found yourself looking at a Shakespeare play, then down at the footnotes, then back up at the play, and still not understanding? You know what the individual words mean, but they don't add up. SparkNotes' *No Fear Shakespeare* will help you break through all that. Put the pieces together with our easy-to-read translations. Soon you'll be reading Shakespeare's own words fearlessly— and actually enjoying it.

*No Fear Shakespeare* puts Shakespeare's language side-by-side with a facing-page translation into modern English— the kind of English people actually speak today. When Shakespeare's words make your head spin, our translation will help you sort out what's happening, who's saying what, and why.

# *spark notes

SPARKNOTES and NO FEAR SHAKESPEARE
are registered trademarks of SparkNotes LLC.

© 2003, 2019, 2020 Spark Publishing

ISBN 978-1-4114-7970-8

Distributed in Canada by Sterling Publishing Co., Inc.
c/o Canadian Manda Group, 664 Annette Street
Toronto, Ontario M6S 2C8, Canada
Distributed in the United Kingdom by GMC Distribution Services
Castle Place, 166 High Street, Lewes, East Sussex BN7 1XU, England
Distributed in Australia by NewSouth Books
University of New South Wales, Sydney, NSW 2052, Australia

For information about custom editions, special sales, and premium
and corporate purchases, please contact Sterling Special Sales at
800-805-5489 or specialsales@sterlingpublishing.com.

Manufactured in Canada

Lot #:

2  4  6  8  10  9  7  5  3  1

09/20

sterlingpublishing.com
sparknotes.com

Cover design by Elizabeth Mihaltse Lindy
Interior design by Sharon Jacobs

# CONTENTS

## PART I

### LITERATURE GUIDE

## PART II

### THE PLAY

## PART III

### STUDY GUIDE

# PART I

---

# LITERATURE
# GUIDE

**NOTES**

# CHAPTER

# 1

# CONTEXT

THE MOST INFLUENTIAL WRITER in all of English literature, William Shakespeare was born in 1564 to a successful middle-class glove-maker in Stratford-upon-Avon, England. Shakespeare attended grammar school, but his formal education proceeded no further. In 1582 he married an older woman, Anne Hathaway, and had three children with her. Around 1590 he left his family behind and traveled to London to work as an actor and playwright. Public and critical acclaim quickly followed, and Shakespeare eventually became the most popular playwright in England and part-owner of the Globe Theatre. His career bridged the reigns of Elizabeth I (ruled 1558–1603) and James I (ruled 1603–1625), and he was a favorite of both monarchs. Indeed, King James granted Shakespeare's company the greatest possible compliment by bestowing upon its members the title of "King's Men." Wealthy and renowned, Shakespeare retired to Stratford-upon-Avon and died in 1616 at the age of fifty-two. At the time of Shakespeare's death, literary luminaries such as Ben Jonson hailed his works as timeless.

Shakespeare's works were collected and printed in various editions in the century following his death, and by the early eighteenth century his reputation as the greatest poet ever to write in English was well established. The unprecedented admiration garnered by his works led to a fierce curiosity about Shakespeare's life, but the dearth of biographical information has left many details of Shakespeare's personal history shrouded in mystery. Some people have concluded from this fact and from Shakespeare's modest education that Shakespeare's plays were actually written by someone else—Francis Bacon and the Earl of Oxford are the two most popular candidates—but the support for this claim is overwhelmingly circumstantial, and the theory is not taken seriously by many scholars.

In the absence of credible evidence to the contrary, Shakespeare must be viewed as the author of the thirty-seven plays and 154 sonnets that bear his name. The legacy of this body of work is immense. A number of Shakespeare's plays seem to have transcended even the category of brilliance, becoming so influential as to affect profoundly the course of Western literature and culture ever since.

*Othello* was first performed by the King's Men at the court of King James I on November 1, 1604. Written during Shakespeare's great tragic period, which also included the composition of *Hamlet* (1600), *King Lear* (1604–1605), *Macbeth* (1606), and *Antony and Cleopatra* (1606–1607), *Othello* is set against the backdrop of the wars between Venice and Turkey that raged in the latter part of the sixteenth century. Cyprus, which is the setting for most of the action, was a Venetian outpost attacked by the Turks in 1570 and conquered the following year. Shakespeare's information on the Venetian-Turkish conflict probably derives from *The History of the Turks* by Richard Knolles, which was published in England in the autumn of 1603. The story of *Othello* is also derived from another source—an Italian prose tale written in 1565 by Giovanni Battista Giraldi Cinzio (usually referred to as Cinthio). The original story contains the bare bones of Shakespeare's plot: A Moorish general is deceived by his ensign into believing that his wife has been unfaithful. To Cinthio's story Shakespeare added supporting characters, such as the rich young dupe Roderigo and the outraged and grief-stricken Brabanzio, Desdemona's father. Shakespeare compressed the action into the space of a few days and set it against the backdrop of military conflict. And, most memorably, he turned the ensign, a minor villain, into the archvillain Iago.

The question of Othello's exact race is open to some debate. The word "Moor" now refers to the Islamic Arabic inhabitants of North Africa who conquered Spain in the eighth century, but the term was used rather broadly in the period and was sometimes applied to Africans from other regions. George Abbott, for example, in his *Brief Description of the Whole World* of 1599, made distinctions between "blackish Moors" and "black Negroes"; a 1600 translation of John Leo's *History and Description of Africa* distinguishes "white or tawny Moors" of the Mediterranean coast of Africa from the "Negroes or black Moors" of the south. Othello's darkness or blackness is alluded to many times in the play, but Shakespeare and other Elizabethans frequently described brunette or darker than average Europeans as black. The opposition of black and white imagery that runs throughout *Othello* is certainly a marker of difference between Othello and his European peers, but the difference is never quite so racially specific as a modern reader might imagine it to be. While Moorish characters abound on the Elizabethan and Jacobean stage, none are given so major or heroic a role as Othello. Perhaps the most vividly stereotypical black character of the period is Aaron, the villain of Shakespeare's early play *Titus Andronicus*. The antithesis of Othello, Aaron is lecherous, cunning, and vicious; his final words are: "If one good deed in all my life I did / I do repent it to my very soul" (*Titus Andronicus*, 5.3.). Othello, by contrast, is a noble figure of great authority, respected and admired by the duke and Senate of Venice as well as by those who serve him, such as Cassio, Montano, and Lodovico. Only Iago voices an explicitly stereotypical view of Othello, depicting him from the beginning as an animalistic, barbarous, and foolish outsider.

**NOTES**

# 2

## PLOT OVERVIEW

OTHELLO BEGINS ON A STREET IN VENICE, in the midst of an argument between Roderigo, a rich man, and Iago. Roderigo has been paying Iago to help him in his suit to win the hand of Desdemona. But Roderigo has just learned that Desdemona has married Othello, a general whom Iago grudgingly serves as ensign. Iago says he hates Othello, who recently passed him over for the position of lieutenant in favor of the inexperienced soldier Michael Cassio.

Unseen, Iago and Roderigo cry out to Brabanzio that his daughter Desdemona has been stolen by and married to Othello, the Moor. Brabanzio finds that his daughter is indeed missing, and he gathers some officers to find Othello. Not wanting his hatred of Othello to become known, Iago leaves Roderigo and hurries back to Othello before Brabanzio sees him. At Othello's lodgings, Cassio arrives with an urgent message from the duke: Othello's help is needed in the matter of the imminent Turkish invasion of Cyprus. Not long afterward, Brabanzio arrives with Roderigo and others, and accuses Othello of stealing his daughter by witchcraft. When he finds out that Othello is on his way to speak with the duke, Brabanzio decides to go along and accuse Othello before the assembled Senate.

Brabanzio's plan backfires. The duke and the Senate are very sympathetic toward Othello. Given a chance to speak for himself, Othello explains that he wooed and won Desdemona not by witchcraft but with stories of his adventures in travel and war. The duke finds Othello's explanation convincing, and Desdemona herself enters at this point to defend her choice in marriage and to announce to her father that her allegiance is now to her husband. Brabanzio is frustrated, but acquiesces and allows the Senate meeting to resume. The duke says that Othello must go to Cyprus to aid in the defense against the Turks, who are headed for the island. Desdemona insists that she accompany her husband on his trip, and preparations are made for them to depart that night.

In Cyprus the following day, two gentlemen stand on the shore with Montano, the governor of Cyprus. A third gentleman arrives and reports that the Turkish fleet has been wrecked in a storm at sea. Cassio, whose ship did not suffer the same fate, arrives soon after, followed by a second ship carrying Iago, Roderigo, Desdemona, and Emilia, Iago's wife. Once they have landed, Othello's ship is sighted, and the group goes to the harbor. As they wait for Othello, Cassio greets Desdemona by clasping her hand. Watching them, Iago tells the audience that he will use "as little a web as this" handholding to ensnare Cassio (2.1.).

Othello arrives, greets his wife, and announces that there will be reveling that evening to celebrate Cyprus's victory over the Turks. Once everyone has left, Roderigo complains to Iago that he has no chance of breaking up Othello's marriage. Iago assures Roderigo that as soon as Desdemona's "blood is made dull with the act of sport," she will lose interest in Othello and seek sexual satisfaction elsewhere (2.1.). However, Iago warns that "elsewhere" will likely be with Cassio. Iago counsels Roderigo that he should cast Cassio into disgrace by starting a fight with Cassio at the evening's revels. In a soliloquy, Iago explains to the audience that eliminating Cassio is the first crucial step in his plan to ruin Othello. That night, Iago gets Cassio drunk and then sends Roderigo to start a fight with him. Apparently provoked by Roderigo, Cassio chases Roderigo across the stage. Governor Montano attempts to hold Cassio down, and Cassio stabs him. Iago sends Roderigo to raise an alarm in the town.

The alarm is rung, and Othello, who had left earlier with plans to consummate his marriage, soon arrives to still the commotion. When Othello demands to know who began the fight, Iago feigns reluctance to implicate his "friend" Cassio, but he ultimately tells the whole story. Othello then strips Cassio of his rank of lieutenant. Cassio is extremely upset, and he laments to Iago, once everyone else has gone, that his reputation has been ruined forever. Iago assures Cassio that he can get back into Othello's good graces by using Desdemona as an intermediary. In a soliloquy, Iago tells us that he will frame Cassio and Desdemona as lovers to make Othello jealous.

In an attempt at reconciliation, Cassio sends some musicians to play beneath Othello's window. Othello, however, sends his clown to tell the musicians to go away. Hoping to arrange a meeting with Desdemona, Cassio asks the clown, a peasant who serves Othello, to send Emilia to him. After the clown departs, Iago passes by and tells Cassio that he will get Othello out of the way so that Cassio can speak privately with Desdemona. Othello, Iago, and a gentleman go to examine some of the town's fortifications.

Desdemona is quite sympathetic to Cassio's request and promises that she will do everything she can to make Othello forgive his former lieutenant. As Cassio is about to leave, Othello and Iago return. Feeling uneasy, Cassio leaves without talking to Othello. Othello inquires whether it was Cassio who just parted from his wife, and Iago, beginning to kindle Othello's fire of jealousy, replies, "No, sure, I cannot think it, / That he would steal away so guilty-like, / Seeing you coming" (3.3.).

Othello becomes upset and moody, and Iago furthers his goal of removing both Cassio and Othello by suggesting that Cassio and Desdemona are involved in an affair. Desdemona's entreaties to Othello to reinstate Cassio as lieutenant add to Othello's almost immediate conviction that his wife has been unfaithful. After Othello's conversation with Iago, Desdemona comes to call Othello to supper and finds him feeling unwell. She offers him her handkerchief to wrap around his head, but he finds it to be "too little" and lets it drop to the floor (3.3.). Desdemona and Othello go to dinner, and Emilia picks up the handkerchief, mentioning to the audience that Iago has always wanted her to steal it for him.

Iago is ecstatic when Emilia gives him the handkerchief, which he plants in Cassio's room as "evidence" of his affair with Desdemona. When Othello demands "ocular proof" (3.3.) that his wife is unfaithful, Iago says that he has seen Cassio "wipe his beard" (3.3.) with Desdemona's handkerchief—the first gift Othello ever gave her. Othello vows to take vengeance on his wife and Cassio, and Iago vows that he will help him. When Othello sees Desdemona later that evening, he demands that she give him the handkerchief, but she tells him that she does not have it with her and attempts to change the subject by pressing Othello to reinstate Cassio as a lieutenant. This drives Othello into a further rage, and he storms out. Later, Cassio comes onstage, wondering about the handkerchief he has just found in his chamber. He is greeted by Bianca, a prostitute, whom he asks to take the handkerchief and copy its embroidery for him.

Through Iago's machinations, Othello becomes so consumed by jealousy that he falls into a trance and has a fit of epilepsy. As he writhes on the ground, Cassio comes by, and Iago tells him to come back in a few minutes to talk. Once Othello recovers, Iago tells him about the meeting he has planned with Cassio. He instructs Othello to hide nearby and watch as Iago extracts from Cassio the story of his affair with Desdemona. While Othello stands out of earshot, Iago pumps Cassio for information about Bianca, causing Cassio to laugh and confirm Othello's suspicions. Bianca herself then enters with Desdemona's handkerchief, reprimanding Cassio for making her copy the embroidery of a love token given to him by another woman. When Desdemona enters with Lodovico and Lodovico subsequently gives Othello a letter from Venice calling him home and installing Cassio as his replacement, Othello goes over the edge, striking Desdemona and then storming out.

That night, Othello accuses Desdemona of being a whore. He ignores her protestations, seconded by Emilia, that she is innocent. Iago assures Desdemona that Othello is simply upset about matters of state. Later that night, however, Othello ominously tells Desdemona to wait for him in bed and to send Emilia away. Meanwhile, Iago assures the still-complaining Roderigo that everything is going as planned: In order to prevent Desdemona and Othello from leaving, Roderigo must kill Cassio. Then he will have a clear avenue to his love.

Iago instructs Roderigo to ambush Cassio, but Roderigo misses his mark and Cassio wounds him instead. Iago wounds Cassio and runs away. When Othello hears Cassio's cry, he assumes that Iago has killed Cassio as he said he would. Lodovico and Graziano enter to see what all the commotion is about. Iago enters shortly thereafter and flies into a pretend rage as he "discovers" Cassio's assailant, Roderigo, whom he murders. Cassio is taken to have his wound dressed.

Meanwhile, Othello stands over his sleeping wife in their bedchamber, preparing to kill her. Desdemona wakes up and attempts to plead with Othello. She asserts her innocence, but Othello smothers her. Emilia enters with the news that Roderigo is dead. Othello asks if Cassio is dead, too, and is mortified when Emilia says he is not. After crying out that she has been murdered, Desdemona changes her story before she dies, claiming that she has committed suicide. Emilia asks Othello what happened, and Othello tells her that he has killed Desdemona for her infidelity, which Iago brought to his attention.

Montano, Graziano, and Iago come into the room. Iago attempts to silence Emilia, who realizes what he has done. At first, Othello insists that Iago has told the truth, citing the handkerchief as evidence. Once Emilia tells him how she found the handkerchief and gave it to Iago, Othello is crushed and begins to weep. He tries to kill Iago but is disarmed. Iago kills Emilia and flees, but he is caught by Lodovico and Montano, who return holding Iago captive. They also bring Cassio, who is now in a chair because of his wound. Othello wounds Iago and is disarmed. Lodovico tells Othello that he must come with them back to Venice to be tried. Othello makes a speech about how he would like to be remembered, then kills himself with a sword he had hidden on his person. The play closes with a speech by Lodovico. He gives Othello's house and goods to Graziano and orders that Iago be executed.

**NOTES**

# 3

# IN-DEPTH REVIEW OF CHARACTERS

## OTHELLO

The play's protagonist and hero. A Christian Moor and a general of the armies of Venice, Othello is an eloquent and physically powerful figure, respected by all those around him. In spite of his elevated status, he is nevertheless easy prey to insecurities because of his age, his life as a soldier, and his race. He possesses a "free and open nature," which his ensign Iago uses to twist his love for his wife, Desdemona, into a powerful and destructive jealousy (1.3.).

## DESDEMONA

The daughter of the Venetian senator Brabanzio. Desdemona and Othello are secretly married before the play begins. While in many ways stereotypically pure and meek, Desdemona is also determined and self-possessed. She is equally capable of defending her marriage, jesting bawdily with Iago, and responding with dignity to Othello's incomprehensible jealousy.

## IAGO

Othello's ensign (a job also known as an ancient or a standard-bearer), and the villain of the play. Iago is twenty-eight years old. While his ostensible reason for desiring Othello's demise is that he has been passed over for promotion to lieutenant, Iago's motivations are never very clearly expressed and seem to originate in an obsessive, almost visceral delight in manipulation and destruction.

### MICHAEL CASSIO

Othello's lieutenant. Cassio is a young and inexperienced soldier, whose high position is much resented by Iago. Truly devoted to Othello, Cassio is extremely ashamed after being implicated in a drunken brawl on Cyprus and being demoted from his rank as lieutenant.

Iago uses Cassio's youth, good looks, and friendship with Desdemona to play on Othello's insecurities about Desdemona's fidelity.

### EMILIA

Iago's wife and Desdemona's attendant. A cynical, worldly woman, Emilia is deeply attached to her mistress and distrustful of her mistress's husband.

### RODERIGO

A jealous suitor of Desdemona. Young, rich, and foolish, Roderigo is convinced that if he gives Iago all his money, Iago will help him win Desdemona's hand. Repeatedly frustrated as Othello marries Desdemona and then takes her to Cyprus, Roderigo is ultimately desperate enough to agree to help Iago kill Cassio after Iago points out that Cassio is another potential rival for Desdemona's affections.

### BIANCA

A courtesan, or prostitute, in Cyprus. Bianca's favorite customer is Cassio, who teases her with promises of marriage.

### BRABANZIO

Desdemona's father, a somewhat blustering and self-important Venetian senator. As a friend of Othello, Brabanzio feels betrayed when the general marries his daughter in secret.

### DUKE OF VENICE

The official authority in Venice, the duke has great respect for Othello as a public servant and military officer. His primary role in the play is to reconcile Othello and Brabanzio in Act 1, scene 3, and then to send Othello to Cyprus.

## MONTANO

The governor of Cyprus before Othello. We see him first in Act 2, as he recounts the status of the war and awaits the Venetian ships.

## LODOVICO

One of Brabanzio's kinsmen, Lodovico acts as a messenger from Venice to Cyprus. He arrives in Cyprus in Act 4 with letters stating that Othello has been replaced by Cassio as governor.

## GRAZIANO

Brabanzio's kinsman, who accompanies Lodovico to Cyprus. Amid the chaos of the final scene, Graziano mentions that Desdemona's father has died.

## CLOWN

Othello's servant. Although the clown appears only in two short scenes, his appearances reflect and distort the action and words of the main plots: His puns on the word "lie" in Act 3, scene 4, for example, foreshadow Othello's confusion as to the two meanings of that word in Act 4, scene 1.

# 4

# ANALYSIS OF MAJOR CHARACTERS

## OTHELLO

Beginning with the opening lines of the play, Othello remains at a distance from much of the action that concerns and affects him. Roderigo and Iago refer ambiguously to a "he" or "him" for much of the first scene. When they begin to specify whom they are talking about, especially once they stand beneath Brabanzio's window, they do so with racial epithets, not names. These include "the Moor" (1.1.), "the Thick-lips" (1.1.), "an old black ram" (1.1.), and "a Barbary horse" (1.1.). Although Othello appears at the beginning of the second scene, we do not hear his name until well into Act 1, scene 3. Later, Othello's will be the last of the three ships to arrive at Cyprus in Act 2, scene 1; Othello will stand apart while Cassio and Iago supposedly discuss Desdemona in Act 4, scene 1; and Othello will assume that Cassio is dead without being present when the fight takes place in Act 5, scene 1. Othello's status as an outsider may be the reason he is such easy prey for Iago.

Although Othello is a cultural and racial outsider in Venice, his skill as a soldier and leader is nevertheless valuable and necessary to the state, and he is an integral part of Venetian civic society. He is in great demand by the duke and the Senate, as evidenced by Cassio's comment that the Senate "sent about three several guests" to look for Othello (1.2.). The Venetian government trusts Othello enough to put him in full martial and political command of Cyprus; indeed, in his dying speech, Othello reminds the Venetians of the "service" he has performed for their state (5.2.).

Those who consider Othello their social and civic peer, such as Desdemona and Brabanzio, nevertheless seem drawn to him because of his exotic qualities. Othello admits as much when he tells the duke about his friendship with Brabanzio. He says, "[Desdemona's] father loved me, oft invited me, / Still questioned me the story of my life / From year to year" (1.3.). Othello is also able to captivate his peers with his speech. The duke's reply to Othello's speech about how he wooed Desdemona with his tales of adventure is: "I think this tale would win my daughter too" (1.3.).

Othello sometimes makes a point of presenting himself as an outsider, whether because he recognizes his exotic appeal or because he is self-conscious of and defensive about his difference from other Venetians. For example, in spite of his obvious eloquence in Act 1, scene 3, he protests, "Rude am I in my speech, / And little blessed with the soft phrase of peace" (1.3.). While Othello is never rude in his speech, his eloquence does suffer as he is put under increasing strain by Iago's plots. In the final moments of the play, Othello regains his composure and, once again, seduces both his onstage and offstage audiences with his words. The speech that precedes his suicide is a tale that could woo almost anyone. It is the tension between Othello's victimization at the hands of a foreign culture and his own willingness to torment himself that makes him a tragic figure, rather than simply Iago's ridiculous puppet.

## IAGO

Possibly the most heinous villain in all of Shakespeare's plays, Iago is fascinating for his most terrible characteristic: his utter lack of convincing motivation for his actions. In the first scene, he claims to be angry at Othello for having passed him over for the position of lieutenant (1.1.). At the end of Act 1, scene 3, Iago says he thinks Othello may have slept with his wife, Emilia: "It is thought abroad that 'twixt my sheets / He's done my office" (1.3.). Iago mentions this suspicion again at the end of Act 2, scene 1, explaining that he lusts after Desdemona because he wants to get even with Othello "wife for wife" (2.1.). None of these claims seems to adequately explain Iago's deep hatred of Othello, and Iago's lack of motivation—or his inability or unwillingness to express his true motivation—makes his actions all the more terrifying. He is willing to take revenge on anyone—Othello, Desdemona, Cassio, Roderigo, even Emilia—at the slightest provocation and enjoys the pain and damage he causes.

Iago is often funny, especially in his scenes with the foolish Roderigo, which serve as a showcase of Iago's manipulative abilities. He seems almost to wink at the audience as he revels in his own skill. As entertained spectators, we find ourselves on Iago's side when he is with Roderigo, but the interactions between the two also reveal a streak of cowardice in Iago—a cowardice that becomes manifest in the final scene, when Iago kills his own wife (5.2.).

Iago's murder of Emilia might also stem from the general hatred of women that he displays. Some readers have suggested that Iago's true, underlying motive for persecuting Othello is his homosexual love for the general. He certainly seems to take great pleasure in preventing Othello from enjoying marital happiness, and he expresses his love for Othello frequently and effusively.

Iago's talent for understanding and manipulating the desires of those around him makes him both a powerful and a compelling figure. Iago is able to take the handkerchief from Emilia and know that he can deflect her questions; he is able to tell Othello about the handkerchief and know that Othello will not doubt him; he is able to tell the audience, "And what's he then that says I play the villain," and know that it will laugh as though he were a clown (2.3.). Though an inveterate liar, Iago inspires a lack of trust for Othello in all the play's characters; this is most dangerous to Othello.

## DESDEMONA

Desdemona is a more plausible, well-rounded figure than much criticism has given her credit for. Arguments that see Desdemona as stereotypically weak and submissive ignore the conviction and authority of her first speech ("My noble father, / I do perceive here a divided duty" [1.3.]) and her terse fury after Othello strikes her ("I have not deserved this" [4.1.]). Similarly, critics who argue that Desdemona's slightly bizarre bawdy jesting with Iago in Act 2, scene 1, is either an interpolation not written by Shakespeare or a mere vulgarity ignore the fact that Desdemona is young, sexual, and recently married. She later displays the same chiding, almost mischievous wit in Act 3, scene 3, when she attempts to persuade Othello to forgive Cassio.

Desdemona is at times a submissive character, most notably in her willingness to take credit for her own murder. In response to Emilia's question, "Oh, who hath done this deed?" Desdemona's final words are, "Nobody. I myself. Farewell. / Commend me to my kind lord. Oh, farewell" (5.2.). The play, then, depicts Desdemona contradictorily as a self-effacing, faithful wife and as a bold, independent personality. This contradiction may be intentional, meant to portray the way Desdemona herself feels after defending to her father her choice of marriage in Act 1, scene 3, and then almost immediately being put in the position of defending her fidelity to her husband. She begins the play as a supremely independent person, but midway through she must struggle against all odds to convince Othello that she is not *too* independent. The manner in which Desdemona is murdered—smothered by a pillow in a bed covered in her wedding sheets—is symbolic: She is literally suffocated beneath the demands put on her fidelity. Since her first lines, Desdemona has seemed capable of meeting or even rising above those demands. In the end, Othello stifles the speech that made Desdemona so powerful.

Tragically, Desdemona is apparently aware of her imminent death. She, not Othello, asks Emilia to put her wedding sheets on the bed, and she asks Emilia to bury her in these sheets should she die first. The last time we see Desdemona before she awakens to find Othello standing over her with murder in his eyes, she sings a song she learned from her mother's maid: "She was in love, and he she loved proved mad / And did forsake her. She had a song of "Willow," / . . . / And she died singing it. That song tonight / Will not go from my mind" (4.3.). Like the audience, Desdemona seems able only to watch as her husband is driven insane with jealousy. Though she maintains to the end that she is "guiltless," Desdemona also forgives her husband (5.2.). Her forgiveness of Othello may help the audience to forgive him as well.

# PART II

---

# THE PLAY

# 5

# Othello

## THE ORIGINAL PLAY
## WITH A MODERN TRANSLATION

William Shakespeare

**NO FEAR** SHAKESPEARE™

# CHARACTER LIST*

**Othello**

**Desdemona**

**Iago**

**Michael Cassio**

**Emilia**

**Roderigo**

**Bianca**

**Brabantio**

**Duke of Venice**

**Montano**

**Lodovico**

**Graziano**

**Clown**

*See page 13 for an in-depth review of the characters.

# ACT ONE

## Scene 1

*Enter* RODERIGO *and* IAGO

**RODERIGO**
Tush! Never tell me. I take it much unkindly
That thou, Iago, who hast had my purse
As if the strings were thine, shouldst know of this.

**IAGO**
'Sblood, but you'll not hear me! If ever I did dream
5    of such a matter, abhor me.

**RODERIGO**
Thou told'st me
Thou didst hold him in thy hate.

**IAGO**
Despise me
If I do not. Three great ones of the city
10    (In personal suit to make me his lieutenant)
Off-capped to him, and by the faith of man
I know my price, I am worth no worse a place.
But he (as loving his own pride and purposes)
Evades them with a bombast circumstance
15    Horribly stuffed with epithets of war,
And in conclusion
Nonsuits my mediators. For "Certes," says he,
"I have already chose my officer."
And what was he?
20    Forsooth, a great arithmetician,
One Michael Cassio, a Florentine
(A fellow almost damned in a fair wife)
That never set a squadron in the field,
Nor the division of a battle knows
25    More than a spinster—unless the bookish theoric,

# ACT ONE

## Scene 1

RODERIGO *and* IAGO *enter.*

**RODERIGO**

Come on, don't tell me that. I don't like it that you knew about this, Iago. All this time I've thought you were such a good friend that I've let you spend my money as if it were yours.

**IAGO**

Damn it, you're not listening to me! I never dreamed this was happening—if you find out I did, you can go ahead and hate me.

**RODERIGO**

You told me you hated him.

**IAGO**

They're talking about Othello, though they never mention his name.

I do hate him, I swear. Three of Venice's most important noblemen took their hats off to him and asked him humbly to make me his lieutenant, the second in command. And I know my own worth well enough to know I deserve that position. But he wants to have things his own way, so he sidesteps the issue with a lot of military talk and refuses their request. "I've already chosen my lieutenant," he says. And who does he choose? A guy who knows more about numbers than fighting! This guy from Florence named Michael Cassio. He has a pretty wife but he can't even control her. And he's definitely never commanded men in battle. He's got no more hands-on knowledge of warfare than an old woman—unless you count what he's read in books,

Wherein the toged consuls can propose
As masterly as he. Mere prattle without practice
Is all his soldiership. But he, sir, had th' election
And I, of whom his eyes had seen the proof
30     At Rhodes, at Cyprus, and on other grounds
Christian and heathen, must be belee'd and calmed
By debitor and creditor. This counter-caster
He (in good time) must his lieutenant be
And I, bless the mark, his Moorship's ancient.

RODERIGO
35     By heaven, I rather would have been his hangman.

IAGO
Why, there's no remedy. 'Tis the curse of service.
Preferment goes by letter and affection,
And not by old gradation, where each second
Stood heir to th' first. Now sir, be judge yourself,
40     Whether I in any just term am affined
To love the Moor.

RODERIGO
I would not follow him then.

IAGO
O sir, content you.
I follow him to serve my turn upon him.
45     We cannot all be masters, nor all masters
Cannot be truly followed. You shall mark
Many a duteous and knee-crooking knave
That (doting on his own obsequious bondage)
Wears out his time much like his master's ass
50     For naught but provender, and when he's old, cashiered.
Whip me such honest knaves. Others there are
Who, trimmed in forms and visages of duty,
Keep yet their hearts attending on themselves
And, throwing but shows of service on their lords,
55     Do well thrive by them. And when they have lined their
          coats,
Do themselves homage. These fellows have some soul,

which any peace-lover can do. His military understanding is all theory, no practice. But Cassio's been
chosen over me. My career is cut short by some book-
keeper, even though the general saw my fighting skills
first-hand in Rhodes and Cyprus. This accountant is
now lieutenant, while I end up as the Moor's flag-
bearer.

*Moor = North African*

**RODERIGO**

By God, I'd rather be his executioner.

**IAGO**

And there's nothing I can do about it. That's the curse
of military service. You get promoted when someone
likes you, not because you're next in line. Now, you
tell me: should I feel loyal to the Moor?

**RODERIGO**

If you don't like him you should quit.

**IAGO**

No, calm down. I'm serving under him to take advantage of him. We can't all be masters, and not all masters should be followed. Look at all the devoted
servants who work for their masters their whole lives
for nothing but their food, and then when they get old
they're terminated. They ought to be whipped for
being so stupid. But then there's another kind of servant who looks dutiful and devoted, but who's really
looking out for himself. By pretending to serve their
lords, these men get rich, and when they've saved up
enough they can be their own masters. Guys like that
have soul, and that's the kind of guy I am. Let me tell

And such a one do I profess myself. For, sir,
It is as sure as you are Roderigo,
Were I the Moor, I would not be Iago.
60    In following him, I follow but myself.
Heaven is my judge, not I for love and duty,
But seeming so, for my peculiar end.
For when my outward action doth demonstrate
The native act and figure of my heart
65    In compliment extern, 'tis not long after
But I will wear my heart upon my sleeve
For daws to peck at. I am not what I am.

**RODERIGO**
What a full fortune does the Thick-lips owe
If he can carry't thus!

**IAGO**
                              Call up her father.
70    Rouse him. Make after him, Poison his delight,
Proclaim him in the streets. Incense her kinsmen,
And, though he in a fertile climate dwell,
Plague him with flies. Though that his joy be joy
Yet throw such changes of vexation on't,
75    As it may lose some color.

**RODERIGO**
Here is her father's house, I'll call aloud.

**IAGO**
Do, with like timorous accent and dire yell
As when, by night and negligence, the fire
Is spied in populous cities.

**RODERIGO**
80    What, ho, Brabantio! Signior Brabantio, ho!

**IAGO**
Awake! What, ho, Brabantio! Thieves! Thieves!
Look to your house, your daughter, and your bags!
Thieves! thieves!

*Enter* **BRABANTIO**, *above*

you, as sure as your name's Roderigo, if I were the Moor I wouldn't want to be Iago. I may seem to love and obey him, but in fact, I'm just serving him to get what I want. If my outward appearance started reflecting what I really felt, soon enough I'd be wearing my heart on my sleeve for birds to peck at. No, it's better to hide it. I'm not who I appear to be.

**RODERIGO**

*"Thick-lips" is a racial slur toward the Moor, Othello.*

Thick-lips sure is lucky if he can pull this off!

**IAGO**

Let's shout up to Desdemona's father, wake him, pester him, spoil his happiness, spread rumors about him in the streets, enrage his relatives, and irritate him endlessly. However real his happiness is, it will vanish in light of this.

**RODERIGO**

Here's her father's house. I'll call out.

**IAGO**

Do it, and shout like the city's on fire.

**RODERIGO**

Hey, Brabantio! Signor Brabantio, hey!

**IAGO**

Wake up, Brabantio! Wake up! Thieves! Thieves! Check on your daughter, your house, your money! Thieves! Thieves!

**BRABANTIO** *enters, above.*

**BRABANTIO**
What is the reason of this terrible summons?
85    What is the matter there?

**RODERIGO**
Signior, is all your family within?

**IAGO**
Are your doors locked?

**BRABANTIO**
                Why, wherefore ask you this?

**IAGO**
Zounds, sir, you're robbed! For shame, put on your gown.
Your heart is burst, you have lost half your soul.
90    Even now, now, very now, an old black ram
Is tupping your white ewe. Arise, arise,
Awake the snorting citizens with the bell
Or else the devil will make a grandsire of you.
Arise, I say!

**BRABANTIO**
             What, have you lost your wits?

**RODERIGO**
95    Most reverend signior, do you know my voice?

**BRABANTIO**
Not I. What are you?

**RODERIGO**
My name is Roderigo.

**BRABANTIO**
The worser welcome.
I have charged thee not to haunt about my doors.
100    In honest plainness thou hast heard me say
My daughter is not for thee. And now in madness,
Being full of supper and distempering drafts,
Upon malicious knavery dost thou come
To start my quiet?

**RODERIGO**
105    Sir, sir, sir—

**BRABANTIO**

What's the reason for this horrible shouting? What's the matter?

**RODERIGO**

Sir, is everyone in your family at home?

**IAGO**

Are your doors locked?

**BRABANTIO**

Why are you asking me that?

**IAGO**

For God's sake, sir, you've been robbed. Get dressed. Your heart's going to break. It's like half your soul's been ripped out. At this very minute an old black ram is having sex with your little white lamb. Wake up, wake up, ring a bell and wake up all the snoring citizens. If you wait too long you'll have black grandchildren. Get up, I tell you!

**BRABANTIO**

Are you crazy?

**RODERIGO**

Do you recognize my voice, noble lord?

**BRABANTIO**

Not me. Who are you?

**RODERIGO**

My name's Roderigo.

**BRABANTIO**

I told you not to hang around my house. I've already told you quite plainly that my daughter will never marry you. Now you come here drunk to make trouble and startle me out of a sound sleep?

**RODERIGO**

Sir, sir, sir—

**BRABANTIO**
But thou must needs be sure
My spirits and my place have in their power
To make this bitter to thee.

**RODERIGO**
Patience, good sir.

**BRABANTIO**
What tell'st thou me of robbing? This is Venice,
110　My house is not a grange.

**RODERIGO**
Most grave Brabantio,
In simple and pure soul I come to you—

**IAGO**
Zounds, sir, you are one of those that will not serve God,
if the devil bid you. Because we come to do you service and
you think we are ruffians, you'll have your daughter
115　covered with a Barbary horse. You'll have your nephews
neigh to you. You'll have coursers for cousins and gennets
for germans.

**BRABANTIO**
What profane wretch art thou?

**IAGO**
I am one, sir, that comes to tell you your daughter
120　and the Moor are now making the beast with two backs.

**BRABANTIO**
Thou art a villain!

**IAGO**
You are a senator!

**BRABANTIO**
This thou shalt answer. I know thee, Roderigo.

**RODERIGO**
Sir, I will answer any thing. But, I beseech you,
If't be your pleasure and most wise consent
125　(As partly I find it is) that your fair daughter
At this odd-even and dull watch o' th' night
Transported with no worse nor better guard

**BRABANTIO**

You know I'm powerful enough to make you pay for this.

**RODERIGO**

Please wait, sir.

**BRABANTIO**

Why are you talking about robbery? This is Venice. My house isn't in some remote countryside.

**RODERIGO**

Brabantio, with all due respect, I'm here out of courtesy and good will. I've come to tell you—

**IAGO**

My God, sir, you're stubborn and suspicious. We come here to help you and you treat us like thugs, but you let an African horse climb all over your daughter. Your grandsons will neigh to you like horses. Your whole family will be ruined.

**BRABANTIO**

What kind of crude jerk are you?

**IAGO**

The kind that tells you that the Moor is having sex with your daughter right now.

**BRABANTIO**

You're a villain!

**IAGO**

You're a senator!

**BRABANTIO**

You're going to pay for this, Roderigo. I know who you are.

**RODERIGO**

I'll answer for everything. I don't know if you know or approve of this, but in the wee hours of the morning your daughter left your house, with no better escort than a hired gondolier, to go into the rough embrace of a lustful Moor. If all of this happened with your

But with a knave of common hire, a gondolier,
To the gross clasps of a lascivious Moor,
130     If this be known to you and your allowance,
We then have done you bold and saucy wrongs.
But if you know not this my manners tell me
We have your wrong rebuke. Do not believe
That, from the sense of all civility,
135     I thus would play and trifle with your reverence.
Your daughter (if you have not given her leave)
I say again, hath made a gross revolt,
Tying her duty, beauty, wit, and fortunes
In an extravagant and wheeling stranger
140     Of here and everywhere. Straight satisfy yourself.
If she be in her chamber or your house,
Let loose on me the justice of the state
For thus deluding you.

**BRABANTIO**
                   Strike on the tinder, ho!
Give me a taper, call up all my people!
145     This accident is not unlike my dream,
Belief of it oppresses me already.
Light, I say, light!

                           *Exit above*

**IAGO**
*(to* **RODERIGO***)*
                 Farewell, for I must leave you.
It seems not meet, nor wholesome to my place,
To be producted (as, if I stay, I shall)
150     Against the Moor. For I do know the state
(However this may gall him with some check)
Cannot with safety cast him, for he's embarked
With such loud reason to the Cyprus wars
(Which even now stand in act) that, for their souls,
155     Another of his fathom they have none
To lead their business. In which regard,
Though I do hate him as I do hell pains,

approval, then we've been very rude to bother you like this. But if you didn't know about it, then you were wrong to get mad at us. I'd never play pranks on you. If you didn't allow your daughter to do what she's doing, then she's rebelling against you. She's throwing her life away on some stranger. Go ahead, see for yourself if she's in her bedroom. If she is, you can sue me for lying to you.

BRABANTIO

Light the candles! Wake up my whole household! I dreamt about this. I'm starting to worry it's true. Give me some light!

BRABANTIO *exits*.

IAGO

*(to* RODERIGO*)* It's time for me to say goodbye to you. It would be inappropriate—dangerous, even—for me to be seen working against the Moor, as I would if I stayed. The Venetian government might reprimand him for this, but it can't safely get rid of him, since it needs him urgently for the imminent Cyprus wars. They couldn't find another man with his abilities to lead their armed forces—not if their souls depended on it. I hate him, but I've got to show him signs of loy-

Yet for necessity of present life
I must show out a flag and sign of love,
160    (Which is indeed but sign). That you shall surely find him,
Lead to the Sagittary the raisèd search,
And there will I be with him. So farewell.

*Exit*

*Enter* BRABANTIO, *with servants and torches*

**BRABANTIO**
It is too true an evil. Gone she is.
And what's to come of my despisèd time
165    Is naught but bitterness. Now, Roderigo,
Where didst thou see her?—Oh, unhappy girl!—
With the Moor, say'st thou?—Who would be a father?—
How didst thou know 'twas she?—Oh, she deceives me
Past thought!—What said she to you?—Get more tapers,
170    Raise all my kindred. Are they married, think you?

**RODERIGO**
Truly, I think they are.

**BRABANTIO**
Oh, heaven, how got she out? Oh, treason of the blood!
Fathers, from hence trust not your daughters' minds
By what you see them act. Is there not charms
175    By which the property of youth and maidhood
May be abused? Have you not read, Roderigo,
Of some such thing?

**RODERIGO**
                    Yes, sir, I have indeed.

**BRABANTIO**
Call up my brother—Oh, would you had had her!
Some one way, some another. Do you know
180    Where we may apprehend her and the Moor?

**RODERIGO**
I think I can discover him, if you please
To get good guard and go along with me.

alty and affection, even if it's just an act. If you want to find him, send the search party to the Sagittarius Inn. He and I will be there.

IAGO *exits.*

BRABANTIO *enters with servants and torches.*

**BRABANTIO**

It's true. She's gone. The rest of my life will be nothing but bitterness. Now, Roderigo, where did you see her?—Oh, that miserable wretch!—You say you saw her with the Moor?—Oh, who would want to be a father?—How did you know it was her?—To think she tricked me so easily!—What did she say to you?—Get me more candles, and wake up all my relatives. Do you think they're married?

**RODERIGO**

Yes, I really think so.

**BRABANTIO**

Oh, heaven, how did she get out? My own flesh and blood rebels against me! Fathers, never trust your daughters just because they act obedient and innocent. Are there magic spells that can lead young virgins astray? Have you ever heard of anything like that, Roderigo?

**RODERIGO**

Yes, sir, I have.

**BRABANTIO**

Call my brother.—Now I wish you'd married her!—Some of you go one way, some the other way.—Do you know where we can find her and the Moor?

**RODERIGO**

I think I can find him. Get together a group of armed men and follow me.

**BRABANTIO**
Pray you lead on. At every house I'll call.
I may command at most.—Get weapons, ho!
185 And raise some special officers of might.—
On, good Roderigo. I will deserve your pains.

*Exeunt*

**BRABANTIO**
Lead the way. I'll stop at every house. I'm respected enough that most of them will do what I say.—Get your weapons! And get the officers who guard the city at night.—Let's go, Roderigo. I'll reward you for your troubles.

*They exit.*

# ACT ONE, Scene 2

*Enter* OTHELLO, IAGO, *and attendants with torches*

IAGO
Though in the trade of war I have slain men,
Yet do I hold it very stuff o' th' conscience
To do no contrived murder. I lack iniquity
Sometimes to do me service. Nine or ten times
5    I had thought t' have yerked him here under the ribs.

OTHELLO
'Tis better as it is.

IAGO
                    Nay, but he prated
And spoke such scurvy and provoking terms
Against your honor
That, with the little godliness I have,
10   I did full hard forbear him. But I pray you, sir,
Are you fast married? Be assured of this:
That the Magnifico is much beloved
And hath in his effect a voice potential
As double as the Duke's. He will divorce you,
15   Or put upon you what restraint and grievance
The law (with all his might to enforce it on)
Will give him cable.

OTHELLO
                  Let him do his spite.
My services which I have done the signiory
Shall out-tongue his complaints. 'Tis yet to know—
20   Which, when I know that boasting is an honor,
I shall promulgate. I fetch my life and being
From men of royal siege, and my demerits
May speak unbonneted to as proud a fortune
As this that I have reached. For know, Iago,
25   But that I love the gentle Desdemona,
I would not my unhousèd free condition
Put into circumscription and confine
For the sea's worth. But look, what lights come yond?

## ACT ONE, Scene 2

OTHELLO *and* IAGO *enter, followed by attendants with torches.*

IAGO

I've killed many men in battle, but I still believe it's deeply wrong to murder someone. Sometimes I worry I'm not cruel enough for this job. Nine or ten times I wanted to stab him under the ribs.

OTHELLO

It's better that you didn't kill him.

IAGO

But he kept chattering so foolishly, talking about you in such insulting and despicable terms, that it was hard for me to restrain myself. But please tell me, sir, is your marriage secure? Brabantio is an important man in this city, almost as powerful as the duke himself. He'll try to annul your marriage, or else inflict whatever punishment the law and his power will allow him to.

Iago may be asking whether Othello has consummated his marriage by sleeping with Desdemona yet. A marriage could be annulled if it had never been consummated.

OTHELLO

Let him do his worst. The services I have done for the Venetian government will count for more than his complaints will. No one knows this yet—and I don't like to brag, but I come from a royal family, and I'm as noble as the woman I've married. And let me tell you, Iago, if I didn't love Desdemona as much as I do, I'd never agree to get married and lose my freedom at all. But look at those lights. Who's coming?

**IAGO**
Those are the raisèd father and his friends.
30 You were best go in.

**OTHELLO**
                              Not I, I must be found.
My parts, my title, and my perfect soul
Shall manifest me rightly. Is it they?

**IAGO**
By Janus, I think no.

*Enter* CASSIO, *with officers and torches*

**OTHELLO**
The servants of the Duke and my lieutenant?
35 The goodness of the night upon you, friends!
What is the news?

**CASSIO**
                              The Duke does greet you, general,
And he requires your haste-post-haste appearance,
Even on the instant.

**OTHELLO**
                              What's the matter, think you?

**CASSIO**
Something from Cyprus as I may divine.
40 It is a business of some heat. The galleys
Have sent a dozen sequent messengers
This very night at one another's heels,
And many of the consuls, raised and met,
Are at the Duke's already. You have been hotly called for.
45 When being not at your lodging to be found
The Senate hath sent about three several guests
To search you out.

**OTHELLO**
                              'Tis well I am found by you.
I will but spend a word here in the house
And go with you.

**IAGO**

That's her father and his friends, who've been roused out of bed. You'd better go inside.

**OTHELLO**

No, I must let them find me. My good qualities, my legal status as Desdemona's husband, and my innocence will protect me. Is it them?

**IAGO**

I don't think so.

*CASSIO enters with officers and men carrying torches.*

**OTHELLO**

The servants of the Duke and my lieutenant? Hello, everyone! What's going on?

**CASSIO**

The Duke sends his regards. He needs to see you right away.

**OTHELLO**

What do you think he wants?

**CASSIO**

Something about Cyprus. I think it's important. The warships have sent a dozen messages tonight, one after the other, and many of the senators have been awakened and are at the Duke's already. They're very anxious for you to get there. When you weren't at home, the Senate sent out three different search parties to find you.

**OTHELLO**

It's good you found me. I'll just speak a word or two here in the house and then I'll go with you.

*Exit*

CASSIO

Ancient, what makes he here?

IAGO

50  Faith, he tonight hath boarded a land carrack.
If it prove lawful prize, he's made for ever.

CASSIO

I do not understand.

IAGO

He's married.

CASSIO

To who?

IAGO

Marry, to—

*Enter* OTHELLO

Come, captain, will you go?

OTHELLO

55  Have with you.

CASSIO

Here comes another troop to seek for you.

*Enter* BRABANTIO, RODERIGO, *and officers with torches and weapons*

IAGO

It is Brabantio. General, be advised,
He comes to bad intent.

OTHELLO

Holla! Stand there!

RODERIGO

Signior, it is the Moor.

BRABANTIO

Down with him, thief!

*They draw their swords*

OTHELLO *exits.*

**CASSIO**

Ensign, what's he doing in there?

**IAGO**

Tonight he boarded a treasure ship. If he can keep it, he'll be set forever.

**CASSIO**

I don't understand.

**IAGO**

He's married.

**CASSIO**

To whom?

**IAGO**

To—

OTHELLO *enters.*

Are you ready?

**OTHELLO**

Yes, I'll go with you now.

**CASSIO**

Here comes another group looking for you.

BRABANTIO *and* RODERIGO *enter, followed by* OFFICERS *and men with torches.*

**IAGO**

It's Brabantio. Look out, sir. He intends to do something bad to you.

**OTHELLO**

Hey! Stop right there!

**RODERIGO**

Sir, it's the Moor.

**BRABANTIO**

Get him, he's a thief!

*Both sides draw their swords.*

**IAGO**

60      You, Roderigo! Come, sir, I am for you.

**OTHELLO**

Keep up your bright swords, for the dew will rust them.
Good signior, you shall more command with years
Than with your weapons.

**BRABANTIO**

O thou foul thief, where hast thou stowed my daughter?
65      Damned as thou art, thou hast enchanted her!
For I'll refer me to all things of sense,
If she in chains of magic were not bound,
Whether a maid so tender, fair, and happy,
So opposite to marriage that she shunned
70      The wealthy curlèd darlings of our nation,
Would ever have, t' incur a general mock,
Run from her guardage to the sooty bosom
Of such a thing as thou—to fear, not to delight.
Judge me the world if 'tis not gross in sense
75      That thou hast practiced on her with foul charms,
Abused her delicate youth with drugs or minerals
That weakens motion. I'll have 't disputed on.
'Tis probable and palpable to thinking.
I therefore apprehend and do attach thee
80      For an abuser of the world, a practicer
Of arts inhibited and out of warrant.—
Lay hold upon him. If he do resist,
Subdue him at his peril!

**OTHELLO**

                              Hold your hands,
Both you of my inclining and the rest.
85      Were it my cue to fight, I should have known it
Without a prompter. Whither will you that I go
To answer this your charge?

**IAGO**

You, Roderigo! Come on, I'll fight you.

**OTHELLO**

Put away your swords. They'll get rusty in the dew. Sir, your age and status inspire more respect than your weapons do.

**BRABANTIO**

You evil thief, where have you hidden my daughter? You devil, you've put a spell on her! Anybody with eyes could tell you that a beautiful and happy young girl like her, who's refused to marry all of the hand-some young men of the city, wouldn't run off with a black thing like you unless she'd been bewitched. You're something to fear, not to love. It's obvious to everyone that you've tricked her, drugged her, or kid-napped her. That's probably what happened, so I'm arresting you.—Arrest this man as a practitioner of black magic. Grab him. If he struggles, use force!

**OTHELLO**

Just a minute. I don't need anyone to tell me when to fight. You've accused me of some serious crimes. Where do you want me to go to respond to these charges?

**BRABANTIO**
                            To prison, till fit time
Of law and course of direct session
Call thee to answer.

**OTHELLO**
                            What if I do obey?
90    How may the Duke be therewith satisfied,
Whose messengers are here about my side
Upon some present business of the state
To bring me to him?

**OFFICER**
                         'Tis true, most worthy signior.
The Duke's in council and your noble self,
95    I am sure, is sent for.

**BRABANTIO**
                      How? The Duke in council?
In this time of the night? Bring him away.
Mine's not an idle cause. The Duke himself,
Or any of my brothers of the state,
Cannot but feel this wrong as 'twere their own.
100   For if such actions may have passage free,
Bond-slaves and pagans shall our statesmen be.

*Exeunt*

**BRABANTIO**

To prison, until you're called into court.

**OTHELLO**

What if I do what you say? How would I satisfy the Duke then? His messengers are waiting here to take me to him immediately, on pressing state business.

**OFFICER**

It's true. The Duke's in a meeting right now, and he's sent for you too.

**BRABANTIO**

The Duke's in a meeting? At this time of night? Bring him with us. The law's on my side. The Duke and any of my fellow senators will take this wrong as seriously as if it were their own. If we let crimes like this happen, slaves and heathens will be our rulers.

*They all exit.*

# ACT ONE, Scene 3

*Enter* DUKE, SENATORS, *and* OFFICERS

DUKE
There's no composition in this news
That gives them credit.

FIRST SENATOR
Indeed, they are disproportioned.
My letters say a hundred and seven galleys.

DUKE
5    And mine a hundred and forty.

SECOND SENATOR
And mine, two hundred.
But though they jump not on a just account—
As in these cases, where the aim reports
'Tis oft with difference—yet do they all confirm
A Turkish fleet, and bearing up to Cyprus.

DUKE
10    Nay, it is possible enough to judgment.
I do not so secure me in the error,
But the main article I do approve
In fearful sense.

SAILOR
*(within)*
What, ho, what, ho, what, ho!

OFFICER
A messenger from the galleys.

*Enter* SAILOR

DUKE
15    Now, what's the business?

SAILOR
The Turkish preparation makes for Rhodes,
So was I bid report here to the state
By Signior Angelo.

## ACT ONE, Scene 3

*The* DUKE *enters with* SENATORS *and* OFFICERS.

DUKE

These reports are inconsistent. You can't trust them.

FIRST SENATOR

It's true, they're inconsistent. My letters say there are a hundred and seven ships.

DUKE

And mine say a hundred and forty.

SECOND SENATOR

And mine say two hundred. But often in these cases, reports are just estimates. The important thing is that they all say a Turkish fleet is approaching Cyprus.

DUKE

Yes, we get the idea. The inconsistency doesn't make me think that the reports are all wrong. I have no doubt about what they're basically saying, and it's frightening.

SAILOR

*(offstage)* Hello! Hey, hello!

OFFICER

It's a messenger from the warships.

A SAILOR *enters.*

DUKE

Why are you here?

SAILOR

Signor Angelo told me to come here and tell you that the Turkish fleet is heading for Rhodes, not Cyprus.

**DUKE**
How say you by this change?

**FIRST SENATOR**
                                        This cannot be,
20      By no assay of reason. 'Tis a pageant,
        To keep us in false gaze. When we consider
        Th' importancy of Cyprus to the Turk,
        And let ourselves again but understand
        That as it more concerns the Turk than Rhodes
25      So may he with more facile question bear it,
        For that it stands not in such warlike brace
        But altogether lacks th' abilities
        That Rhodes is dressed in. If we make thought of this
        We must not think the Turk is so unskillful
30      To leave that latest which concerns him first,
        Neglecting an attempt of ease and gain
        To wake and wage a danger profitless.

**DUKE**
Nay, in all confidence, he's not for Rhodes.

**OFFICER**
Here is more news.

*Enter a* MESSENGER

**MESSENGER**
35      The Ottomites, reverend and gracious,
        Steering with due course toward the isle of Rhodes,
        Have there injointed them with an after fleet.

**FIRST SENATOR**
Ay, so I thought. How many, as you guess?

**MESSENGER**
        Of thirty sail. And now they do re-stem
40      Their backward course, bearing with frank appearance
        Their purposes toward Cyprus. Signior Montano,
        Your trusty and most valiant servitor,
        With his free duty recommends you thus,
        And prays you to believe him.

**DUKE**
What do you think about this change?

**FIRST SENATOR**
They can't have changed; there's no way this could be true. It's a trick to confuse us. Think about how important Cyprus is to the Turks, and remember that they could capture Cyprus more easily, since it isn't as well protected as Rhodes is. If we keep these things in mind, we can't possibly imagine that the Turks would be so incompetent as to put off for last what they want to achieve first, setting aside something easy and profitable to do something dangerous and pointless.

**DUKE**
No, I think we can be confident that the Turks aren't really headed for Rhodes.

**OFFICER**
Here's some more news coming in.

A **MESSENGER** *enters.*

**MESSENGER**
Sir, the Turks sailed to Rhodes, where they joined with another fleet.

**FIRST SENATOR**
That's just what I thought. How many, can you guess?

**MESSENGER**
Thirty ships. Now they've turned around and are clearly heading for Cyprus. Signor Montano, your brave and loyal servant, gives you this information and asks you to send reinforcements to relieve him.

**DUKE**
                                        'Tis certain then for Cyprus.
45      Marcus Luccicos, is not he in town?

**FIRST SENATOR**
        He's now in Florence.

**DUKE**
        Write from us to him. Post-post-haste, dispatch.

**FIRST SENATOR**
        Here comes Brabantio and the valiant Moor.

        *Enter* BRABANTIO, OTHELLO, CASSIO, IAGO, RODERIGO, *and*
        *officers*

**DUKE**
        Valiant Othello, we must straight employ you
50      Against the general enemy Ottoman—
        *(to* BRABANTIO*)* I did not see you. Welcome, gentle signior.
        We lacked your counsel and your help tonight.

**BRABANTIO**
        So did I yours. Good your grace, pardon me.
        Neither my place nor aught I heard of business
55      Hath raised me from my bed, nor doth the general care
        Take hold on me, for my particular grief
        Is of so flood-gate and o'erbearing nature
        That it engluts and swallows other sorrows
        And it is still itself.

**DUKE**
60      Why, what's the matter?

**BRABANTIO**
        My daughter! Oh, my daughter!

**ALL**
                                        Dead?

**BRABANTIO**
                                                Ay, to me.
        She is abused, stol'n from me, and corrupted
        By spells and medicines bought of mountebanks.

**DUKE**

Then it's certain they're heading for Cyprus. Is Marcus Luccicos in town?

**FIRST SENATOR**

No, he's in Florence.

**DUKE**

Write to him immediately. Hurry.

**FIRST SENATOR**

Here come Brabantio and the brave Moor.

BRABANTIO, OTHELLO, CASSIO, IAGO, RODERIGO *and the officers enter.*

**DUKE**

Brave Othello, I have to send you right away to fight the Turks, our great enemy.—*(to* BRABANTIO*)* Oh, I didn't see you there. Welcome, sir. I could have used your wisdom and help tonight.

**BRABANTIO**

I could have used yours as well. Forgive me, your grace. I didn't get out of bed and come here in the dead of night because I heard about the war or because I was worried about the city's defense. I have a personal problem so painful and gut-wrenching that it overwhelms everything else.

**DUKE**

Why, what's the matter?

**BRABANTIO**

It's my daughter! Oh, my daughter!

**ALL**

Is she dead?

**BRABANTIO**

She's dead to me. She's been tricked and stolen from me, enchanted by black magic spells. She must've

For nature so prepost'rously to err,
65    Being not deficient, blind, or lame of sense,
Sans witchcraft could not.

**DUKE**
Whoe'er he be that in this foul proceeding
Hath thus beguiled your daughter of herself
And you of her, the bloody book of law
70    You shall yourself read in the bitter letter,
After your own sense, yea, though our proper son
Stood in your action.

**BRABANTIO**
                              Humbly I thank your grace.
Here is the man, this Moor, whom now it seems,
Your special mandate for the state affairs
75    Hath hither brought.

**ALL**
                              We are very sorry for't.

**DUKE**
(to OTHELLO) What, in your own part, can you say to this?

**BRABANTIO**
Nothing, but this is so.

**OTHELLO**
Most potent, grave, and reverend signiors,
My very noble and approved good masters,
80    That I have ta'en away this old man's daughter,
It is most true. True, I have married her.
The very head and front of my offending
Hath this extent, no more. Rude am I in my speech,
And little blessed with the soft phrase of peace,
85    For since these arms of mine had seven years' pith
Till now some nine moons wasted, they have used
Their dearest action in the tented field,
And little of this great world can I speak,

been tricked or drugged, because there's no way she could have made this mistake on her own.

**DUKE**

Whoever tricked your daughter and stole her from you will pay for it. And you yourself will determine the sentence as you see fit, and impose the death penalty if you choose to, even if the criminal were my own son.

**BRABANTIO**

I humbly thank you, sir. Here is the man, the Moor. It seems you had your own reasons for summoning him here.

**ALL**

We're sorry to hear this.

**DUKE**

*(to* OTHELLO*)* What do you have to say for yourself?

**BRABANTIO**

Nothing, but this is true.

**OTHELLO**

Noble, honorable gentlemen whom I serve: it's true that I've taken this man's daughter from him and married her. But that's my only offense. There's nothing more. I'm awkward in my speech and I'm not a smooth talker. From the time I was seven years old until nine months ago I've been fighting in battles. I don't know much about the world apart from fighting. So I won't do myself much good by speaking in my own defense. But if you'll let me, I'll tell you the plain

More than pertains to feats of broils and battle,
90    And therefore little shall I grace my cause
In speaking for myself. Yet, by your gracious patience,
I will a round unvarnished tale deliver
Of my whole course of love. What drugs, what charms,
What conjuration and what mighty magic—
95    For such proceeding I am charged withal—
I won his daughter.

**BRABANTIO**
                              A maiden never bold,
Of spirit so still and quiet that her motion
Blushed at herself. And she, in spite of nature,
Of years, of country, credit, everything,
100    To fall in love with what she feared to look on?
It is a judgment maimed and most imperfect
That will confess perfection so could err.
Against all rules of nature, and must be driven
To find out practices of cunning hell
105    Why this should be. I therefore vouch again
That with some mixtures powerful o'er the blood
Or with some dram, conjured to this effect,
He wrought upon her.

**DUKE**
                                    To vouch this is no proof,
Without more wider and more overt test
110    Than these thin habits and poor likelihoods
Of modern seeming do prefer against him.

**FIRST SENATOR**
But, Othello, speak.
Did you by indirect and forcèd courses
Subdue and poison this young maid's affections?
115    Or came it by request and such fair question
As soul to soul affordeth?

**OTHELLO**
                                    I do beseech you,
Send for the lady to the Sagittary,

story of how we fell in love, and what drugs, charms, spells, and powerful magic—because that's what I'm being accused of—I used to win his daughter.

BRABANTIO

She's a good girl, quiet and obedient. She blushes at the slightest thing. And you want me to believe that despite her young age and proper upbringing she fell in love with a man she'd be afraid to look at? The very thought of it is ridiculous. You'd have to be stupid to think that someone so perfect could make such an unnatural mistake as that. The devil must be behind this. Therefore I say again that he must have used some powerful drug or magic potion on her.

DUKE

Your saying this isn't proof. There has to be clear evidence that he's done this, not just these accusations.

FIRST SENATOR

Tell us, Othello. Did you trick or deceive this lady in some way? Or did you agree to this as equals?

OTHELLO

Please, send for Desdemona to come here from the Sagittarius Inn and ask her to speak about me in front

And let her speak of me before her father.
If you do find me foul in her report
120 The trust, the office I do hold of you,
Not only take away, but let your sentence
Even fall upon my life.

DUKE

       Fetch Desdemona hither.

OTHELLO

Ancient, conduct them. You best know the place.

*Exeunt* IAGO *and attendants*

And till she come, as truly as to heaven
125 I do confess the vices of my blood
So justly to your grave ears I'll present
How I did thrive in this fair lady's love
And she in mine.

DUKE

     Say it, Othello.

OTHELLO

Her father loved me, oft invited me,
130 Still questioned me the story of my life
From year to year, the battles, sieges, fortunes,
That I have passed.
I ran it through, even from my boyish days,
To th' very moment that he bade me tell it,
135 Wherein I spoke of most disastrous chances,
Of moving accidents by flood and field,
Of hair-breadth 'scapes i' th' imminent deadly breach,
Of being taken by the insolent foe
And sold to slavery, of my redemption thence
140 And portance in my traveler's history.
Wherein of antres vast and deserts idle,
Rough quarries, rocks, hills whose heads touch heaven
It was my hint to speak—such was my process—
And of the Cannibals that each others eat,

of her father. If she has anything bad to say about me, then you can sentence me to death.

**DUKE**

Bring Desdemona here.

**OTHELLO**

Iago, bring Desdemona here. You know where she is.

*IAGO and attendants exit.*

In the meantime I'll tell you all, as honestly as I confess my sins to God, how I wooed this beautiful lady, and how she came to love me.

**DUKE**

Tell us, Othello.

**OTHELLO**

Her father loved me and used to invite me to his house often, continually asking me about my life and all the battles I've fought. I told him everything, from my boyhood up until the time when I was talking to him. I told him about unfortunate disasters, hair-raising adventures on sea and on land, and near-catastrophes and dangerous adventures I've been through. I told him how I was captured and sold as a slave, how I bought my freedom, and how I wandered through caves and deserts. I was able to tell him about cannibals who eat each other, and men with heads growing below their shoulders. When I talked about all these things, Desdemona used to listen attentively. If she had to go do some household chore, I noticed that she'd always come back quickly to hear more of my stories.

145   The Anthropophagi, and men whose heads
Grew beneath their shoulders. These things to hear
Would Desdemona seriously incline.
But still the house affairs would draw her hence,
Which ever as she could with haste dispatch,
150   She'd come again, and with a greedy ear
Devour up my discourse, which I, observing,
Took once a pliant hour and found good means
To draw from her a prayer of earnest heart
That I would all my pilgrimage dilate,
155   Whereof by parcels she had something heard
But not intentively. I did consent,
And often did beguile her of her tears
When I did speak of some distressful stroke
That my youth suffered. My story being done
160   She gave me for my pains a world of sighs.
She swore, in faith, 'twas strange, 'twas passing strange,
'Twas pitiful, 'twas wondrous pitiful.
She wished she had not heard it, yet she wished
That heaven had made her such a man. She thanked me
165   And bade me, if I had a friend that loved her,
I should but teach him how to tell my story
And that would woo her. Upon this hint I spake.
She loved me for the dangers I had passed,
And I loved her that she did pity them.
170   This only is the witchcraft I have used.
Here comes the lady. Let her witness it.

*Enter* DESDEMONA, IAGO, *and attendants*

DUKE
I think this tale would win my daughter too.
Good Brabantio. Take up this mangled matter at the best.
Men do their broken weapons rather use
175   Than their bare hands.

When I was relaxing, she'd pull me aside and ask to hear some part of a story she had missed. Her eyes would fill with tears at the bad things I went through in my younger years. When my stories were done, she'd sigh and tell me how strangely wonderful and sad my life had been. She said she wished she hadn't heard it, but she also wished there was a man like me for her. She thanked me and told me that if a friend of mine had a story like mine to tell, she'd fall in love with him. I took the hint and spoke to her. She said she loved me for the dangers I'd survived, and I loved her for feeling such strong emotions about me. That's the only witchcraft I ever used. Here comes my wife now. She'll confirm everything.

DESDEMONA, IAGO, *and attendants enter.*

DUKE

I think a story like that would win my own daughter over. Brabantio, I urge you to make the best of this. Try to accept what's happened.

**BRABANTIO**
                              I pray you, hear her speak.
If she confess that she was half the wooer,
Destruction on my head if my bad blame
Light on the man.—Come hither, gentle mistress.
Do you perceive in all this noble company
180     Where most you owe obedience?

**DESDEMONA**
                              My noble father,
I do perceive here a divided duty.
To you I am bound for life and education.
My life and education both do learn me
How to respect you. You are the lord of duty.
185     I am hitherto your daughter. But here's my husband.
And so much duty as my mother showed
To you, preferring you before her father,
So much I challenge that I may profess
Due to the Moor my lord.

**BRABANTIO**
                              God be with you. I have done.
190     Please it your grace, on to the state affairs.
I had rather to adopt a child than get it.—
Come hither, Moor.
I here do give thee that with all my heart
Which, but thou hast already, with all my heart
195     I would keep from thee. For your sake, jewel,
I am glad at soul I have no other child.
For thy escape would teach me tyranny,
To hang clogs on them.—I have done, my lord.

**DUKE**
Let me speak like yourself and lay a sentence
200     Which, as a grise or step, may help these lovers.
When remedies are past, the griefs are ended
By seeing the worst, which late on hopes depended.

**BRABANTIO**

Please let her speak. If she admits she wanted this, then I won't blame Othello.—Come here, my child. Who do you obey here?

**DESDEMONA**

Father, this isn't easy for me. I'm torn. I owe you respect because you gave me life and education. You're the one I have to obey. I'm your daughter. But this man here is my husband now, and I owe him as much as my mother owed you, just as she preferred you to her own father. So I have to give my obedience to the Moor, my husband.

**BRABANTIO**

I'm finished, then. Duke, please go ahead with your state business. I'd rather adopt a child than have one of my own.—Come here, Moor. I'm forced to give my blessing to this marriage. With all my heart, I give you that thing which, if you didn't already have it, I'd try with all my heart to keep from you. Desdemona, I'm glad you're my only child, since if I had others I'd keep them all locked up. You would have made me treat them like a tyrant.—I'm done, my lord.

**DUKE**

Let me refer to a proverb that may help you forgive these lovers: if you can't change something, don't cry about it. When you lament something bad that's already happened, you're setting yourself up for more

To mourn a mischief that is past and gone
Is the next way to draw new mischief on.
205   What cannot be preserved when fortune takes,
Patience her injury a mock'ry makes.
The robbed that smiles steals something from the thief,
He robs himself that spends a bootless grief.

**BRABANTIO**
So let the Turk of Cyprus us beguile,
210   We lose it not, so long as we can smile.
He bears the sentence well that nothing bears
But the free comfort which from thence he hears.
But he bears both the sentence and the sorrow
That, to pay grief, must of poor patience borrow.
215   These sentences to sugar or to gall,
Being strong on both sides, are equivocal.
But words are words. I never yet did hear
That the bruised heart was piercèd through the ears.
I humbly beseech you, proceed to th' affairs of state.

**DUKE**
220   The Turk with a most mighty preparation makes for
Cyprus. Othello, the fortitude of the place is best known
to you, and though we have there a substitute of most
allowed sufficiency, yet opinion, a sovereign mistress of
effects, throws a more safer voice on you. You must therefore
225   be content to slubber the gloss of your new fortunes with
this more stubborn and boist'rous expedition.

**OTHELLO**
The tyrant custom, most grave senators,
Hath made the flinty and steel couch of war
My thrice-driven bed of down. I do agnize
230   A natural and prompt alacrity
I find in hardness, and do undertake
These present wars against the Ottomites.
Most humbly therefore bending to your state,

bad news. A robbery victim who can smile about his losses is superior to the thief who robbed him, but if he cries he's just wasting time.

BRABANTIO

So if the Turks steal Cyprus from us, it won't be bad as long as we keep smiling. It's easy to accept platitudes like that if you haven't lost anything. But I've lost something precious, and I have to put up with the platitude as well as suffering my loss. Talk is cheap. I've never heard of someone feeling better because of someone else's words. Please, I'm asking you, go ahead and get back to your state affairs.

DUKE

The Turks are heading for Cyprus with a powerful fleet. Othello, you understand better than anyone how the defenses for Cyprus work. Even though we have a very good officer in charge there already, everyone says you're the better man for the job. So I'll have to ask you to put a damper on your marriage celebrations and take part in this dangerous expedition.

OTHELLO

I've gotten used to the hardships of a military life. I rise to the occasion when faced with difficulties. I will take charge of this war against the Turks. But I humbly ask you to make appropriate arrangements for my

I crave fit disposition for my wife.
235 Due reference of place and exhibition,
With such accommodation and besort
As levels with her breeding.

**DUKE**
Why, at her father's.

**BRABANTIO**
I'll not have it so.

**OTHELLO**
240 Nor I.

**DESDEMONA**
Nor would I there reside,
To put my father in impatient thoughts
By being in his eye. Most gracious Duke,
To my unfolding lend your prosperous ear
245 And let me find a charter in your voice,
T' assist my simpleness.

**DUKE**
What would you, Desdemona?

**DESDEMONA**
That I did love the Moor to live with him,
My downright violence and storm of fortunes
250 May trumpet to the world. My heart's subdued
Even to the very quality of my lord.
I saw Othello's visage in his mind,
And to his honors and his valiant parts
Did I my soul and fortunes consecrate.
255 So that, dear lords, if I be left behind
A moth of peace and he go to the war,
The rites for which I love him are bereft me,
And I a heavy interim shall support
By his dear absence. Let me go with him.

**OTHELLO**
260 Let her have your voice.
Vouch with me, heaven, I therefore beg it not
To please the palate of my appetite,

wife, giving her a place to live and people to keep her company that suit her high rank.

**DUKE**

She can stay at her father's house.

**BRABANTIO**

I won't allow it.

**OTHELLO**

Neither will I.

**DESDEMONA**

And I wouldn't stay there. I don't want to upset my father by being in his house. Dear Duke, please listen to what I have to say.

**DUKE**

What do you want to do, Desdemona?

**DESDEMONA**

When I fell in love with Othello I made up my mind that I wanted to live with him. You can see how much I wanted to be with him by how violently I threw away my old life. I feel like I'm a part of him now, and that means I'm part of a soldier. I saw Othello's true face when I saw his mind. I gave my whole life to him because of his honor and bravery. If I were left at home uselessly while he went off to war, then I'm separated from my husband in his natural element. I'd be miserable without him. Let me go with him.

**OTHELLO**

Please allow her to do this. I'm not asking to have her near me for sex—I'm too old for that, and my sexual

Nor to comply with heat the young affects
In my defunct and proper satisfaction,
265 But to be free and bounteous to her mind,
And heaven defend your good souls, that you think
I will your serious and great business scant
When she is with me. No, when light-winged toys
Of feathered Cupid seel with wanton dullness
270 My speculative and officed instrument,
That my disports corrupt and taint my business,
Let housewives make a skillet of my helm
And all indign and base adversities
Make head against my estimation.

**DUKE**
275 Be it as you shall privately determine,
Either for her stay or going. Th' affair cries haste
And speed must answer it.

**FIRST SENATOR**
                              You must away tonight.

**OTHELLO**
With all my heart.

**DUKE**
At nine i' th' morning here we'll meet again.
280 Othello, leave some officer behind
And he shall our commission bring to you,
And such things else of quality and respect
As doth import you.

**OTHELLO**
                              So please your grace, my ancient.
A man he is of honesty and trust.
285 To his conveyance I assign my wife,
With what else needful your good grace shall think
To be sent after me.

urges are dead. I want this because she wants it—I love her for her mind. And I'd never want you to think that I'd neglect my serious official duties while she was there with me. If I ever let love blind me so that I choose to lounge around in bed with my loved one instead of going off to war, then you can let a house-wife use my helmet as a frying pan. My reputation would be disgraced if I ever acted like that.

**DUKE**

You can decide that privately. I don't care whether she stays or goes. What's important is the urgency of this mission. You've got to act fast.

**FIRST SENATOR**

You'll have to leave tonight.

**OTHELLO**

With all my heart, I'll go right away.

**DUKE**

We'll meet again at nine in the morning. Othello, have one of your officers stay behind to bring you your commission and whatever else is important to you.

**OTHELLO**

My lord, my ensign is an honest and trustworthy man. He'll accompany my wife, and bring whatever else you think I might need.

**DUKE**
                        Let it be so.
Good night to every one.—*(to* BRABANTIO*)*
And, noble signior,
290    If virtue no delighted beauty lack,
Your son-in-law is far more fair than black.

**FIRST SENATOR**
Adieu, brave Moor. Use Desdemona well.

**BRABANTIO**
Look to her, Moor, if thou hast eyes to see.
She has deceived her father, and may thee.

          *Exeunt* DUKE, BRABANTIO, CASSIO, SENATORS, *and*
                                  *officers*

**OTHELLO**
295    My life upon her faith!—Honest Iago,
My Desdemona must I leave to thee.
I prithee, let thy wife attend on her,
And bring them after in the best advantage.
Come, Desdemona, I have but an hour
300    Of love, of worldly matter and direction,
To spend with thee. We must obey the time.

                 *Exeunt* OTHELLO *and* DESDEMONA

**RODERIGO**
Iago.

**IAGO**
What say'st thou, noble heart?

**RODERIGO**
What will I do, think'st thou?

**IAGO**
305    Why, go to bed, and sleep.

**RODERIGO**
I will incontinently drown myself.

**DUKE**

All right, then. Good night, everyone.—*(to* BRABANTIO*)* Sir, if goodness is beautiful, your son-in-law is beautiful, not black.

**FIRST SENATOR**

Goodbye, black Moor. Treat Desdemona well.

**BRABANTIO**

Keep an eye on her, Moor. She lied to me, and she may lie to you.

*The* DUKE, BRABANTIO, CASSIO, SENATORS, *and officers exit.*

**OTHELLO**

I'd bet my life she'd never lie to me. Iago, I'm leaving my dear Desdemona with you. Have your wife attend to her, and bring them along as soon as you can. Come on, Desdemona, I've only got an hour of love to spend with you, to tell you what you need to do. We're on a tight schedule.

OTHELLO *and* DESDEMONA *exit.*

**RODERIGO**

Iago.

**IAGO**

What do you have to say, noble friend?

**RODERIGO**

What do you think I should do?

**IAGO**

Go to bed, and sleep.

**RODERIGO**

I'm going to go drown myself.

ACT ONE

**IAGO**

If thou dost I shall never love thee after. Why, thou silly
gentleman!

**RODERIGO**

It is silliness to live when to live is torment, and then have
310     we a prescription to die when death is our physician.

**IAGO**

Oh, villainous! I have looked upon the world for four
times seven years, and since I could distinguish betwixt a
benefit and an injury I never found man that knew how to
love himself. Ere I would say I would drown myself for the
315     love of a guinea hen, I would change my humanity with a
baboon.

**RODERIGO**

What should I do? I confess it is my shame to be so fond,
but it is not in my virtue to amend it.

**IAGO**

Virtue? A fig! 'Tis in ourselves that we are thus or thus.
320     Our bodies are our gardens, to the which our wills are
gardeners. So that if we will plant nettles or sow lettuce,
set hyssop and weed up thyme, supply it with one gender
of herbs or distract it with many—either to have it sterile
with idleness, or manured with industry—why, the power
325     and corrigible authority of this lies in our wills. If the
balance of our lives had not one scale of reason to poise
another of sensuality, the blood and baseness of our
natures would conduct us to most prepost'rous
conclusions. But we have reason to cool our raging
330     motions, our carnal stings, our unbitted lusts. Whereof I
take this that you call love to be a sect or scion.

**RODERIGO**

It cannot be.

**IAGO**

It is merely a lust of the blood and a permission of the will.
Come, be a man. Drown thyself? Drown cats and blind
335.     puppies! I have professed me thy friend, and I confess me

**IAGO**

If you do that, I'll never respect you again. Why, you silly man!

**RODERIGO**

It's silly to live when life is torture. The only cure is death.

**IAGO**

Oh, how stupid! I've been alive for twenty-eight years, and I've never met a man who knew what was good for him. I'd rather be a baboon than kill myself out of love for some woman I can't have.

**RODERIGO**

What should I do? I know it's foolish to be so much in love, but I can't help it.

**IAGO**

Can't help it? Nonsense! What we are is up to us. Our bodies are like gardens and our willpower is like the gardener. Depending on what we plant—weeds or lettuce, or one kind of herb rather than a variety, the garden will either be barren and useless, or rich and productive. If we didn't have rational minds to counterbalance our emotions and desires, our bodily urges would take over. We'd end up in ridiculous situations. Thankfully, we have reason to cool our raging lusts. In my opinion, what you call love is just an offshoot of lust.

**RODERIGO**

I don't believe it.

**IAGO**

You feel love because you feel lust and you have no willpower. Come on, be a man. Drown yourself? Drowning is for cats or blind puppies—don't drown yourself! I've told you I'm your friend, and I'll stick by

knit to thy deserving with cables of perdurable toughness.
I could never better stead thee than now. Put money in thy
purse. Follow thou the wars, defeat thy favor with an
usurped beard. I say, put money in thy purse. It cannot be
340 long that Desdemona should continue her love to the
Moor—put money in thy purse—nor he his to her. It was
a violent commencement in her, and thou shalt see an
answerable sequestration—put but money in thy purse.
These Moors are changeable in their wills—fill thy purse
345 with money. The food that to him now is as luscious as
locusts shall be to him shortly as bitter as coloquintida.
She must change for youth. When she is sated with his
body she will find the errors of her choice. Therefore, put
money in thy purse. If thou wilt needs damn thyself, do it
350 a more delicate way than drowning. Make all the money
thou canst. If sanctimony and a frail vow betwixt an erring
barbarian and supersubtle Venetian be not too hard for my
wits and all the tribe of hell, thou shalt enjoy her.
Therefore make money. A pox of drowning thyself! 'Tis
355 clean out of the way. Seek thou rather to be hanged in
compassing thy joy than to be drowned and go without her.

**RODERIGO**
Wilt thou be fast to my hopes, if I depend on the issue?

**IAGO**
Thou art sure of me. Go, make money. I have told thee
often, and I re-tell thee again and again, I hate the Moor.
360 My cause is hearted. Thine hath no less reason. Let us be
conjunctive in our revenge against him. If thou canst
cuckold him, thou dost thyself a pleasure, me a sport.
There are many events in the womb of time which will be
delivered. Traverse, go, provide thy money. We will have
365 more of this tomorrow. Adieu.

**RODERIGO**
Where shall we meet i' th' morning?

you. I've never been more useful to you than I will be now. Here's what you'll do. Sell all your assets and your land, and turn it into cash. Desdemona can't continue loving the Moor any more than he can continue loving her. She fell in love with him very suddenly, and they'll break up just as suddenly. Moors are moody people.—So sell your lands and raise a lot of cash. What seems sweet to him now will soon turn bitter. She'll dump Othello for a younger man. When she's had enough of the Moor's body, she'll realize her mistake. She'll need to have a new lover. She'll have to have it. So have your money ready. If you want to go to hell, there are better ways to do it than killing yourself. Raise all the money you can. I can get the better of religion and a few flimsy vows between a misguided barbarian and a depraved Venetian girl. You'll get to sleep with her—just put together some money. And to hell with drowning yourself! That's completely beside the point. If you're ready to die, you can risk death by committing crimes in an attempt to get the woman you want. Don't just give up on her and drown yourself.

**RODERIGO**

Can I count on you if I wait to see what happens?

**IAGO**

You can trust me. Go now and get cash. I told you before, and I'll tell you again and again: I hate the Moor. I'm devoted to my cause of hating him, just as devoted as you are to yours. So let's join forces and get revenge. If you seduce Desdemona and make a fool out of him, it'll be fun for both of us. Many things may happen. Go get money. We'll speak again tomorrow. Goodbye.

**RODERIGO**

Where will we meet in the morning?

IAGO

                               At my lodging.

RODERIGO

I'll be with thee betimes.

IAGO

                        Go to, farewell.
Do you hear, Roderigo?

RODERIGO

What say you?

IAGO

370    No more of drowning, do you hear?

RODERIGO

I am changed.

IAGO

Go to, farewell. Put money enough in your purse.

RODERIGO

I'll sell all my land.

*Exit*

IAGO

Thus do I ever make my fool my purse.
375    For I mine own gained knowledge should profane
If I would time expend with such a snipe
But for my sport and profit. I hate the Moor,
And it is thought abroad that 'twixt my sheets
He's done my office. I know not if 't be true,
380    But I, for mere suspicion in that kind,
Will do as if for surety. He holds me well.
The better shall my purpose work on him.
Cassio's a proper man. Let me see now,

**IAGO**

At my house.

**RODERIGO**

I'll be there early.

**IAGO**

Go home. Goodbye. Oh, and one more thing—

**RODERIGO**

What is it?

**IAGO**

No more talk about killing yourself, okay?

**RODERIGO**

I've changed my mind about that.

**IAGO**

Go then, goodbye. Put a lot of cash together.

**RODERIGO**

I'm going to sell all my land.

*RODERIGO exits.*

**IAGO**

That's how I always do it, getting money from fools. I'd be wasting my skills dealing with an idiot like that if I couldn't get something useful out of him. I hate the Moor, and there's a widespread rumor that he's slept with my wife. I'm not sure it's true, but just the suspicion is enough for me. He thinks highly of me. That'll help. Cassio's a handsome man. Let's see, how

To get his place and to plume up my will
385 In double knavery. How? How? Let's see.
After some time, to abuse Othello's ear
That he is too familiar with his wife.
He hath a person and a smooth dispose
To be suspected, framed to make women false.
390 The Moor is of a free and open nature
That thinks men honest that but seem to be so,
And will as tenderly be led by th' nose
As asses are.
I have 't. It is engendered! Hell and night
395 Must bring this monstrous birth to the world's light.

*Exit*

can I get his position and use him to hurt Othello at the same time? How? How? Let's see. After a while I'll start telling Othello that Cassio is too intimate with Desdemona. Cassio is a smooth talker and a good-looking guy, the sort of man that people would expect to be a seducer. The Moor is open and straightforward. He thinks any man who seems honest is honest. People like that are easy to manipulate. So it's all decided. I've worked it out. With a little help from the devil, I'll bring this monstrous plan to success.

*He exits.*

# ACT TWO

## Scene 1

*Enter* MONTANO *and two* GENTLEMEN

**MONTANO**
What from the cape can you discern at sea?

**FIRST GENTLEMAN**
Nothing at all. It is a high-wrought flood.
I cannot 'twixt the heaven and the main
5 Descry a sail.

**MONTANO**
Methinks the wind hath spoke aloud at land,
A fuller blast ne'er shook our battlements.
If it hath ruffianed so upon the sea
What ribs of oak, when mountains melt on them,
10 Can hold the mortise? What shall we hear of this?

**SECOND GENTLEMAN**
A segregation of the Turkish fleet.
For do but stand upon the foaming shore,
The chidden billow seems to pelt the clouds,
The wind-shaked surge, with high and monstrous mane,
15 Seems to cast water on the burning bear,
And quench the guards of th' ever-fixèd pole.
I never did like molestation view
On the enchafèd flood.

**MONTANO**
If that the Turkish fleet
20 Be not ensheltered and embayed, they are drowned.
It is impossible they bear it out.

*Enter a* THIRD GENTLEMAN

# ACT TWO

## Scene 1

MONTANO *and two* GENTLEMEN *enter.*

**MONTANO**
What can you see out on the ocean?

**FIRST GENTLEMAN**
Nothing. The water's so rough that I can't see any sails, either in the bay or on the ocean.

**MONTANO**
It was windy on shore too. A big blast of wind shook our fortifications. How could a ship made out of wood hold together in those mountainous waves? What do you think will be the result of this storm?

**SECOND GENTLEMAN**
The Turkish navy will be broken up. The wind's whipping up the waves so high you expect them to reach the clouds and splash against the stars in the sky. I've never seen the waters so disturbed.

**MONTANO**
If the Turkish fleet isn't protected in some harbor, their men must all be drowned. No ship could survive this storm.

*A* THIRD GENTLEMAN *enters.*

**THIRD GENTLEMAN**
News, lads, Our wars are done!
The desperate tempest hath so banged the Turks,
That their designment halts. A noble ship of Venice
25    Hath seen a grievous wreck and sufferance
On most part of their fleet.

**MONTANO**
How? Is this true?

**THIRD GENTLEMAN**
                              The ship is here put in,
A Veronesa. Michael Cassio,
Lieutenant to the warlike Moor Othello,
30    Is come on shore. The Moor himself at sea
And is in full commission here for Cyprus.

**MONTANO**
I am glad on 't. 'Tis a worthy governor.

**THIRD GENTLEMAN**
But this same Cassio, though he speak of comfort
Touching the Turkish loss, yet he looks sadly
35    And prays the Moor be safe. For they were parted
With foul and violent tempest.

**MONTANO**
                              Pray heavens he be,
For I have served him, and the man commands
Like a full soldier. Let's to the seaside, ho!
As well to see the vessel that's come in
40    As to throw out our eyes for brave Othello,
Even till we make the main and th' aerial blue
An indistinct regard.

**THIRD GENTLEMAN**
                    Come, let's do so.
For every minute is expectancy
Of more arrivance.

*Enter* CASSIO

**THIRD GENTLEMAN**

I've got news, boys, the war's over! This terrible storm has smashed the Turks so badly that their plans are ruined. One of our ships has reported that it saw most of their fleet shipwrecked.

**MONTANO**

What? Is this true?

**THIRD GENTLEMAN**

The ship's sailing into harbor now; it's from Verona. Michael Cassio, lieutenant of the Moor Othello, has arrived on shore. The Moor himself is still at sea. He's been commissioned to come here to Cyprus.

**MONTANO**

I'm happy about that. He'll be a good governor.

**THIRD GENTLEMAN**

Cassio brings good news about the Turkish defeat, but he's worried about Othello's safety. The two of them were separated during the storm.

**MONTANO**

I hope to God Othello's all right. I served under him, and I know what an excellent commander he is. Let's go to the shore to get a look at the ship that came in, and to look out for Othello's ship. We'll stare out at the sea until the sea and the sky blur together.

**THIRD GENTLEMAN**

Let's do that. Every minute we expect more ships to arrive.

CASSIO *enters.*

**CASSIO**

45      Thanks, you the valiant of this warlike isle
        That so approve the Moor. Oh, let the heavens
        Give him defense against the elements,
        For I have lost him on a dangerous sea.

**MONTANO**

        Is he well shipped?

**CASSIO**

50      His bark is stoutly timbered and his pilot
        Of very expert and approved allowance
        Therefore my hopes, not surfeited to death,
        Stand in bold cure.

**A VOICE**

        *(within)* A sail, a sail, a sail!

        *Enter a* MESSENGER

**CASSIO**

55      What noise?

**MESSENGER**

        The town is empty. On the brow o' th' sea
        Stand ranks of people, and they cry "A sail!"

**CASSIO**

        My hopes do shape him for the governor.

        *A shot*

**SECOND GENTLEMAN**

        They do discharge their shot of courtesy.
60      Our friends at least.

**CASSIO**

        I pray you sir, go forth
        And give us truth who 'tis that is arrived.

**SECOND GENTLEMAN**

        I shall.

                                                    *Exit*

CASSIO

Thanks, you brave men who defend this island and respect Othello. I hope heaven protects him from the weather, because I lost sight of him on the stormy sea.

MONTANO

Is his ship sturdy?

CASSIO

Yes, it's well built, and the ship's pilot is very expert and experienced. For that reason I still have some hope for him, even though I don't have my hopes up too high.

A VOICE

*(offstage)* A sail! A sail! A sail!

A MESSENGER *enters.*

CASSIO

What's all that shouting about?

MESSENGER

Everybody in town is down at the shore shouting "A sail!"

CASSIO

I hope it's Othello.

*A shot is heard.*

SECOND GENTLEMAN

They've fired a greeting shot, so at least it's a friendly ship.

CASSIO

Please go find out for certain who has arrived.

SECOND GENTLEMAN

I'll do that.

SECOND GENTLEMAN *exits.*

**MONTANO**
But good lieutenant, is your general wived?

**CASSIO**
65    Most fortunately. He hath achieved a maid
That paragons description and wild fame,
One that excels the quirks of blazoning pens,
And in th' essential vesture of creation
Does tire the ingener.

*Enter* SECOND GENTLEMAN

70    How now? Who has put in?

**SECOND GENTLEMAN**
'Tis one Iago, ancient to the general.

**CASSIO**
He's had most favorable and happy speed.
Tempests themselves, high seas, and howling winds,
The guttered rocks and congregated sands,
75    Traitors ensteeped to enclog the guiltless keel,
As having sense of beauty, do omit
Their mortal natures, letting go safely by
The divine Desdemona.

**MONTANO**
What is she?

**CASSIO**
80    She that I spake of, our great captain's captain,
Left in the conduct of the bold Iago,
Whose footing here anticipates our thoughts
A se'nnight's speed. Great Jove, Othello guard,
And swell his sail with thine own powerful breath,
85    That he may bless this bay with his tall ship,
Make love's quick pants in Desdemona's arms,
Give renewed fire to our extincted spirits
And bring all Cyprus comfort!

**MONTANO**

Good lieutenant, is your general married?

**CASSIO**

Yes, and he's very lucky to have married the woman he did. His wife defies description. She's God's master-piece, and she'd exhaust whoever tried to do her justice while praising her.

*The* SECOND GENTLEMAN *enters.*

Who's arrived in the harbor?

**SECOND GENTLEMAN**

A man named Iago, the general's ensign.

**CASSIO**

He made good time. You see how the storm, the jagged rocks, and the sand banks that trap ships all appreciate a beautiful woman. They let the heavenly Desdemona arrive safe and sound.

**MONTANO**

Who's that?

**CASSIO**

She's the one I was talking about, the general's wife. The brave Iago was put in charge of bringing her here, and he's arrived a week sooner than we expected. Dear God, please protect Othello and help him arrive here safely, so he and Desdemona can be in each other's arms, and Othello can cheer us up and bring comfort to Cyprus.

*Enter* DESDEMONA, EMILIA, IAGO, RODERIGO *with attendants*

                                        Oh, behold,
The riches of the ship is come on shore!
90      You men of Cyprus, let her have your knees.
Hail to thee, lady, and the grace of heaven,
Before, behind thee, and on every hand,
Enwheel thee round!

**DESDEMONA**
I thank you, valiant Cassio.
95      What tidings can you tell me of my lord?

**CASSIO**
He is not yet arrived. Nor know I aught
But that he's well and will be shortly here.

**DESDEMONA**
Oh, but I fear. How lost you company?

**CASSIO**
The great contention of the sea and skies
100    Parted our fellowship—

**A VOICE**
*(within)* A sail, a sail!

**CASSIO**
But, hark! a sail.

*A shot*

**SECOND GENTLEMAN**
They give this greeting to the citadel.
This likewise is a friend.

**CASSIO**
                        See for the news.

*Exit a* SECOND GENTLEMEN

DESDEMONA, IAGO, RODERIGO *and* EMILIA *enter.*

Look, the precious Desdemona has arrived on shore. We should all kneel before her, men of Cyprus! Greetings, my lady, and may God always be with you.

DESDEMONA

Thank you, brave Cassio. Is there any news about my husband?

CASSIO

He hasn't arrived yet. As far as I know, he's okay and will arrive here soon.

DESDEMONA

Oh, but I'm worried. How did you two get separated?

CASSIO

The storm separated us.

A VOICE

*(offstage)* A sail! A sail!

CASSIO

Listen, they've spotted another ship!

*A gunshot is heard.*

SECOND GENTLEMAN

They fired a greeting shot too, so this is also a friendly ship.

CASSIO

Go find out the news.

SECOND GENTLEMAN *exits.*

105    Good ancient, you are welcome.—Welcome, mistress.
       *(kisses* EMILIA*)*
       Let it not gall your patience, good Iago,
       That I extend my manners. 'Tis my breeding
       That gives me this bold show of courtesy.

IAGO
       Sir, would she give you so much of her lips
110    As of her tongue she oft bestows on me,
       You'll have enough.

DESDEMONA
       Alas, she has no speech!

IAGO
       In faith, too much.
       I find it still, when I have leave to sleep.
115    Marry, before your ladyship, I grant,
       She puts her tongue a little in her heart
       And chides with thinking.

EMILIA
                              You have little cause to say so.

IAGO
       Come on, come on. You are pictures out of door, bells in
       your parlors, wild-cats in your kitchens, saints in your
120    injuries, devils being offended, players in your
       housewifery, and housewives in your beds.

DESDEMONA
       Oh, fie upon thee, slanderer!

IAGO
       Nay, it is true, or else I am a Turk.
       You rise to play and go to bed to work.

EMILIA
125    You shall not write my praise.

IAGO
                                    No, let me not.

Ensign Iago, welcome.—And welcome to you, too, madam. *(he kisses* EMILIA*)* Don't be upset that I kissed your wife hello, Iago. It's a courtesy where I come from.

IAGO

If she gave you as much lip as she gives me, you'd be sick of her by now.

DESDEMONA

On the contrary, she's a soft-spoken woman.

IAGO

No, she talks too much. She's always talking when I want to sleep. I admit that in front of you, my lady, she keeps a bit quiet. But she's scolding me silently.

EMILIA

You have no reason to say that.

IAGO

Come on, come on. You women are all the same. You're as pretty as pictures when you're out in public, but in your own houses you're as noisy as jangling bells. In your own kitchens you act like wildcats. You make yourselves sound like saints when you're complaining about something, but you act like devils when someone offends you. You don't take your jobs as housewives seriously, and you're shameless hussies in bed.

DESDEMONA

Shame on you, you slanderer!

IAGO

No, it's true, or if it's not, I'm a villain. You wake up to have fun, and you start work when you go to bed.

EMILIA

You clearly have nothing good to say about me.

IAGO

No, I don't.

**DESDEMONA**
What wouldst thou write of me, if thou should'st
praise me?

**IAGO**
O gentle lady, do not put me to 't,
For I am nothing, if not critical.

**DESDEMONA**
130    Come on, assay. There's one gone to the harbor?

**IAGO**
Ay, madam.

**DESDEMONA**
I am not merry, but I do beguile
The thing I am by seeming otherwise.
Come, how wouldst thou praise me?

**IAGO**
135    I am about it, but indeed my invention
Comes from my pate as birdlime does from frieze,
It plucks out brains and all. But my Muse labors
And thus she is delivered:
If she be fair and wise, fairness and wit,
140    The one's for use, the other useth it.

**DESDEMONA**
Well praised! How if she be black and witty?

**IAGO**
If she be black, and thereto have a wit,
She'll find a white that shall her blackness fit.

**DESDEMONA**
Worse and worse!

**EMILIA**
How if fair and foolish?

**IAGO**
145    She never yet was foolish that was fair,
For even her folly helped her to an heir.

**DESDEMONA**
These are old fond paradoxes to make fools laugh i' th'
alehouse. What miserable praise hast thou for her
That's foul and foolish?

**DESDEMONA**

But if you had to say something nice about me, what would you say?

**IAGO**

Don't make me do it, my lady. I'm critical by nature.

**DESDEMONA**

Come on, just try.—By the way, has someone gone down to the harbor?

**IAGO**

Yes, madam.

**DESDEMONA**

I'm not as happy as I seem. I'm just trying not to show how worried I am about Othello's safety. Come on, what would you say about me?

**IAGO**

I'm trying to think of something, but I'm not good at inventing clever things. It takes time. Ah, I've got it. If a woman is pretty and smart, she uses her good looks to get what she wants.

**DESDEMONA**

Very clever! But what if the woman is smart but ugly?

**IAGO**

Even if she's ugly, she'll be smart enough to find a guy to sleep with her.

**DESDEMONA**

This is getting worse and worse!

**EMILIA**

What if she's pretty but stupid?

**IAGO**

No pretty woman is stupid, because her stupidity will make her more attractive to men.

**DESDEMONA**

These are stupid old jokes that men tell each other in bars. What horrible thing do you have to say about a woman who's both ugly and stupid?

**IAGO**

150     There's none so foul and foolish thereunto,
But does foul pranks which fair and wise ones do.

**DESDEMONA**

Oh, heavy ignorance! Thou praisest the worst best. But
what praise couldst thou bestow on a deserving woman
indeed, one that in the authority of her merit did justly put

155     on the vouch of very malice itself?

**IAGO**

She that was ever fair and never proud,
Had tongue at will and yet was never loud,
Never lacked gold and yet went never gay,
Fled from her wish and yet said "Now I may,"

160     She that being angered, her revenge being nigh,
Bade her wrong stay and her displeasure fly,
She that in wisdom never was so frail
To change the cod's head for the salmon's tail,
She that could think and ne'er disclose her mind,

165     See suitors following and not look behind,
She was a wight, if ever such wights were—

**DESDEMONA**

To do what?

**IAGO**

To suckle fools and chronicle small beer.

**DESDEMONA**

Oh, most lame and impotent conclusion! Do not learn of

170     him, Emilia, though he be thy husband. How say you,
Cassio? Is he not a most profane and liberal counselor?

**CASSIO**

He speaks home, madam. You may relish him more in the
soldier than in the scholar.

CASSIO *takes* DESDEMONA'S *hand*

**IAGO**

*(aside)* He takes her by the palm. Ay, well said, whisper!

175.     With as little a web as this will I ensnare as great a fly as

**IAGO**

No matter how ugly or stupid the woman is, she plays the same dirty tricks that the smart and pretty ones do.

**DESDEMONA**

You don't know a thing! You give your best praise to the worst women. But how would you praise a truly good woman, someone who had no reason to worry about what anyone said about her?

**IAGO**

A woman who was beautiful but never proud, who could speak well but knew when to be quiet, who dressed well but was never overdressed, who had self-restraint even when she could get what she wanted, a woman who never took revenge, who overlooked it when people hurt her, who was too wise to do anything stupid, who could think without revealing her thoughts, and who could refrain from flirting with men in love with her, that kind of woman, if she ever existed, would—

**DESDEMONA**

Would do what?

**IAGO**

Would raise babies and clip coupons.

**DESDEMONA**

Oh, that's pathetic! Don't listen to him, Emilia, even though he's your husband. What do you think about him, Cassio? Isn't he a horrible man?

**CASSIO**

He speaks bluntly, madam. He's more of a soldier than a wise man.

CASSIO *takes* DESDEMONA'S *hand.*

**IAGO**

*(to himself)* He's taking her hand. That's right, go ahead and whisper together. This is all I need to get

ACT TWO

Cassio. Ay, smile upon her, do, I will gyve thee in thine own
courtship. You say true, 'Tis so, indeed. If such tricks as these
strip you out of your lieutenantry, it had been better you had
not kissed your three fingers so oft, which now again you are
180 most apt to play the sir in. Very good, well kissed, and
excellent courtesy! 'tis so, indeed. Yet again your fingers to
your lips? Would they were clyster-pipes for your sake!—

*Trumpet within*

The Moor! I know his trumpet.

CASSIO

                                                        'Tis truly so.

DESDEMONA
Let's meet him and receive him.

CASSIO

                                                  Lo, here he comes!

*Enter* OTHELLO *and attendants*

OTHELLO
185 Oh my fair warrior!

DESDEMONA

                                        My dear Othello!

OTHELLO
It gives me wonder great as my content
To see you here before me. Oh, my soul's joy!
If after every tempest come such calms,
May the winds blow till they have wakened death,
190 And let the laboring bark climb hills of seas
Olympus-high, and duck again as low
As hell's from heaven! If it were now to die,
'Twere now to be most happy, for I fear
My soul hath her content so absolute
195 That not another comfort like to this
Succeeds in unknown fate.

Cassio. Yes, keep smiling at her, Cassio. Your fine manners around women will be your downfall. Oh, I'm sure you're saying something very clever. If you lose your job because of little flirtations like this, you'll wish you hadn't been so courteous with her. Oh, how nice, you're kissing your own hand, one finger at a time? I wish those fingers were enema tubes!—

*A gentleman's kissing his own fingers was considered a polite gesture.*

*A trumpet plays offstage.*

That's the Moor! I recognize his trumpet.

CASSIO
Yes, it is.

DESDEMONA
Let's go greet him when he lands.

CASSIO
Look, here he comes.

OTHELLO *enters with attendants.*

OTHELLO
My beautiful warrior!

DESDEMONA
My darling Othello!

OTHELLO
I'm amazed you got here before me. But I'm overjoyed! My love, if the calm after the storm could always be this wonderful, I'd want the wind to blow until it waked the dead, and whipped up waves as tall as mountains! If I died right now I'd be completely happy, since I'll probably never be as happy as this again in my life.

**DESDEMONA**
         The heavens forbid
But that our loves and comforts should increase,
Even as our days do grow.

**OTHELLO**
        Amen to that, sweet powers!
I cannot speak enough of this content.
200 It stops me here, it is too much of joy.
And this, and this, the greatest discords be *(kissing her)*
That e'er our hearts shall make!

**IAGO**
*(aside)*
        Oh, you are well tuned now,
But I'll set down the pegs that make this music,
As honest as I am.

**OTHELLO**
       Come, let us to the castle.
205 News, friends! Our wars are done, the Turks
    are drowned.
How does my old acquaintance of this isle?—
Honey, you shall be well desired in Cyprus,
I have found great love amongst them. O my sweet,
I prattle out of fashion, and I dote
210 In mine own comforts.—I prithee, good Iago,
Go to the bay and disembark my coffers.
Bring thou the master to the citadel.
He is a good one, and his worthiness
Does challenge much respect.—Come, Desdemona,
215 Once more, well met at Cyprus.

*Exeunt* OTHELLO, DESDEMONA, *and attendants*

**IAGO**
Do thou meet me presently at the harbor.—Come hither.
If thou be'st valiant, as they say base men being in love
have then a nobility in their natures more than is native to
them, list me. The lieutenant tonight watches on the court

**DESDEMONA**

God willing, our love and our happiness will only increase as we get older.

**OTHELLO**

Amen to that! I can't talk about my happiness anymore. It's too much. I hope these kisses I'm about to give you are the closest we ever come to fighting. *(they kiss)*

**IAGO**

*(to himself)* Oh, you're happy now, but I'll ruin your happiness, for all my supposed honesty.

**OTHELLO**

Let's go up to the castle. Good news, friends. The war's over and the Turks are drowned. How are my old friends from this island doing?—Honey, they'll love you here in Cyprus. They've been very good to me here. Oh, my dear, I'm blabbing on and on because I'm so happy.—Iago, would you be good enough to go get my trunks from the ships? And bring the ship's captain to the castle. He's a good man.—Let's go, Desdemona. I'll say it again: I'm so happy to see you here in Cyprus!

**OTHELLO**, **DESDEMONA**, *and attendants exit.*

**IAGO**

Meet me down at the harbor.—Come here. They say love makes cowards brave. So if you're brave, listen to me. Lieutenant Cassio will be on guard duty tonight.

220 of guard. First, I must tell thee this: Desdemona is directly
in love with him.

**RODERIGO**
With him? Why, 'tis not possible.

**IAGO**
Lay thy finger thus, and let thy soul be instructed. Mark
me with what violence she first loved the Moor, but for
225 bragging and telling her fantastical lies. To love him still
for prating? Let not thy discreet heart think it. Her eye
must be fed, and what delight shall she have to look on the
devil? When the blood is made dull with the act of sport,
there should be a game to inflame it and to give satiety a
230 fresh appetite, loveliness in favor, sympathy in years,
manners and beauties. All which the Moor is defective in.
Now for want of these required conveniences, her delicate
tenderness will find itself abused, begin to heave the gorge,
disrelish and abhor the Moor. Very nature will instruct
235 her in it and compel her to some second choice. Now sir,
this granted—as it is a most pregnant and unforced
position—who stands so eminent in the degree of this
fortune as Cassio does? A knave very voluble, no further
conscionable than in putting on the mere form of civil and
240 humane seeming, for the better compassing of his salt and
most hidden loose affection. Why, none, why, none! A
slipper and subtle knave, a finder of occasions that has an
eye, can stamp and counterfeit advantages, though true
advantage never present itself. A devilish knave. Besides,
245 the knave is handsome, young, and hath all those requisites
in him that folly and green minds look after. A pestilent
complete knave, and the woman hath found him already.

**RODERIGO**
I cannot believe that in her. She's full of most blessed
condition.

**IAGO**
250. Blessed fig's-end! The wine she drinks is made of grapes.
If she had been blessed, she would never have loved the

But first, I have to tell you that Desdemona's completely in love with him.

**RODERIGO**

With Cassio? That's impossible.

**IAGO**

Be quiet and listen to me. Remember how she fell madly in love with the Moor because he bragged and told her made-up stories? Did you expect her to keep on loving him for his chattering? You're too smart to think that. No, she needs someone nice-looking. Othello's ugly, what pleasure could she find in him? Lovemaking gets boring after a while. To keep things hot, she'll need to see someone with a handsome face, someone close to her in age, someone who looks and acts like her. Othello isn't any of those things. Since he doesn't have these advantages to make him attractive to her, she'll get sick of him until he makes her want to puke. She'll start looking around for a second choice. Now, if that's true—and it's obviously true—who's in a better position than Cassio? He's a smooth talker, and uses sophistication and fine manners to hide his lust. Nobody's as crafty as he is. Besides, he's young and handsome, and he's got all the qualities that naïve and silly girls go for. He's a bad boy, and Desdemona's got her eye on him already.

**RODERIGO**

I can't believe that. She's not that kind of woman. She's very moral.

**IAGO**

Like hell she is! She's made of the same flesh and blood as everyone else. If she were so moral, she would never have fallen in love with the Moor in the first place.

Moor. Blessed pudding! Didst thou not see her paddle
with the palm of his hand? Didst not mark that?

RODERIGO

Yes, that I did, but that was but courtesy.

IAGO

255    Lechery, by this hand, an index and obscure prologue to
the history of lust and foul thoughts. They met so near
with their lips that their breaths embraced together.
Villainous thoughts, Roderigo! When these mutabilities
so marshal the way, hard at hand comes the master and
260    main exercise, th' incorporate conclusion. Pish! But, sir,
be you ruled by me. I have brought you from Venice.
Watch you tonight for the command, I'll lay 't upon you.
Cassio knows you not. I'll not be far from you. Do you
find some occasion to anger Cassio, either by speaking too
265    loud, or tainting his discipline, or from what other course
you please, which the time shall more favorably minister.

RODERIGO

Well.

IAGO

Sir, he's rash and very sudden in choler, and haply may
strike at you. Provoke him that he may. For even out of that
270    will I cause these of Cyprus to mutiny, whose qualification
shall come into no true taste again but by the displanting of
Cassio. So shall you have a shorter journey to your desires
by the means I shall then have to prefer them, and the
impediment most profitably removed, without the
275    which there were no expectation of our prosperity.

RODERIGO

I will do this, if you can bring it to any opportunity.

IAGO

I warrant thee. Meet me by and by at the citadel. I must
fetch his necessaries ashore. Farewell.

RODERIGO

Adieu.

*Exit*

Good lord! Did you notice how she and Cassio were fondling each other's hands? Did you see that?

**RODERIGO**

Yes, I did. But that wasn't romantic, it was just polite manners.

**IAGO**

They were lusting after each other. You could tell by how they were acting that they're going to be lovers. They were so close that their breath was mingling. When two people get that intimate, sex will soon follow. Disgusting! But listen to me; let me guide you. I brought you here from Venice. Be on guard duty tonight. I'll put you in charge. Cassio doesn't know you. I'll be nearby. Make Cassio angry somehow, either by speaking too loud, or insulting his military skills, or however else you want.

**RODERIGO**

All right.

**IAGO**

He's hot-tempered, and he might try to hit you with his staff. Try to get him to do that. That'll allow me to stir up public sentiment against him here in Cyprus. I'll get them so riled up that they'll only calm down when Cassio's fired. To get what you want, you need to get Cassio out of the way. If you don't do that, things are hopeless for you.

**RODERIGO**

I'll do it, if you help me out.

**IAGO**

I promise I will. Meet me in a little while at the citadel. I need to get Othello's things from the ship. Goodbye.

**RODERIGO**

Goodbye.

**RODERIGO** *exits.*

**IAGO**

280   That Cassio loves her, I do well believe 't.
      That she loves him, 'tis apt and of great credit.
      The Moor, howbeit that I endure him not,
      Is of a constant, loving, noble nature,
      And I dare think he'll prove to Desdemona
285   A most dear husband. Now, I do love her too,
      Not out of absolute lust—though peradventure
      I stand accountant for as great a sin—
      But partly led to diet my revenge,
      For that I do suspect the lusty Moor
290   Hath leaped into my seat. The thought whereof
      Doth, like a poisonous mineral, gnaw my inwards,
      And nothing can or shall content my soul
      Till I am evened with him, wife for wife.
      Or, failing so, yet that I put the Moor
295   At least into a jealousy so strong
      That judgment cannot cure. Which thing to do,
      If this poor trash of Venice, whom I trace
      For his quick hunting, stand the putting on,
      I'll have our Michael Cassio on the hip,
300   Abuse him to the Moor in the right garb
      (For I fear Cassio with my night-cape too)
      Make the Moor thank me, love me, and reward me
      For making him egregiously an ass
      And practicing upon his peace and quiet
305   Even to madness. 'Tis here, but yet confused.
      Knavery's plain face is never seen till used.

                                                   *Exit*

**IAGO**

I think Cassio really does love her, and it's perfectly likely that she loves him too. I can't stand the Moor, but I have to admit that he's a reliable, loving, and good-natured man. He'd probably be a good husband to Desdemona. I love her too, not simply out of lust, but also to feed my revenge. I have a feeling the Moor slept with my wife. That thought keeps gnawing at me, eating me up inside. I won't be satisfied until I get even with him, wife for wife. If I can't do that, I can at least make the Moor so jealous that he can't think straight. If that piece of Venetian trash Roderigo can do what I need to carry out my plan, I'll have power over Cassio. I'll say bad things about him to the Moor. I have a feeling Cassio seduced my wife as well. I'll make the Moor thank me, love me, and reward me, even though the joke will be on him the whole time. I've got a good plan, though I haven't worked out the details yet. You can never see the end of an evil plan until the moment comes.

IAGO *exits.*

## ACT TWO, Scene 2

*Enter Othello's* HERALD, *with a proclamation*

HERALD
It is Othello's pleasure, our noble and valiant general,
that, upon certain tidings now arrived, importing the
mere perdition of the Turkish fleet, every man put himself
into triumph: some to dance, some to make bonfires, each
man to what sport and revels his addiction leads him. For
besides these beneficial news, it is the celebration of his
nuptial. So much was his pleasure should be proclaimed.
All offices are open, and there is full liberty of feasting
from this present hour of five till the bell have told eleven.
Bless the isle of Cyprus and our noble general Othello!

*Exit*

## ACT TWO, Scene 2

*Othello's* HERALD *enters with a proclamation.*

HERALD

Our noble and courageous general Othello having been informed that the Turkish fleet has been completely destroyed, invites every man to celebrate our victory. Some of you dance, some of you make bonfires, and every man celebrate in whatever way he likes to. For besides the good news, we are also celebrating his marriage. That's the end of the announcement. There will be a feast from five o'clock until eleven. God bless the island of Cyprus and our noble general Othello!

*The* HERALD *exits.*

## ACT TWO, Scene 3

*Enter* OTHELLO, DESDEMONA, CASSIO, *and attendants*

OTHELLO
Good Michael, look you to the guard tonight.
Let's teach ourselves that honorable stop
Not to outsport discretion.

CASSIO
Iago hath direction what to do,
5    But notwithstanding with my personal eye
Will I look to 't.

OTHELLO
             Iago is most honest.
Michael, good night. Tomorrow with your earliest
Let me have speech with you.—
Come, my dear love,
10   The purchase made, the fruits are to ensue:
That profit's yet to come 'tween me and you.
Good night.

        *Exeunt* OTHELLO, DESDEMONA, *and attendants*
*Enter* IAGO

CASSIO
Welcome, Iago. We must to the watch.

IAGO
Not this hour, lieutenant, 'tis not yet ten o' the clock. Our
15   general cast us thus early for the love of his Desdemona—
who let us not therefore blame. He hath not yet made
wanton the night with her, and she is sport for Jove.

CASSIO
She's a most exquisite lady.

IAGO
And, I'll warrant her, full of game.

## ACT TWO, Scene 3

OTHELLO, DESDEMONA, CASSIO *and attendants enter.*

**OTHELLO**

Good Michael, keep a careful eye on the guards tonight. Let's exercise restraint and not let the party get too wild.

**CASSIO**

Iago has orders what to do. But I'll see to it personally anyway.

**OTHELLO**

Iago's a good man. Goodnight, Michael. Come talk to me tomorrow as early as you can.—Come with me, my dear love. Now that the wedding's over, we can have the pleasure of consummating our marriage. Good night, everyone.

OTHELLO *and* DESDEMONA *exit with their attendants.* IAGO *enters.*

**CASSIO**

Hello, Iago. It's time for us to stand guard.

**IAGO**

*Jove is the head of the gods in Roman mythology*

Not yet, lieutenant. It's not even ten o'clock. The general got rid of us early tonight so he could be with Desdemona.—I can't blame him. He hasn't spent the night with her yet, and she's beautiful enough to be Jove's lover.

**CASSIO**

She's an exquisitely beautiful lady.

**IAGO**

And I bet she's good in bed too.

**CASSIO**
20      Indeed she's a most fresh and delicate creature.

**IAGO**
What an eye she has! Methinks it sounds a parley to provocation.

**CASSIO**
An inviting eye, and yet methinks right modest.

**IAGO**
And when she speaks, is it not an alarum to love?

**CASSIO**
25      She is indeed perfection.

**IAGO**
Well, happiness to their sheets! Come, lieutenant, I have a stoup of wine, and here without are a brace of Cyprus gallants that would fain have a measure to the health of black Othello.

**CASSIO**
30      Not tonight, good Iago. I have very poor and unhappy brains for drinking. I could well wish courtesy would invent some other custom of entertainment.

**IAGO**
Oh, they are our friends. But one cup. I'll drink for you.

**CASSIO**
I have drunk but one cup tonight, and that was craftily
35      qualified too, and behold what innovation it makes here. I am unfortunate in the infirmity, and dare not task my weakness with any more.

**IAGO**
What, man, 'tis a night of revels! The gallants desire it.

**CASSIO**
Where are they?

**IAGO**
40      Here at the door. I pray you call them in.

**CASSIO**
I'll do 't, but it dislikes me.

*Exit*

**CASSIO**

Yes, she's young and tender.

**IAGO**

And such pretty eyes! Like an invitation.

**CASSIO**

Yes, she's pretty. But she's modest and ladylike too.

**IAGO**

And when she speaks, doesn't her voice stir up passion?

**CASSIO**

She's a perfect woman, it's true.

**IAGO**

Well, good luck to them tonight in bed! Come with us, lieutenant. I've got a jug of wine, and these two Cyprus gentlemen want to drink a toast to the black Othello.

**CASSIO**

Not tonight, Iago. I'm not much of a drinker. I wish there was less social pressure to drink.

**IAGO**

Oh, but these are our friends. Just one glass. I'll do most of the drinking for you.

**CASSIO**

I've already had a glass of wine tonight, watered down, but look how drunk I am. I'm not a heavy drinker. I wouldn't dare drink much more than that.

**IAGO**

What are you talking about, man? Tonight is for celebrating! The gentlemen are waiting.

**CASSIO**

Where are they?

**IAGO**

By the door. Please invite them in.

**CASSIO**

I'll do it, but I don't like it.

CASSIO *exits.*

IAGO
    If I can fasten but one cup upon him,
    With that which he hath drunk tonight already,
    He'll be as full of quarrel and offense
45  As my young mistress' dog. Now my sick fool Roderigo,
    Whom love hath turned almost the wrong side out,
    To Desdemona hath tonight caroused
    Potations pottle-deep, and he's to watch.
    Three lads of Cyprus, noble swelling spirits
50  (That hold their honors in a wary distance,
    The very elements of this warlike isle)
    Have I tonight flustered with flowing cups,
    And they watch too. Now 'mongst this flock of drunkards
    Am I to put our Cassio in some action
55  That may offend the isle.
                                    But here they come.
    If consequence do but approve my dream
    My boat sails freely, both with wind and stream.

    *Enter* CASSIO, MONTANO *and gentlemen*


CASSIO
    'Fore heaven, they have given me a rouse already.
MONTANO
    Good faith, a little one, not past a pint,
60  As I am a soldier.
IAGO
                            Some wine, ho!
    *(sings)*
            *And let me the cannikin clink,  clink,*
            *And let me the cannikin clink.*
            *A soldier's a man,*
            *A life's but a span,*
65          *Why then let a soldier drink.*
            *Some wine, boys!*

IAGO

If I can just get him to drink one more glass after what he's drunk already, he'll be as argumentative and eager to fight as a little dog. That fool Roderigo, all twisted up inside with love, has been drinking toasts to Desdemona by the gallon, and he's on guard duty. I've gotten the rest of the guards drunk, as well as several gentlemen from Cyprus who are quick to take offense. Now I'll get Cassio to do something in front of all these drunkards that will offend everyone on the island. Here they come. If the future turns out as I hope it will, I'm all set for success.

CASSIO, MONTANO, *and* GENTLEMEN *enter, followed by servants with wine.*

CASSIO

My God, they've given me a lot to drink.

MONTANO

No, it was a little one, not more than a pint.

IAGO

Bring in more wine!
*(he sings)*
> *And clink your glasses together,*
> *And clink your glasses together.*
> *A soldier's a man,*
> *And a man's life is short,*
> *So let the soldier drink.*
> *Have some more wine, boys!*

**CASSIO**
'Fore heaven, an excellent song.

**IAGO**
I learned it in England where indeed they are most potent in potting. Your Dane, your German, and your swag-bellied Hollander—Drink, ho!—are nothing to your English.

**CASSIO**
Is your Englishman so expert in his drinking?

**IAGO**
Why, he drinks you with facility your Dane dead drunk; he sweats not to overthrow your Almain. He gives your Hollander a vomit ere the next pottle can be filled.

**CASSIO**
To the health of our general!

**MONTANO**
I am for it, lieutenant, and I'll do you justice.

**IAGO**
Oh, sweet England!
*(sings)*
> *King Stephen was a worthy peer,*
> *His breeches cost him but a crown,*
> *He held them sixpence all too dear,*
> *With that he called the tailor lown.*
> *He was a wight of high renown,*
> *And thou art but of low degree,*
> *'Tis pride that pulls the country down,*
> *Then take thine auld cloak about thee.*
> *Some wine, ho!*

**CASSIO**
Why, this is a more exquisite song than the other.

**IAGO**
Will you hear 't again?

**CASSIO**
No, for I hold him to be unworthy of his place that does those things. Well, heaven's above all, and there be souls must be saved, and there be souls must not be saved.

**IAGO**
It's true, good lieutenant.

**CASSIO**

My God, what a great song!

**IAGO**

I learned it England, where they have a talent for drinking. The Danes, the Germans, and the Dutch—come on, drink, drink!—are nothing compared to the English.

**CASSIO**

Are Englishmen really such heavy drinkers?

**IAGO**

They drink Danes under the table, and it takes them no effort at all to out-drink Germans. And the Dutch are vomiting while the English are asking for refills.

**CASSIO**

Let's drink to our general!

**MONTANO**

Hear, hear! I'll drink as much as you do!

**IAGO**

Oh, sweet England!
*(he sings)*
> *King Stephen was a good king, and his pants were*
> *    very cheap,*
> *But he thought his tailor overcharged him, so he*
> *    called him a peasant.*
> *And that was a man of noble rank, much higher than*
> *    you are.*
> *So be happy with your worn-out cloak,*
> *Since pride is ruining the nation.*
> *More wine!*

**CASSIO**

God, that song's even better than the other one.

**IAGO**

Do you want to hear it again?

**CASSIO**

No, because we shouldn't be doing that— stuff. Oh well, God's in charge, and some people have to go to heaven, while other people have to go to hell.

**IAGO**

That's true, lieutenant.

**CASSIO**
For mine own part, no offence to the general nor any man
of quality, I hope to be saved.

**IAGO**
95   And so do I too, lieutenant.

**CASSIO**
Ay, but (by your leave) not before me. The lieutenant is to
be saved before the ancient. Let's have no more of this,
let's to our affairs.—Forgive us our sins!—Gentlemen,
let's look to our business. Do not think, gentlemen, I am
100   drunk. This is my ancient, this is my right hand, and this
is my left. I am not drunk now. I can stand well enough,
and I speak well enough.

**ALL**
Excellent well!

**CASSIO**
Why, very well then. You must not think then that I am
105   drunk.

*Exit*

**MONTANO**
To th' platform, masters. Come, let's set the watch.

*Exit* GENTLEMEN

**IAGO**
You see this fellow that is gone before,
He is a soldier fit to stand by Caesar
And give direction. And do but see his vice,
110   'Tis to his virtue a just equinox,
The one as long as th' other. 'Tis pity of him.
I fear the trust Othello puts him in
On some odd time of his infirmity
Will shake this island.

**MONTANO**
                                But is he often thus?

CASSIO

Speaking for myself—and no offense to the general or anyone else—I hope I'm going to heaven.

IAGO

Me too, lieutenant.

CASSIO

Okay, but please not before me. The lieutenant has to get to heaven before the ensign. But let's stop this drinking and get down to business.—God forgive our sins!—Gentlemen, let's get down to business. By the way, I don't want anyone thinking I'm drunk. This is my ensign. This is my right hand, and this is my left hand.
I'm not drunk. I can stand well enough, and I can speak just fine.

ALL

Yes, you're speaking very well.

CASSIO

Yes, very well. So don't think that I'm drunk.

*CASSIO exits.*

MONTANO

Let's go to the platform where we'll stand guard. Come on.

*GENTLEMEN exit.*

IAGO

You see that man who just left? He's a good soldier, good enough to be Caesar's right-hand man. But he has a serious weakness. It's too bad. I'm worried that Othello trusts him too much, and it'll be bad for Cyprus eventually.

MONTANO

But is he often like this?

**IAGO**

115 'Tis evermore the prologue to his sleep.
He'll watch the horologe a double set
If drink rock not his cradle.

**MONTANO**

It were well
The general were put in mind of it.
Perhaps he sees it not, or his good nature
120 Prizes the virtue that appears in Cassio
And looks not on his evils. Is not this true?

*Enter* RODERIGO

**IAGO**

*(aside)* How now, Roderigo?
I pray you, after the lieutenant, go!

*Exit* RODERIGO

**MONTANO**

And 'tis great pity that the noble Moor
125 Should hazard such a place as his own second
With one of an ingraft infirmity.
It were an honest action to say
So to the Moor.

**IAGO**

Not I, for this fair island.
I do love Cassio well, and would do much
130 To cure him of this evil—

*Cry within "Help! help!"*

**IAGO**

But, hark! What noise?

*Enter* CASSIO, *pursuing* RODERIGO

**IAGO**

He drinks like this every night before he goes to sleep. He'd stay up all night and all day if he didn't drink himself to sleep.

**MONTANO**

The general should be informed about this. Maybe he's never noticed, or he only wants to see Cassio's good side. Don't you think so?

RODERIGO *enters.*

**IAGO**

(*speaking so that only* RODERIGO *can hear*) Hello, Roderigo. Please, follow the lieutenant. Hurry! Go!

RODERIGO *exits.*

**MONTANO**

And it's too bad that the Moor chose a man with such a deep-rooted drinking problem as his second-in-command. We should definitely say something to the Moor.

**IAGO**

I wouldn't say anything, not if you gave me the whole island for doing so. I respect Cassio and I'd like to help cure his alcoholism—

*A voice offstage calls "Help! Help!"*

**IAGO**

What's that noise?

CASSIO *enters, chasing* RODERIGO.

**CASSIO**
Zounds! You rogue! You rascal!

**MONTANO**
What's the matter, lieutenant?

**CASSIO**
A knave teach me my duty?
135     I'll beat the knave into a twiggen bottle.

**RODERIGO**
Beat me?

**CASSIO**
Dost thou prate, rogue? *(strikes him)*

**MONTANO**
Nay, good lieutenant! I pray you, sir, hold your hand.
*(stays him)*

**CASSIO**
Let me go, sir, or I'll knock you o'er the mazzard.

**MONTANO**
140     Come, come, you're drunk.

**CASSIO**
Drunk?

*They fight*

**IAGO**
*(aside to* RODERIGO*)*
Away, I say, go out, and cry a mutiny.—

*Exit* RODERIGO

Nay, good lieutenant! Alas, gentlemen—
Help, ho!— Lieutenant—sir, Montano—
145     Help, masters!—Here's a goodly watch indeed!

*Bell rings*

**CASSIO**

Damn you, you villain, you rascal!

**MONTANO**

What's the matter, lieutenant?

**CASSIO**

To think that fool had the nerve to try to teach me manners! I'll beat him until the welts look like basket-weave!

**RODERIGO**

You'll beat me?

**CASSIO**

Are you talking, you villain? *(he hits* **RODERIGO***)*

**MONTANO**

No, don't hit him, lieutenant! Please, sir, restrain yourself. *(he restrains* **CASSIO***)*

**CASSIO**

Let me go, or I'll knock you on the head.

**MONTANO**

Come on, you're drunk.

**CASSIO**

Drunk?

**MONTANO** *and* **CASSIO** *fight.*

**IAGO**

*(speaking so that only* **RODERIGO** *can hear)* Go tell everyone there's a riot.—

**RODERIGO** *exits.*

No, lieutenant—God, gentlemen—Help—Lieutenant—sir, Montano—Help, men!—The night guard is coming!

*Someone rings a bell.*

Who's that which rings the bell?—Diablo, ho!
The town will rise. Fie, Fie, lieutenant,
You'll be ashamed for ever.

*Enter* OTHELLO *and attendants*

OTHELLO
What is the matter here?

MONTANO
150 I bleed still,
I am hurt to the death. He dies!

OTHELLO
Hold, for your lives!

IAGO
Hold, ho! Lieutenant—sir, Montano—gentlemen,
Have you forgot all place of sense and duty?
155 Hold! The general speaks to you. Hold, for shame!

OTHELLO
Why, how now, ho! From whence ariseth this?
Are we turned Turks? And to ourselves do that
Which heaven hath forbid the Ottomites?
For Christian shame, put by this barbarous brawl.
160 He that stirs next to carve for his own rage
Holds his soul light, he dies upon his motion.
Silence that dreadful bell, it frights the isle
From her propriety. What is the matter, masters?—
Honest Iago, that looks dead with grieving,
165 Speak, who began this? On thy love, I charge thee.

IAGO
I do not know. Friends all but now, even now,
In quarter, and in terms like bride and groom
Divesting them for bed. And then, but now,
As if some planet had unwitted men,

Who's sounding that alarm? The whole town will riot!
God, lieutenant, please stop! You'll be ashamed of this
forever!

OTHELLO *enters with attendants.*

OTHELLO

What is the matter here?

MONTANO

My God, I'm bleeding! I've been mortally wounded.
I'll kill him!

OTHELLO

Stop right now!

IAGO

Stop! Lieutenant—sir, Montano—gentlemen! Have
you forgotten your duty and your sense of decorum?
Stop! The general is talking to you! Stop, for God's
sake!

OTHELLO

How did this all start? Have we all become as savage as
the Turks, treating each other as badly as they would
have treated us? For heaven's sake, stop this savage
brawl! The next man who swings his sword must not
care about his life, because the instant he strikes, he
dies. Stop that alarm from ringing, it's scaring the
islanders. What's the matter here, gentlemen?—Honest Iago, you look upset. Speak up and tell me who
started this. Answer me.

IAGO

I don't know. We were all having fun until just a
minute ago; we were as happy as a bride and groom
taking off their clothes. But then the mood suddenly
changed. It was as if something had driven the men

170     Swords out, and tilting one at other's breasts
In opposition bloody. I cannot speak
Any beginning to this peevish odds,
And would in action glorious I had lost
Those legs that brought me to a part of it.

**OTHELLO**
175     How comes it, Michael, you are thus forgot?

**CASSIO**
I pray you pardon me, I cannot speak.

**OTHELLO**
Worthy Montano, you were wont be civil.
The gravity and stillness of your youth
The world hath noted, and your name is great
180     In mouths of wisest censure. What's the matter
That you unlace your reputation thus
And spend your rich opinion for the name
Of a night-brawler? Give me answer to it.

**MONTANO**
Worthy Othello, I am hurt to danger.
185     Your officer Iago can inform you,
While I spare speech, which something now offends me,
Of all that I do know. Nor know I aught
By me that's said or done amiss this night,
Unless self-charity be sometimes a vice,
190     And to defend ourselves it be a sin
When violence assails us.

**OTHELLO**
                      Now, by heaven,
My blood begins my safer guides to rule,
And passion, having my best judgment collied,
Assays to lead the way. If I once stir,

insane and made them point their swords at one
another. I don't know what could have started this. I'd
rather have lost my legs in battle than be a part of this!

**OTHELLO**

How did you manage to lose your self-control like
this, Michael?

**CASSIO**

Please, excuse me, sir. I can't speak.

**OTHELLO**

Montano, you're supposed to be calm and collected.
You're famous for it. Wise people respect you. What
in the world made you risk your reputation like this
and become a street brawler? Tell me.

**MONTANO**

Othello, I've been seriously hurt. Your officer Iago can
tell you what happened. I should save my breath,
since it hurts to talk. I didn't do anything wrong that
I know of, unless it was a sin to defend myself when
someone attacked me.

**OTHELLO**

All right, now I'm starting to lose my cool.
By God, if you don't tell me what happened you'll all
suffer. Tell me how this fight began, who started it.
Whoever is guilty, even if he were my twin brother, I

195 Or do but lift this arm, the best of you
Shall sink in my rebuke. Give me to know
How this foul rout began, who set it on,
And he that is approved in this offence,
Though he had twinned with me, both at a birth,
200 Shall lose me. What, in a town of war
Yet wild, the people's hearts brimful of fear,
To manage private and domestic quarrel?
In night, and on the court and guard of safety?
'Tis monstrous. Iago, who began 't?

**MONTANO**
205 If partially affined or leagued in office
Thou dost deliver more or less than truth
Thou art no soldier.

**IAGO**
                              Touch me not so near.
I had rather have this tongue cut from my mouth
Than it should do offence to Michael Cassio.
210 Yet I persuade myself to speak the truth
Shall nothing wrong him. This it is, general:
Montano and myself being in speech,
There comes a fellow crying out for help
And Cassio following him with determined sword
215 To execute upon him. Sir, this gentleman
Steps in to Cassio and entreats his pause,
Myself the crying fellow did pursue,
Lest by his clamor—as it so fell out—
The town might fall in fright. He, swift of foot,
220 Outran my purpose, and I returned then rather
For that I heard the clink and fall of swords
And Cassio high in oath, which till tonight
I ne'er might say before. When I came back—
For this was brief— I found them close together
225 At blow and thrust, even as again they were
When you yourself did part them.
More of this matter cannot I report.

swear I'm through with him. We're in a town that's just avoided a war, everyone's still on edge, and you're getting into private fights while you're supposed to be on guard duty? That's unbelievably bad. Iago, who started it?

MONTANO

I know you're close to Cassio, but if you diverge from the truth in any way, you're not a true soldier.

IAGO

You're hitting close to home there. I'd rather cut my tongue out of my mouth than say anything bad about Michael Cassio. But I don't think it'll hurt him to tell the truth. This is what happened, General. Montano and I were talking when a man came running, crying for help. Cassio was chasing him with his sword out, trying to kill the guy. This gentleman stopped Cassio and told him to put away his sword. I followed the guy who was crying for help, to keep him from scaring the public. But he was fast and outran me. When I got back, I heard the swords clinking and Cassio swearing. I'd never heard him swear before. They were nearly killing each other, as you saw when you pulled them apart. I can't tell you anything else.

But men are men, the best sometimes forget.
Though Cassio did some little wrong to him,
230 As men in rage strike those that wish them best,
Yet surely Cassio, I believe, received
From him that fled some strange indignity
Which patience could not pass.

OTHELLO

                          I know, Iago,
Thy honesty and love doth mince this matter,
235 Making it light to Cassio. Cassio, I love thee
But never more be officer of mine.—

*Enter* DESDEMONA, *attended*

Look, if my gentle love be not raised up!
I'll make thee an example.

DESDEMONA

What's the matter, dear?

OTHELLO

240 All's well, sweeting,
Come away to bed.—*(to* MONTANO*)* Sir, for your hurts
Myself will be your surgeon. Lead him off.

                        MONTANO *is led off*

Iago, look with care about the town
And silence those whom this vile brawl distracted.—
245 Come, Desdemona, 'tis the soldiers' life
To have their balmy slumbers waked with strife.

                *Exeunt all but* IAGO *and* CASSIO

IAGO

What, are you hurt, lieutenant?

CASSIO

Ay, past all surgery.

IAGO

Marry, heaven forbid!

But nobody's perfect, and even the best man sometimes loses control and strikes out in rage. Cassio was wrong to hurt Montano, who was only trying to help him, but I'm sure the guy who ran away must have offended Cassio in some terrible way, and Cassio couldn't let it pass.

OTHELLO

Iago, I know you're fond of Cassio and are downplaying this for his benefit. Cassio, I love you, but you're never again going to be one of my officers.—

DESDEMONA *enters with attendants.*

Look, you've woken my wife! I'll make you an example for the others to learn from.

DESDEMONA

What's the matter, dear?

OTHELLO

Everything's fine, now, sweetheart. Go back to bed.— *(to MONTANO)* I'll see to it personally that your wounds are treated. Lead him off.

> MONTANO *is carried off.*

Iago, go and calm down the townspeople.—Come with me, Desdemona. Unfortunately, it's part of the soldier's life to be woken up by trouble.

> *Everyone except CASSIO and IAGO exits.*

IAGO

Are you hurt, lieutenant?

CASSIO

Yes, but no doctor can help me.

IAGO

Oh I hope that's not true!

**CASSIO**

250     Reputation, reputation, reputation! Oh, I have lost my
        reputation! I have lost the immortal part of myself, and
        what remains is bestial. My reputation, Iago, my
        reputation!

**IAGO**

        As I am an honest man, I thought you had received some
255     bodily wound. There is more sense in that than in
        reputation. Reputation is an idle and most false
        imposition, oft got without merit and lost without
        deserving. You have lost no reputation at all unless you
        repute yourself such a loser. What, man, there are ways to
260     recover the general again. You are but now cast in his
        mood, a punishment more in policy than in malice, even
        so as one would beat his offenseless dog to affright an
        imperious lion. Sue to him again and he's yours.

**CASSIO**

        I will rather sue to be despised than to deceive so good a
265     commander with so slight, so drunken, and so indiscreet
        an officer. Drunk? And speak parrot? And squabble?
        Swagger? Swear? And discourse fustian with one's own
        shadow? O thou invisible spirit of wine, if thou hast no
        name to be known by, let us call thee devil!

**IAGO**

270     What was he that you followed with your sword? What
        had he done to you?

**CASSIO**

        I know not.

**IAGO**

        Is 't possible?

**CASSIO**

        I remember a mass of things, but nothing distinctly. A
275     quarrel, but nothing wherefore. Oh, that men should put
        an enemy in their mouths to steal away their brains! That
        we should, with joy, pleasance revel and applause,
        transform ourselves into beasts!

CASSIO

My reputation, my reputation! I've lost my reputation, the longest-living and truest part of myself! Everything else in me is just animal-like. Oh, my reputation, Iago, my reputation!

IAGO

I swear I thought you meant you'd been hurt physically. Your physical health matters more than your reputation. A reputation is a useless and fake quality that others impose on us. You haven't lost it unless you think you have. There are lots of ways to get on the general's good side again. You've been discharged because he's angry, and because he's obliged to do so for policy reasons, not because he dislikes you. He's got to beat up the weak to frighten the strong. Go to him, petition him. He'll change his mind.

CASSIO

I'd rather ask him to hate me than ask such a good commander to accept such a worthless, drunk, stupid officer as myself. Drunk? Babbling senselessly? Squabbling? Swaggering? Swearing? Ranting and raving to my own shadow! Oh, wine is the devil!

IAGO

Who were you chasing with your sword? What did he do to you?

CASSIO

I don't know.

IAGO

Is that possible?

CASSIO

I remember a jumble of impressions, but nothing distinctly. I remember a fight, but not why we were fighting. Oh God, why do men drink and lose their minds? Why do we party until we're like animals?

**IAGO**

Why, but you are now well enough. How came you thus
280   recovered?

**CASSIO**

It hath pleased the devil drunkenness to give place to the
devil wrath. One unperfectness shows me another, to
make me frankly despise myself.

**IAGO**

Come, you are too severe a moraler. As the time, the place,
285   and the condition of this country stands, I could heartily
wish this had not befallen. But since it is as it is, mend it
for your own good.

**CASSIO**

I will ask him for my place again, he shall tell me I am a
drunkard. Had I as many mouths as Hydra, such an
290   answer would stop them all. To be now a sensible man, by
and by a fool, and presently a beast! Oh, strange! Every
inordinate cup is unblessed and the ingredient is a devil.

**IAGO**

Come, come, good wine is a good familiar creature, if it be
well used. Exclaim no more against it. And, good
295   lieutenant, I think you think I love you.

**CASSIO**

I have well approved it, sir. I drunk!

**IAGO**

You or any man living may be drunk at a time, man. I tell you
what you shall do. Our general's wife is now the general. I
may say so in this respect, for that he hath devoted and given
300.   up himself to the contemplation, mark, and denotement of
her parts and graces. Confess yourself freely to her,
importune her help to put you in your place again. She is of
so free, so kind, so apt, so blessed a disposition, she holds it
a vice in her goodness not to do more than she is requested.
305.   This broken joint between you and her husband entreat her
to splinter, and, my fortunes against any lay worth naming,
this crack of your love shall grow stronger than it was before.

**IAGO**

You seem all right now. How did you get better?

**CASSIO**

My drunkenness went away when anger took over.
One weakness led to another, to make me hate myself.

**IAGO**

Come on, you're being too hard on yourself. I wish
none of this had happened, given the situation here,
and your rank. But since this has happened, you
should fix it for your own good.

**CASSIO**

I'll ask him for my position back again, and he'll tell
me I'm a drunk. Even if I had a whole bunch of
mouths, I wouldn't be able to answer that. I was a reasonable man, then I became a fool, and finally a beast!
Oh, how strange! Every glass of liquor is damned, and
the devil's the main ingredient!

**IAGO**

Come on now, wine is good for you, if you know how
to use it. Don't say anything bad about wine anymore.
Lieutenant, I think you know I'm your friend.

**CASSIO**

I know that, sir. Imagine, me, a drunk!

**IAGO**

Any man can get drunk sometime. I'll tell you what to
do. Othello's wife has a lot of influence now. He's
completely devoted to her. Go open your heart to her.
Ask her to help you get back your position. She is so
generous, kind, and ready to help that she thinks it's
wrong not to do everything she can, even more than
she is asked to do. Ask her to help you heal the rift
between her husband and you. I'd bet my lucky stars
your problem will be forgotten, and your relationship
will be stronger than ever.

**ACT TWO**

**CASSIO**

You advise me well.

**IAGO**

I protest, in the sincerity of love and honest kindness.

**CASSIO**

310    I think it freely, and betimes in the morning I will beseech
the virtuous Desdemona to undertake for me. I am
desperate of my fortunes if they check me.

**IAGO**

You are in the right. Good night, lieutenant, I must to the
watch.

**CASSIO**

315    Good night, honest Iago.

*Exit*

**IAGO**

And what's he then that says I play the villain?
When this advice is free I give and honest,
Probal to thinking and indeed the course
To win the Moor again? For 'tis most easy
320    Th' inclining Desdemona to subdue
In any honest suit. She's framed as fruitful
As the free elements. And then for her
To win the Moor, were to renounce his baptism,
All seals and symbols of redeemèd sin,
325    His soul is so enfettered to her love,
That she may make, unmake, do what she list,
Even as her appetite shall play the god
With his weak function. How am I then a villain
To counsel Cassio to this parallel course,
330    Directly to his good? Divinity of hell!
When devils will the blackest sins put on
They do suggest at first with heavenly shows
As I do now. For whiles this honest fool
Plies Desdemona to repair his fortune
335    And she for him pleads strongly to the Moor,
I'll pour this pestilence into his ear:

**CASSIO**

That's good advice.

**IAGO**

I'm helping you because I like and respect you.

**CASSIO**

I believe it completely. Early in the morning I'll go visit Desdemona and plead my case. My situation is desperate.

**IAGO**

You're doing the right thing. Good night, lieutenant. I've got to go to the guard tower.

**CASSIO**

Good night, honest Iago.

**CASSIO** *exits.*

**IAGO**

Who can say I'm evil when my advice is so good? That's really the best way to win the Moor back again. It's easy to get Desdemona on your side. She's full of good intentions. And the Moor loves her so much he would renounce his Christianity to keep her happy. He's so enslaved by love that she can make him do whatever she wants. How am I evil to advise Cassio to do exactly what'll do him good? That's the kind of argument you'd expect from Satan! When devils are about to commit their biggest sins they put on their most heavenly faces, just like I'm doing now. And while this fool is begging Desdemona to help him, and while she's pleading his case to the Moor, I'll poison the Moor's ear against her, hinting that she's taking Cassio's side because of her lust for him. The more she

That she repeals him for her body's lust.
And by how much she strives to do him good
She shall undo her credit with the Moor.
340     So will I turn her virtue into pitch
And out of her own goodness make the net
That shall enmesh them all.

*Enter* RODERIGO

                     How now, Roderigo!

RODERIGO
I do follow here in the chase not like a hound that hunts,
but one that fills up the cry. My money is almost spent, I
345     have been tonight exceedingly well cudgeled, and I think
the issue will be I shall have so much experience for my
pains. And so, with no money at all and a little more wit,
return again to Venice.

IAGO
How poor are they that have not patience!
350     What wound did ever heal but by degrees?
Thou know'st we work by wit and not by witchcraft,
And wit depends on dilatory time.
Does't not go well? Cassio hath beaten thee.
And thou, by that small hurt, hath cashiered Cassio.
355     Though other things grow fair against the sun,
Yet fruits that blossom first will first be ripe.
Content thyself awhile. In troth, 'tis morning.
Pleasure and action make the hours seem short.
Retire thee, go where thou art billeted.
360     Away, I say, thou shalt know more hereafter.
Nay, get thee gone.
                       *Exit* RODERIGO

tries to help Cassio, the more she'll shake Othello's confidence in her. And that's how I'll turn her good intentions into a big trap to snag them all.

RODERIGO *enters.*

Hello, Roderigo!

RODERIGO

I'm totally worn out. My chase is too much for me. I've spent most of my money, and tonight I got beaten up. The upshot is that I've got a little more experience. So with no money, but a little more wisdom, I'm going back to Venice.

IAGO

You're a poor man if you're this impatient! If you get hurt, does your wound heal immediately? No, it heals gradually. We achieve things with our intelligence, not by magic, and intelligent planning takes time. Aren't things going well? Cassio's beaten you up, but with that tiny sacrifice on your part, you got Cassio discharged! If we're patient, we'll be rewarded with the fruits of our labors. My God, it's morning. All this excitement has made the time fly by. Go back to where you're staying and go to sleep. Go on, I'm telling you. You'll understand better later. Go.

RODERIGO *exits.*

        Two things are to be done:
My wife must move for Cassio to her mistress.
I'll set her on.
Myself, the while, to draw the Moor apart
And bring him jump when he may Cassio find
Soliciting his wife. Ay, that's the way.
Dull not device by coldness and delay.

              *Exit*

365

Now two things still need to be done. My wife has to help make Desdemona take Cassio's side. I'll put her on that. And I need to take the Moor aside right at the moment when Cassio's talking to Desdemona, so he'll see them together. Yes, that's the way I'll do it. Let's not ruin a brilliant plan by being slow to act.

IAGO *exits.*

# ACT THREE

## Scene 1

*Enter* CASSIO *and* MUSICIANS

**CASSIO**
Masters, play here, I will content your pains.
Something that's brief, and bid "Good morrow, general."

*They play. Enter* CLOWN

**CLOWN**
Why masters, have your instruments been in Naples, that
they speak i' th' nose thus?

**MUSICIAN**
5    How, sir? How?

**CLOWN**
Are these, I pray you, wind instruments?

**MUSICIAN**
Ay, marry, are they, sir.

**CLOWN**
Oh, thereby hangs a tale.

**MUSICIAN**
Whereby hangs a tale, sir?

**CLOWN**
10    Marry sir, by many a wind instrument that I know. But,
masters, here's money for you, and the general so likes
your music that he desires you, for love's sake, to make no
more noise with it.

**MUSICIAN**
Well, sir, we will not.

# ACT THREE

## Scene 1

CASSIO *enters with* MUSICIANS.

**CASSIO**

Musicians, start playing here. I'll pay you for your trouble. Play something short that will put the general in a good mood.

*The* MUSICIANS *play. The* CLOWN *enters.*

**CLOWN**

Your instruments all have a nasal twang. Have they been to Naples?

Naples was considered a likely place to contract syphilis, which eats away at the bridge of the nose.

**MUSICIAN**

Excuse me?

**CLOWN**

Are these wind instruments?

**MUSICIAN**

Yes, they are.

**CLOWN**

Oh, there's the problem.

**MUSICIAN**

What's the problem?

**CLOWN**

Anyone full of hot air is a problem. But here's some money. The general likes your music a lot, but he asks you to stop playing now.

**MUSICIAN**

Well, we'll stop, then.

**CLOWN**

15      If you have any music that may not be heard, to 't again. But,
        as they say, to hear music the general does not greatly care.

**MUSICIAN**

        We have none such, sir.

**CLOWN**

        Then put up your pipes in your bag, for I'll away. Go,
        vanish into air, away!

                                    *Exeunt* MUSICIANS

**CASSIO**

20      Dost thou hear, my honest friend?

**CLOWN**

        No, I hear not your honest friend, I hear you.

**CASSIO**

        Prithee, keep up thy quillets. There's a poor piece of gold
        for thee. If the gentlewoman that attends the general's
        wife be stirring, tell her there's one Cassio entreats her a
25      little favour of speech. Wilt thou do this?

**CLOWN**

        She is stirring, sir. If she will stir hither, I shall seem to
        notify unto her.

                                    *Exit* CLOWN

        *Enter* IAGO

              In happy time, Iago.

**IAGO**

        You have not been abed, then?

**CASSIO**

                        Why, no. The day had broke
        Before we parted. I have made bold, Iago,
30      To send in to your wife. My suit to her
        Is that she will to virtuous Desdemona
        Procure me some access.

**CLOWN**

If you've got any music that can't be heard, then play that. But as I said, the general isn't really in the mood to hear music now.

**MUSICIAN**

We don't have any music that can't be heard.

**CLOWN**

Then pack up your instruments and go away. Go!

*The* MUSICIANS *exit.*

**CASSIO**

Do you hear, my friend?

**CLOWN**

No, I don't hear your friend. I hear you.

**CASSIO**

Please don't play games. (CASSIO *gives* CLOWN *money*). There's a bit of gold for you. When the woman taking care of the general's wife wakes up, could you please tell her that Cassio asks to speak with her?

**CLOWN**

She's awake, sir. If she feels like coming over here, I'll give her your message.

*The* CLOWN *exits.*

IAGO *enters.*

Good to see you, Iago.

**IAGO**

You didn't go to sleep, then?

**CASSIO**

No. When I left you it was already morning. I've been bold, Iago. I've asked to talk to your wife. I'm going to ask her to let me talk to Desdemona.

**IAGO**
I'll send her to you presently,
And I'll devise a mean to draw the Moor
35 Out of the way, that your converse and business
May be more free.

**CASSIO**
I humbly thank you for't.

*Exit* IAGO

I never knew a Florentine more kind and honest.

*Enter* EMILIA

**EMILIA**
Good morrow, good Lieutenant. I am sorry
40 For your displeasure, but all will sure be well.
The general and his wife are talking of it,
And she speaks for you stoutly. The Moor replies
That he you hurt is of great fame in Cyprus
And great affinity, and that in wholesome wisdom
45 He might not but refuse you. But he protests he loves you
And needs no other suitor but his likings
To take the safest occasion by the front
To bring you in again.

**CASSIO**
                                    Yet I beseech you,
If you think fit, or that it may be done,
50 Give me advantage of some brief discourse
With Desdemona alone.

**EMILIA**
                              Pray you come in.
I will bestow you where you shall have time
To speak your bosom freely.

**CASSIO**
                              I am much bound to you.
                                    *Exeunt*

**IAGO**

I'll send her out to you now. I'll think of a plan to get the Moor out of the way, so you can speak more openly.

**CASSIO**

I humbly thank you.

*IAGO exits.*

The citizens of Florence (who included Machiavelli) were not known for kindness and honesty, but Michael Cassio seems unaware of Florence's bad reputation.

Even for a Florentine, I never knew someone so kind and honest.

*EMILIA enters.*

**EMILIA**

Good morning, lieutenant. I'm sorry about what happened, but I'm sure everything will turn out all right. The general and his wife are talking about it now, and she's defending you strongly. The Moor says the man you hurt is very important in Cyprus, and that under the circumstances he has no choice but to refuse to reinstate you. But he says he still loves and respects you, and based on his own feelings alone he's looking for an opportunity to safely take you back.

**CASSIO**

Please find a way to give me some time alone with Desdemona, if you think that's all right.

**EMILIA**

Please come in. I'll take you to a place where you can speak freely.

**CASSIO**

Thank you very much.

*They exit.*

## ACT THREE, Scene 2

*Enter* OTHELLO, IAGO, *and* GENTLEMEN

OTHELLO
These letters give, Iago, to the pilot,
And by him do my duties to the senate.
That done, I will be walking on the works,
Repair there to me.

IAGO
5    Well, my good lord, I'll do 't.

OTHELLO
This fortification, gentlemen, shall we see 't?

GENTLEMEN
We'll wait upon your lordship.

*Exeunt*

## ACT THREE, Scene 2

OTHELLO, IAGO *and* GENTLEMEN *enter.*

OTHELLO

> Iago, give these letters to the ship's captain who brought me here, and ask him to pay my respects to the Senate of Venice. Now that's done, I'm going to walk on the fortification walls. Look for me there when you come back.

IAGO

> I will, my lord.

OTHELLO

> Shall we go see this fortification, men?

GENTLEMEN

> We're at your service, my lord.

*They all exit.*

## ACT THREE, Scene 3

*Enter* DESDEMONA, CASSIO, *and* EMILIA

**DESDEMONA**
    Be thou assured, good Cassio, I will do
    All my abilities in thy behalf.

**EMILIA**
    Good madam, do. I warrant it grieves my husband
    As if the cause were his.

**DESDEMONA**
5    Oh, that's an honest fellow. Do not doubt, Cassio,
    But I will have my lord and you again
    As friendly as you were.

**CASSIO**
                      Bounteous madam,
    Whatever shall become of Michael Cassio,
    He's never anything but your true servant.

**DESDEMONA**
10    I know 't, I thank you. You do love my lord.
    You have known him long, and be you well assured
    He shall in strangeness stand no farther off
    Than in a polite distance.

**CASSIO**
                      Ay, but, lady,
    That policy may either last so long,
15    Or feed upon such nice and waterish diet,
    Or breed itself so out of circumstances,
    That, I being absent and my place supplied,
    My general will forget my love and service.

**DESDEMONA**
    Do not doubt that. Before Emilia here
20    I give thee warrant of thy place. Assure thee,
    If I do vow a friendship, I'll perform it
    To the last article. My lord shall never rest,
    I'll watch him tame and talk him out of patience.

# ACT THREE, Scene 3

DESDEMONA, CASSIO *and* EMILIA *enter.*

**DESDEMONA**
> I'll do everything I can for you, Cassio.

**EMILIA**
> Please do, madam. My husband's so upset about Cassio's problem you'd think it was his own.

**DESDEMONA**
> Your husband's such a good man. Don't worry, Cassio. I'm sure you and my husband will be as friendly as you were before.

**CASSIO**
> My dear beautiful lady, whatever happens to Michael Cassio, he'll always be your humble servant.

**DESDEMONA**
> I know that. Thank you. You're my husband's friend and you've known him a long time. I assure you the only reason he's keeping away from you now is political.

**CASSIO**
> Yes, my lady. But those political considerations might last such a long time that the general will forget my love and service, especially if I'm gone and someone else has my job.

**DESDEMONA**
> That'll never happen. Emilia here will be my witness: I promise you that you'll get your position back again. And if I promise to help someone, I do everything I can. My husband will never get a moment's rest, I'll keep him up at night talking about you until he runs

His bed shall seem a school, his board a shrift,
25  I'll intermingle everything he does
With Cassio's suit. Therefore be merry, Cassio,
For thy solicitor shall rather die
Than give thy cause away.

*Enter* OTHELLO *and* IAGO

EMILIA
                              Madam, here comes my lord.

CASSIO
Madam, I'll take my leave.

DESDEMONA
                              Why, stay and hear me speak.

CASSIO
30  Madam, not now. I am very ill at ease,
Unfit for mine own purposes.

DESDEMONA
Well, do your discretion.

                                        *Exit* CASSIO

IAGO
Ha! I like not that.

OTHELLO
What dost thou say?

IAGO
35  Nothing, my lord, or if—I know not what.

OTHELLO
Was not that Cassio parted from my wife?

IAGO
Cassio, my lord? No, sure, I cannot think it
That he would steal away so guilty-like
Seeing you coming.

OTHELLO
40  I do believe 'twas he.

out of patience. He will think that his bed has become a conference table for discussing your problem—he won't be able to get away from it. I'll bring up your name at every moment. So cheer up. I'm your advocate, and I'd rather die than give up on you.

OTHELLO *and* IAGO *enter.*

EMILIA

Madam, here comes your husband.

CASSIO

Madam, I'd better leave now.

DESDEMONA

Why not stay and hear me talk to him?

CASSIO

No, madam. I'm very uncomfortable, and that won't help my case.

DESDEMONA

Well, do whatever you think best.

CASSIO *exits.*

IAGO

Hey! I don't like that.

OTHELLO

What did you say?

IAGO

Nothing, my lord, or if I did—I don't know what.

OTHELLO

Wasn't that Cassio leaving my wife?

IAGO

Cassio, my lord? No, I don't think so. He wouldn't sneak away looking so guilty when he saw you coming.

OTHELLO

I really think it was him.

**DESDEMONA**
                         How now, my lord?
I have been talking with a suitor here,
A man that languishes in your displeasure.

**OTHELLO**
Who is 't you mean?

**DESDEMONA**
Why, your lieutenant, Cassio. Good my lord,
45    If I have any grace or power to move you
His present reconciliation take.
For if he be not one that truly loves you,
That errs in ignorance and not in cunning,
I have no judgment in an honest face.
50    I prithee, call him back.

**OTHELLO**
Went he hence now?

**DESDEMONA**
Ay, sooth, so humbled
That he hath left part of his grief with me
To suffer with him. Good love, call him back.

**OTHELLO**
55    Not now, sweet Desdemona. Some other time.

**DESDEMONA**
But shall 't be shortly?

**OTHELLO**
                              The sooner, sweet, for you.

**DESDEMONA**
Shall 't be tonight at supper?

**OTHELLO**
                                   No, not tonight.

**DESDEMONA**
Tomorrow dinner, then?

**OTHELLO**
                              I shall not dine at home,
I meet the captains at the citadel.

**DESDEMONA**

What's this, my lord? I was talking to a petitioner here just now, someone who's suffering from your anger.

**OTHELLO**

Who do you mean?

**DESDEMONA**

Your lieutenant, Cassio. Oh, if I've got any influence over you at all, please patch things up with him. In my judgment, this man truly loves you, and his mistake was innocent rather than wicked. Please call him and tell him to come back here.

**OTHELLO**

Was that him just now?

**DESDEMONA**

Yes. He feels so bad and humble that I feel bad along with him. My love, call him back in here.

**OTHELLO**

Not now, my sweet Desdemona. Some other time.

**DESDEMONA**

But will it be soon?

**OTHELLO**

Very soon, because you want it.

**DESDEMONA**

Will it be tonight at supper?

**OTHELLO**

No, not tonight.

**DESDEMONA**

Then tomorrow at dinner?

**OTHELLO**

I won't be eating dinner at home. I'll be meeting the captains at the citadel.

**DESDEMONA**

60    Why, then, tomorrow night, or Tuesday morn.
On Tuesday noon, or night, or Wednesday morn.
I prithee name the time, but let it not
Exceed three days. In faith, he's penitent,
And yet his trespass, in our common reason

65    (Save that, they say, the wars must make example
Out of her best) is not, almost, a fault
T' incur a private check. When shall he come?
Tell me, Othello. I wonder in my soul
What you would ask me that I should deny

70    Or stand so mamm'ring on. What? Michael Cassio
That came a-wooing with you, and so many a time,
When I have spoke of you dispraisingly,
Hath ta'en your part, to have so much to do
To bring him in? Trust me, I could do much—

**OTHELLO**

75    Prithee, no more. Let him come when he will,
I will deny thee nothing.

**DESDEMONA**

                            Why, this is not a boon,
'Tis as I should entreat you wear your gloves,
Or feed on nourishing dishes, or keep you warm,
Or sue to you to do a peculiar profit

80    To your own person. Nay, when I have a suit
Wherein I mean to touch your love indeed
It shall be full of poise and difficult weight
And fearful to be granted.

**OTHELLO**

                            I will deny thee nothing!
Whereon I do beseech thee, grant me this,

85    To leave me but a little to myself.

**DESDEMONA**

Shall I deny you? No. Farewell, my lord.

**OTHELLO**

Farewell, my Desdemona. I'll come to thee straight.

**DESDEMONA**

Well then, tomorrow night, or Tuesday morning. Or Tuesday noon or at night, or Wednesday morning. Please just name a time, but don't wait more than three days. He's very sorry. His mistake was hardly worth punishing him for in the first place—though in wartime it is sometimes necessary to make examples out of even the best soldiers. So when should he come? Tell me, Othello. I can't imagine you asking me for something and me telling you no or standing there muttering. Michael Cassio came with you when you were trying to win my love. Sometimes I'd criticize you to him, and he'd defend you. And now I have to make this big fuss about bringing him back? I swear, I could do so much—

**OTHELLO**

Please, no more. He can come whenever he wants. I won't refuse you anything.

**DESDEMONA**

Don't act like you're doing me a favor! This is like if I asked you to wear your gloves when it's cold outside, or eat nutritious food, or do something that's good for you. If I ever have to ask you for something that will put your luck to the test, it'll be something difficult and terrible.

**OTHELLO**

I won't deny you anything! But in return, please, do one thing for me: leave me alone for a little while.

**DESDEMONA**

Would I ever deny you anything? No. Goodbye, my husband.

**OTHELLO**

Goodbye, my Desdemona. I'll come see you right away.

**DESDEMONA**
    Emilia, come.—Be as your fancies teach you.
    Whate'er you be, I am obedient.

                *Exeunt* DESDEMONA *and* EMILIA

**OTHELLO**
90    Excellent wretch! Perdition catch my soul
    But I do love thee! And when I love thee not
    Chaos is come again.

**IAGO**
    My noble lord—

**OTHELLO**
    What dost thou say, Iago?

**IAGO**
95    Did Michael Cassio, when you wooed my lady,
    Know of your love?

**OTHELLO**
    He did, from first to last.
    Why dost thou ask?

**IAGO**
    But for a satisfaction of my thought,
100    No further harm.

**OTHELLO**
                        Why of thy thought, Iago?

**IAGO**
    I did not think he had been acquainted with her.

**OTHELLO**
    Oh, yes, and went between us very oft.

**IAGO**
    Indeed?

**OTHELLO**
    Indeed? Ay, indeed! Discern'st thou aught in that?
105    Is he not honest?

**IAGO**
    Honest, my lord?

**DESDEMONA**

Come here, Emilia.—Do whatever you feel like doing, my husband, and I'll obey you.

*DESDEMONA and EMILIA exit.*

**OTHELLO**

What a wonderful girl! God help me, I love you! And when I stop loving you, the universe will fall back into the chaos that was there when time began.

**IAGO**

My noble lord—

**OTHELLO**

What is it, Iago?

**IAGO**

When you were wooing Desdemona, did Michael Cassio know about it?

**OTHELLO**

Yes, he knew about it the whole time. Why do you ask?

**IAGO**

I was just curious. No reason.

**OTHELLO**

Why are you curious, Iago?

**IAGO**

I didn't realize he knew her.

**OTHELLO**

Oh, yes. He carried messages back and forth between us very often.

**IAGO**

Oh, really?

**OTHELLO**

Oh, really? Yes, really. Do you see something wrong with that? Isn't he an honest man?

**IAGO**

Honest, my lord?

**OTHELLO**
Honest, ay, honest.

**IAGO**
My lord, for aught I know.

**OTHELLO**
                                    What dost thou think?

**IAGO**
Think, my lord?

**OTHELLO**
110   "Think, my lord?" Alas, thou echo'st me
As if there were some monster in thy thought
Too hideous to be shown. Thou dost mean something.
I heard thee say even now thou lik'st not that
When Cassio left my wife. What didst not like?
115   And when I told thee he was of my counsel
Of my whole course of wooing, thou cried'st "Indeed?"
And didst contract and purse thy brow together
As if thou then hadst shut up in thy brain
Some horrible conceit. If thou dost love me
120   Show me thy thought.

**IAGO**
My lord, you know I love you.

**OTHELLO**
I think thou dost.
And for I know thou 'rt full of love and honesty
And weigh'st thy words before thou giv'st them breath,
125   Therefore these stops of thine fright me the more.
For such things in a false disloyal knave
Are tricks of custom, but in a man that's just
They are close dilations, working from the heart,
That passion cannot rule.

**IAGO**
                                    For Michael Cassio,
130   I dare be sworn, I think, that he is honest.

**OTHELLO**
I think so too.

**OTHELLO**

Honest, yes, honest.

**IAGO**

As far as I know, sir.

**OTHELLO**

What are you thinking?

**IAGO**

Thinking, my lord?

**OTHELLO**

"Thinking, my lord?" My God, you keep repeating everything I say as if you were thinking something too horrible to say out loud. You're thinking something. Just a minute ago I heard you say you didn't like it when Cassio left my wife. What didn't you like? And when I told you he was involved the whole time I was trying to get Desdemona, you replied, "Oh, really?" And then you frowned and wrinkled up your forehead as if you were imagining something horrible. If you're my friend, tell me what you're thinking.

**IAGO**

My lord, you know I'm your friend.

**OTHELLO**

I think you are. And I know you're full of love and honesty, and you think carefully before you speak. That's why these pauses of yours frighten me. If some fool were withholding things from me, I wouldn't think twice about it. If some lying, cheating villain acted like that, it would just be a trick. But when an honest man acts like that, you know he's wrestling with bad thoughts and can't help it.

**IAGO**

As for Michael Cassio, I think it would be safe for me to swear that he's honest.

**OTHELLO**

I think so too.

**IAGO**
> Men should be what they seem,
> Or those that be not, would they might seem none!

**OTHELLO**
> Certain, men should be what they seem.

**IAGO**
> Why then I think Cassio's an honest man.

**OTHELLO**
135
> Nay, yet there's more in this.
> I prithee speak to me as to thy thinkings,
> As thou dost ruminate, and give thy worst of thoughts
> The worst of words.

**IAGO**
> Good my lord, pardon me,
> Though I am bound to every act of duty
140
> I am not bound to that all slaves are free to.
> Utter my thoughts? Why, say they are vile and false,
> As where's that palace whereinto foul things
> Sometimes intrude not? Who has that breast so pure
> Wherein uncleanly apprehensions
145
> Keep leets and law-days and in sessions sit
> With meditations lawful?

**OTHELLO**
> Thou dost conspire against thy friend, Iago,
> If thou but think'st him wronged and mak'st his ear
> A stranger to thy thoughts.

**IAGO**
> I do beseech you,
150
> Though I perchance am vicious in my guess,
> As, I confess, it is my nature's plague
> To spy into abuses, and oft my jealousy
> Shapes faults that are not, that your wisdom,
> From one that so imperfectly conceits,
155
> Would take no notice, nor build yourself a trouble
> Out of his scattering and unsure observance.
> It were not for your quiet nor your good,

IAGO

People should be what they appear to be. If they're not honest, they shouldn't look like they are!

OTHELLO

Absolutely, people should be what they appear to be.

IAGO

In that case, I think Cassio's an honest man.

OTHELLO

No, I think there's more to this than you're letting on. Please tell me what you're thinking—even your worst suspicions.

IAGO

Please don't make me do that, sir. I have to obey all your orders, but surely I'm not obligated to reveal my deepest thoughts—even slaves aren't expected to do that. You want me to say what I'm thinking? What if my thoughts are disgusting and wrong? Even good people think horrible things sometimes. Who is so pure that they never think a bad thought?

OTHELLO

You're not being a good friend, Iago, if you even *think* your friend has been wronged and you don't tell him about it.

IAGO

Please don't ask me to tell you. I might be completely wrong. I have a bad tendency to be suspicious of people and to look too closely into what they're doing. Often I imagine crimes that aren't really there. You would be wise to ignore my weak guesses and imaginary suspicions, and don't worry yourself about the meaningless things I've noticed. For me to tell you my thoughts would only destroy your peace of mind, and

Nor for my manhood, honesty, and wisdom
To let you know my thoughts.

OTHELLO

What dost thou mean?

IAGO

160 Good name in man and woman, dear my lord,
Is the immediate jewel of their souls.
Who steals my purse steals trash. 'Tis something, nothing:
'Twas mine, 'tis his, and has been slave to thousands.
But he that filches from me my good name
165 Robs me of that which not enriches him
And makes me poor indeed.

OTHELLO

I'll know thy thoughts.

IAGO

You cannot, if my heart were in your hand,
Nor shall not, whilst 'tis in my custody.

OTHELLO
Ha!

IAGO

Oh, beware, my lord, of jealousy!
170 It is the green-eyed monster which doth mock
The meat it feeds on. That cuckold lives in bliss
Who, certain of his fate, loves not his wronger,
But, oh, what damnèd minutes tells he o'er
Who dotes, yet doubts— suspects, yet soundly loves!

OTHELLO
175 Oh, misery!

IAGO

Poor and content is rich, and rich enough,
But riches fineless is as poor as winter
To him that ever fears he shall be poor.
Good heaven, the souls of all my tribe defend
180 From jealousy!

it wouldn't be wise, honest, or responsible for me to tell them.

OTHELLO

What are you talking about?

IAGO

A good reputation is the most valuable thing we have—men and women alike. If you steal my money, you're just stealing trash. It's something, it's nothing: it's yours, it's mine, and it'll belong to thousands more. But if you steal my reputation, you're robbing me of something that doesn't make you richer, but makes me much poorer.

OTHELLO

I'm going to find out what you're thinking.

IAGO

You can't find that out, even if you held my heart in your hand you couldn't make me tell you. And as long as my heart's inside my body, you never will.

OTHELLO

What?

IAGO

Beware of jealousy, my lord! It's a green-eyed monster that makes fun of the victims it devours. The man who knows his wife is cheating on him is happy, because at least he isn't friends with the man she's sleeping with. But think of the unhappiness of a man who worships his wife, yet doubts her faithfulness. He suspects her, but still loves her.

OTHELLO

Oh, what misery!

IAGO

The person who's poor and contented is rich enough. But infinite riches are nothing to someone who's always afraid he'll be poor. God, help us not be jealous!

**OTHELLO**
Why, why is this?
Think'st thou I'd make a life of jealousy,
To follow still the changes of the moon
With fresh suspicions? No! To be once in doubt
Is to be resolved. Exchange me for a goat
185 When I shall turn the business of my soul
To such exsufflicate and blowed surmises,
Matching thy inference. 'Tis not to make me jealous
To say my wife is fair, feeds well, loves company,
Is free of speech, sings, plays, and dances.
190 Where virtue is, these are more virtuous.
Nor from mine own weak merits will I draw
The smallest fear or doubt of her revolt,
For she had eyes and chose me. No, Iago,
I'll see before I doubt, when I doubt, prove,
195 And on the proof there is no more but this:
Away at once with love or jealousy!

**IAGO**
I am glad of this, for now I shall have reason
To show the love and duty that I bear you
With franker spirit. Therefore, as I am bound,
200 Receive it from me. I speak not yet of proof.
Look to your wife, observe her well with Cassio.
Wear your eyes thus, not jealous nor secure.
I would not have your free and noble nature
Out of self-bounty be abused. Look to 't.
205 I know our country disposition well.
In Venice they do let God see the pranks
They dare not show their husbands. Their best conscience
Is not to leave 't undone, but keep't unknown.

**OTHELLO**
Dost thou say so?

**OTHELLO**

Why are you telling me this? Do you think I would live a life of jealousy, tormented by new suspicions every hour? No. If there's any doubt, there is no doubt. I might as well be a goat if I ever let myself become obsessed with the kind of suspicions you're implying. If you say my wife is beautiful, eats well, loves good company, speaks freely, sings, plays music, and dances well, you're not making me jealous. When a woman is virtuous, talents like these just make her better. And I'm not going to start feeling inferior. She had her eyes wide open when she chose me. No, Iago, I'll have to see some real evidence before I start suspecting her of anything bad, and when I suspect her, I'll look for proof, and if there's proof, that's when I'll let go of my love and my jealousy.

**IAGO**

I'm glad to hear you say that. Now I can show you my devotion and my duty with more honesty. So please listen to me. I'm not talking about proof yet. Watch your wife. Watch how she is with Cassio. Just watch— don't be either completely suspicious or completely trustful. I wouldn't want to see you taken advantage of because you're such an open and trusting guy. Watch out! I know the people of Venice well. They let God see things they wouldn't show their husbands. They don't avoid doing things that are wrong, they just try not to get caught.

**OTHELLO**

Do you really think so?

**IAGO**

210    She did deceive her father, marrying you,
     And when she seemed to shake and fear your looks,
     She loved them most.

**OTHELLO**

                      And so she did.

**IAGO**

                             Why, go to then.
     She that, so young, could give out such a seeming,
     To seel her father's eyes up close as oak,
215    He thought 'twas witchcraft. But I am much to blame.
     I humbly do beseech you of your pardon
     For too much loving you.

**OTHELLO**

                    I am bound to thee forever.

**IAGO**

     I see this hath a little dashed your spirits.

**OTHELLO**

     Not a jot, not a jot.

**IAGO**

                Trust me, I fear it has.
220    I hope you will consider what is spoke
     Comes from my love. But I do see you're moved.
     I am to pray you not to strain my speech
     To grosser issues nor to larger reach
     Than to suspicion.

**OTHELLO**

225    I will not.

**IAGO**

     Should you do so, my lord,
     My speech should fall into such vile success
     Which my thoughts aimed not at. Cassio's my worthy
          friend—
     My lord, I see you're moved.

**IAGO**

She lied to her father to marry you. And when she pretended to be afraid of you, she loved you the most.

**OTHELLO**

That's right, she did.

**IAGO**

Well, there you go. She was so young, but she deceived her father so thoroughly he thought it was witchcraft! But I'm sorry I've blurted all this out. I beg your pardon for loving you too much.

**OTHELLO**

I'm indebted to you forever.

**IAGO**

You seem a little depressed about this.

**OTHELLO**

Not at all, not at all.

**IAGO**

Really, I'm afraid you are. I hope you remember that I said all this because I love you. But I see you're troubled. Please don't take what I said more seriously than it deserves to be taken.

**OTHELLO**

I won't.

**IAGO**

If you take it too seriously, it'll have bad effects that I didn't want it to have. Cassio's a good friend of mine—My lord, I can see you're upset.

ACT THREE

**OTHELLO**
                                        No, not much moved.
230     I do not think but Desdemona's honest.

**IAGO**
        Long live she so. And long live you to think so.

**OTHELLO**
        And yet how nature, erring from itself—

**IAGO**
        Ay, there's the point. As, to be bold with you,
        Not to affect many proposèd matches
235     Of her own clime, complexion, and degree,
        Whereto we see in all things nature tends—
        Foh! One may smell in such a will most rank,
        Foul disproportions, thoughts unnatural.
        But—pardon me—I do not in position
240     Distinctly speak of her, though I may fear
        Her will, recoiling to her better judgment,
        May fall to match you with her country forms,
        And happily repent.

**OTHELLO**
                                Farewell, farewell.
        If more thou dost perceive, let me know more.
245     Set on thy wife to observe. Leave me, Iago.

**IAGO**
        My lord, I take my leave. *(going)*

**OTHELLO**
        *(aside)* Why did I marry? This honest creature doubtless
        Sees and knows more, much more, than he unfolds.

**IAGO**
        *(returns)* My lord, I would I might entreat your honor
250     To scan this thing no farther. Leave it to time.
        Although 'tis fit that Cassio have his place,
        For sure, he fills it up with great ability,
        Yet, if you please to hold him off awhile,
        You shall by that perceive him and his means.
255     Note if your lady strain his entertainment

OTHELLO

No, not too upset. I'm sure Desdemona would never cheat on me.

IAGO

I hope she never does! And I hope you keep on thinking she wouldn't.

OTHELLO

But still, it's true that good things can go bad, away from their true natures—

IAGO

That's the point I'm trying to make. If I can be frank with you, she veered away from her own nature in turning down all those young men from her own country, with her skin color, with her status—everything her nature would have drawn her to—Ugh! You can almost smell the dark and ugly desires inside her, the unnatural thoughts—But—I'm sorry—I didn't mean to refer to her specifically just now. I only worry that she might snap back to her natural taste in men one day, and compare you unfavorably to other Italians.

OTHELLO

Goodbye, goodbye. If you see anything else, let me know. Tell your wife to watch her. Leave me alone now, Iago.

IAGO

My lord, I'll say goodbye now. *(beginning to exit)*

OTHELLO

*(to himself)* Why did I ever get married? I'm sure this good and honest man sees and knows more, much more, than he's telling me.

IAGO

*(returning)* My lord, please don't think about this any more. Time will tell. It's right for Cassio to have his lieutenancy back—he's very talented. But keep him away for a while, and you'll see how he goes about getting it back. Notice whether your wife insists on your

With any strong or vehement importunity.
Much will be seen in that. In the meantime,
Let me be thought too busy in my fears—
As worthy cause I have to fear I am—
260    And hold her free, I do beseech your honor.

**OTHELLO**
Fear not my government.

**IAGO**
                   I once more take my leave.

*Exit*

**OTHELLO**
This fellow's of exceeding honesty
And knows all quantities, with a learnèd spirit,
Of human dealings. If I do prove her haggard,
265    Though that her jesses were my dear heartstrings,
I'd whistle her off and let her down the wind
To prey at fortune. Haply, for I am black
And have not those soft parts of conversation
That chamberers have, or for I am declined
270    Into the vale of years—yet that's not much—
She's gone, I am abused, and my relief
Must be to loathe her. Oh, curse of marriage
That we can call these delicate creatures ours
And not their appetites! I had rather be a toad
275    And live upon the vapor of a dungeon
Than keep a corner in the thing I love
For others' uses. Yet 'tis the plague to great ones,
Prerogatived are they less than the base.
'Tis destiny unshunnable, like death.
280    Even then this forkèd plague is fated to us
When we do quicken. Look where she comes.

*Enter* DESDEMONA *and* EMILIA

If she be false, heaven mocked itself.
I'll not believe 't.

giving it back to him. That will tell you a lot. But in the meantime, just assume that I'm paranoid—as I'm pretty sure I am—and keep thinking she's innocent, please.

OTHELLO

Don't worry about how I handle it.

IAGO

I'll say goodbye once more.

IAGO *exits.*

OTHELLO

This Iago is extremely honest and good, and he knows a lot about human behavior. If it turns out that she really is running around on me, I'll send her away, even though it'll break my heart. Maybe because I'm black, and I don't have nice manners like courtiers do, or because I'm getting old—but that's not much— She's gone, and I've been cheated on. I have no choice but to hate her. Oh what a curse marriage is! We think our beautiful wives belong to us, but their desires are free! I'd rather be a toad in a moldy basement than to have only a part of someone I love, sharing the rest of her with others. This is the plague of important men—our wives betray us more than those of poor men. It's our destiny, like death. We are destined to be betrayed when we are born. Oh, here she comes.

DESDEMONA *and* EMILIA *enter.*

If she's cheated on me, then heaven itself is a fake. I don't believe it.

**DESDEMONA**

How now, my dear Othello?
Your dinner, and the generous islanders
285   By you invited, do attend your presence.

**OTHELLO**

I am to blame.

**DESDEMONA**

Why do you speak so faintly?
Are you not well?

**OTHELLO**

I have a pain upon my forehead, here.

**DESDEMONA**

290   Why that's with watching, 'twill away again.
Let me but bind it hard, within this hour
It will be well. *(pulls out a handkerchief)*

**OTHELLO**

Your napkin is too little,
Let it alone.

*Her handkerchief drops*

295   Come, I'll go in with you.

**DESDEMONA**

I am very sorry that you are not well.

*Exeunt* OTHELLO *and* DESDEMONA

**EMILIA**

*(picks up the handkercheif)*
I am glad I have found this napkin,
This was her first remembrance from the Moor.
My wayward husband hath a hundred times

**DESDEMONA**
What's going on, Othello, darling? The nobles of Cyprus whom you invited to dinner are waiting for you.

**OTHELLO**
I'm sorry.

**DESDEMONA**
Why are you whispering? Are you sick?

**OTHELLO**
I have a headache, right here in my forehead.

In Shakespeare's day, cuckolds, or men whose wives cheated on them, were imagined to have horns growing from their heads. Othello is alluding to this.

**DESDEMONA**
That's from lack of sleep. It'll go away. Let me wrap up your head, and it will feel okay in less than an hour. *(she pulls out a handkerchief)*

**OTHELLO**
No, your handkerchief's too little. Leave my head alone.

*The handkerchief falls.*

Come on, I'll escort you to dinner.

**DESDEMONA**
I'm very sorry you're not feeling well.

OTHELLO *and* DESDEMONA *exit.*

**EMILIA**
*(picking up the handkerchief)* I'm glad I found this handkerchief. It's the first keepsake the Moor gave her. My stubborn husband has asked me to steal it a

300    Wooed me to steal it, but she so loves the token
       (For he conjured her she should ever keep it)
       That she reserves it evermore about her
       To kiss and talk to. I'll have the work ta'en out
       And give 't Iago. What he will do with it
305    Heaven knows, not I.
       I nothing but to please his fantasy.

       *Enter* IAGO

IAGO
       How now! What do you here alone?

EMILIA
       Do not you chide. I have a thing for you.

IAGO
       A thing for me? It is a common thing—

EMILIA
310    Ha?

IAGO
       To have a foolish wife.

EMILIA
       Oh, is that all? What will you give me now
       For the same handkerchief?

IAGO
       What handkerchief?

EMILIA
315    What handkerchief?
       Why, that the Moor first gave to Desdemona,
       That which so often you did bid me steal.

IAGO
       Hast stolen it from her?

EMILIA
       No, but she let it drop by negligence
320    And, to th' advantage, I being here, took 't up.
       Look, here it is.

hundred times. But she loves it so much (since Othello told her she should always keep it with her) that she always keeps it near her to kiss it and talk to it. I'll copy the embroidery pattern and then give it to Iago. Heaven knows what he's going to do with it. I only try to satisfy his whims.

IAGO *enters.*

IAGO

What's going on? What are you doing here alone?

EMILIA

Don't snap at me. I've got something for you.

IAGO

You've got something for me? It's a common thing—

*"Thing" was slang for vagina. By saying that Emilia's "thing" is "common," Iago implies that she lets anyone have sex with her*

EMILIA

What?

IAGO

—to have a stupid wife.

EMILIA

Oh, is that so? And what would you give me for the handkerchief?

IAGO

What handkerchief?

EMILIA

What handkerchief? The one the Moor gave to Desdemona, which you asked me to steal so many times.

IAGO

You stole it from her?

EMILIA

No, actually. She dropped it carelessly, and, seizing the opportunity, since I was here, I picked it up. Look, here it is.

ACT THREE

IAGO
                    A good wench, give it me.

EMILIA
        What will you do with 't, that you have been so earnest
        To have me filch it?

IAGO
                              Why, what is that to you?

EMILIA
        If it be not for some purpose of import,
325     Give 't me again. Poor lady, she'll run mad
        When she shall lack it.

IAGO
        Be not acknown on 't,
        I have use for it. Go, leave me.

                                        *Exit* EMILIA

        I will in Cassio's lodging lose this napkin
330     And let him find it. Trifles light as air
        Are to the jealous confirmations strong
        As proofs of holy writ. This may do something.
        The Moor already changes with my poison.
        Dangerous conceits are in their natures poisons
335     Which at the first are scarce found to distaste,
        But with a little act upon the blood
        Burn like the mines of sulfur.

        *Enter* OTHELLO

                              I did say so.
        Look, where he comes. Not poppy nor mandragora
        Nor all the drowsy syrups of the world,
340     Shall ever medicine thee to that sweet sleep
        Which thou owedst yesterday.

OTHELLO
                              Ha! Ha! False to me?

IAGO
        Why, how now, general? No more of that.

**IAGO**

Good girl, give it to me.

**EMILIA**

And what are you going to do with it? Why did you want it so much that you begged me to steal it?

**IAGO**

What's it to you?

**EMILIA**

If you don't need it for some important reason, then give it back to me. Poor lady, she'll go crazy when she sees it's missing.

**IAGO**

Don't admit to knowing anything about it. I need it. Now go, leave me.

> **EMILIA** *exits.*

I'll leave this handkerchief at Cassio's house and let him find it. To a jealous man, a meaningless little thing like this looks like absolute proof. This handkerchief may be useful to me. The Moor's mind has already become infected with my poisonous suggestions. Ideas can be like poisons. At first they hardly even taste bad, but once they get into your blood they start burning like hot lava.

**OTHELLO** *enters.*

Here he comes. No drugs or sleeping pills will ever give you the restful sleep that you had last night.

**OTHELLO**

Argh! She's cheating on me?

**IAGO**

Oh, general, please, no more of that!

**OTHELLO**
Avaunt! Be gone! Thou hast set me on the rack.
I swear 'tis better to be much abused
345    Than but to know 't a little.

**IAGO**
How now, my lord!

**OTHELLO**
What sense had I in her stol'n hours of lust?
I saw 't not, thought it not, it harmed not me.
I slept the next night well, fed well, was free and merry.
I found not Cassio's kisses on her lips.
350    He that is robbed, not wanting what is stol'n,
Let him not know't, and he's not robbed at all.

**IAGO**
I am sorry to hear this.

**OTHELLO**
I had been happy if the general camp,
Pioneers and all, had tasted her sweet body,
355    So I had nothing known. Oh, now forever
Farewell the tranquil mind! Farewell content!
Farewell the plumèd troops and the big wars
That makes ambition virtue! Oh, farewell!
Farewell the neighing steed and the shrill trump,
360    The spirit-stirring drum, th' ear-piercing fife,
The royal banner, and all quality,
Pride, pomp, and circumstance of glorious war!
And O you mortal engines, whose rude throats
The immortal Jove's dead clamors counterfeit,
365    Farewell! Othello's occupation's gone.

**IAGO**
Is 't possible, my lord?

**OTHELLO**
Villain, be sure thou prove my love a whore,
Be sure of it. Give me the ocular proof
Or by the worth of mine eternal soul
370    Thou hadst been better have been born a dog
Than answer my waked wrath!

**OTHELLO**

Get lost! You've tortured me with these thoughts. It is better to be tricked completely than to only suspect a little.

**IAGO**

What's with you, my lord?

**OTHELLO**

I had no idea she was cheating on me. I never saw it or suspected it, so it never hurt me. I slept well, ate well, and was happy. I never saw Cassio's kisses on her lips. A man who's robbed, but doesn't miss what's stolen, isn't robbed at all.

**IAGO**

I'm sorry to hear this.

**OTHELLO**

I would've been happy if the whole army had had sex with her, the lowest-ranking grunts and all, as long as I didn't know anything about it. Oh, goodbye to my peace of mind! Goodbye to my happiness! Goodbye to the soldiers and to the wars that make men great! Goodbye! Goodbye to the horses and the trumpets and the drums, the flute and the splendid banners, and all those proud displays and pageantry of war! And you deadly cannons that roar like thunderbolts thrown by the gods, goodbye! Othello's career is over.

**IAGO**

Is this possible, my lord?

**OTHELLO**

You villain, you'd better be able to prove my wife's a whore! Be sure of it. Get me proof I can see. If you can't, trust me, you won't want to feel my rage!

IAGO

                                         Is 't come to this?

OTHELLO

    Make me to see 't, or at the least so prove it
    That the probation bear no hinge nor loop
    To hang a doubt on, or woe upon thy life!

IAGO

375    My noble lord—

OTHELLO

    If thou dost slander her and torture me,
    Never pray more. Abandon all remorse.
    On horror's head horrors accumulate,
    Do deeds to make heaven weep, all earth amazed,
380    For nothing canst thou to damnation add
    Greater than that.

IAGO

                        Oh, grace! Oh, heaven forgive me!
    Are you a man? Have you a soul or sense?
    God buy you, take mine office. O wretched fool
    That lov'st to make thine honesty a vice!
385    O monstrous world! Take note, take note, O world,
    To be direct and honest is not safe.
    I thank you for this profit, and from hence
    I'll love no friend, sith love breeds such offence.

OTHELLO

    Nay, stay. Thou shouldst be honest.

IAGO

390    I should be wise, for honesty's a fool
    And loses that it works for.

OTHELLO

                    By the world,
    I think my wife be honest and think she is not.
    I think that thou art just and think thou art not.
    I'll have some proof. Her name, that was as fresh
395    As Dian's visage, is now begrimed and black
    As mine own face. If there be cords or knives,

**IAGO**

Has it come to this?

**OTHELLO**

Show me, or at least prove it beyond the shadow of a doubt. If you can't, your life is worthless!

**IAGO**

My noble lord—

**OTHELLO**

If you're slandering her just to torture me, then it'll be no use to pray for mercy or say you're sorry. You might as well go ahead and commit every unspeakable crime you can think of, because there's nothing you could that would top what you've already done!

**IAGO**

Oh, heaven help me! Aren't you a rational human being? Don't you have any sense at all? Goodbye. I resign my official position. I'm such an idiot for always telling the truth! What a horrible world we live in! Listen, pay attention, everybody. It's not safe to be straightforward and honest. I'm glad you've taught me this valuable lesson. From now on, I'll never try to help a friend when it hurts him so much to hear the truth.

**OTHELLO**

No, stop. You should always be honest.

**IAGO**

I should always be wise. Honesty's stupid, it makes me lose my friends even when I'm trying to help them.

**OTHELLO**

*By referring to instruments of death, Othello implies that he wants to commit either suicide or murder*

I swear, I think my wife's faithful, and I think she's not. I think you're trustworthy one minute and then not the next. I need proof! Her reputation was as pure as the snow, but now it's as dirty and black as my own face. As long as there are ropes, knives, poison, fire, or

ACT THREE

Poison, or fire, or suffocating streams,
I'll not endure it. Would I were satisfied!

IAGO

I see, sir, you are eaten up with passion.
400   I do repent me that I put it to you.
You would be satisfied?

OTHELLO

                    Would? Nay, and I will.

IAGO

And may, but how? How satisfied, my lord?
Would you, the supervisor, grossly gape on,
Behold her tupped?

OTHELLO

                    Death and damnation! Oh!

IAGO

405   It were a tedious difficulty, I think,
To bring them to that prospect. Damn them then,
If ever mortal eyes do see them bolster
More than their own! What then? How then?
What shall I say? Where's satisfaction?
410   It is impossible you should see this,
Were they as prime as goats, as hot as monkeys,
As salt as wolves in pride, and fools as gross
As ignorance made drunk. But yet, I say,
If imputation and strong circumstances
415   Which lead directly to the door of truth
Will give you satisfaction, you may have 't.

OTHELLO

Give me a living reason she's disloyal.

IAGO

I do not like the office.
But, sith I am entered in this cause so far,
420   Pricked to 't by foolish honesty and love,
I will go on. I lay with Cassio lately
And, being troubled with a raging tooth,
I could not sleep. There are a kind of men
So loose of soul that in their sleeps will mutter

streams to drown in, I won't stand for this. Oh, how I wish I knew the truth!

IAGO

I see you're all eaten up with emotion. I'm sorry I said anything. You want proof?

OTHELLO

Want? Yes, I want it, and I'll get it.

IAGO

But how? How will you get proof? Are you going to hide and watch them having sex?

OTHELLO

Death and damnation! Oh!

IAGO

I think it would be very hard to arrange for them to have sex while you watched. If anyone sees them in bed together besides themselves, I guess we could damn them then. So what can we do? What can I say? What proof is there? It'd be impossible for you to watch them, even if they were as horny as animals in heat and as stupid as drunks. But if you would be willing to accept circumstantial evidence as proof, we can get that.

OTHELLO

Give me one good reason to think she's cheating on me.

IAGO

I don't like what you're asking me to do. But since I've gotten myself involved this far, because I'm so stupidly honest and because I like you so much, I'll keep going. I recently shared a bed with Cassio, and I couldn't sleep because of a raging toothache. Well, some people talk in their sleep, and Cassio is one of

425 Their affairs. One of this kind is Cassio.
In sleep I heard him say "Sweet Desdemona,
Let us be wary, let us hide our loves."
And then, sir, would he gripe and wring my hand,
Cry "O sweet creature!" and then kiss me hard,
430 As if he plucked up kisses by the roots
That grew upon my lips, lay his leg
Over my thigh, and sigh, and kiss, and then
Cry "Cursed fate that gave thee to the Moor!"

OTHELLO
Oh, monstrous! Monstrous!

IAGO
435 Nay, this was but his dream.

OTHELLO
But this denoted a foregone conclusion.

IAGO
'Tis a shrewd doubt, though it be but a dream.
And this may help to thicken other proofs
That do demonstrate thinly.

OTHELLO
I'll tear her all to pieces!

IAGO
440 Nay, yet be wise, yet we see nothing done,
She may be honest yet. Tell me but this,
Have you not sometimes seen a handkerchief
Spotted with strawberries in your wife's hand?

OTHELLO
I gave her such a one, 'twas my first gift.

IAGO
445 I know not that, but such a handkerchief—
I am sure it was your wife's—did I today
See Cassio wipe his beard with.

OTHELLO
If it be that—

IAGO
If it be that, or any that was hers,
It speaks against her with the other proofs.

them. I heard him saying, "Sweet Desdemona, let's be careful and hide our love," in his sleep. And then he grabbed my hand and said, "Oh, my darling!" and kissed me hard, as if he were trying to suck my lips off. Then he put his leg over mine, and sighed and kissed me, and said, "Damn fate for giving you to the Moor!"

OTHELLO

Oh, that's monstrous! Monstrous!

IAGO

No, it was just a dream.

OTHELLO

But it shows that something has already happened.

IAGO

It's a reason for suspicion, even though it's just a dream. And it might back up other evidence that may seem too flimsy.

OTHELLO

I'll tear her to pieces!

IAGO

No, be reasonable. We don't have any proof yet. She might still be faithful. Just tell me this: have you ever seen her holding a handkerchief with an embroidered strawberry pattern on it?

OTHELLO

Yes, I gave her one like that. It was my first gift to her.

IAGO

I don't know about that, but I saw a handkerchief like that today. I'm sure it belongs to your wife, and I saw Cassio use it to wipe his beard.

OTHELLO

If it's the same one—

IAGO

If it's the same one, or any one that belongs to her, then together with the other evidence it's pretty strong.

**OTHELLO**

450 Oh, that the slave had forty thousand lives!
One is too poor, too weak for my revenge.
Now do I see 'tis true. Look here, Iago,
All my fond love thus do I blow to heaven.
'Tis gone.
455 Arise, black vengeance, from the hollow hell!
Yield up, O love, thy crown and hearted throne
To tyrannous hate! Swell, bosom, with thy fraught,
For 'tis of aspics' tongues!

**IAGO**

Yet be content.

**OTHELLO**

Oh, blood, blood, blood!

**IAGO**

Patience, I say. Your mind may change.

**OTHELLO**

460 Never, Iago. Like to the Pontic sea,
Whose icy current and compulsive course
Ne'er keeps retiring ebb but keeps due on
To the Propontic and the Hellespont,
Even so my bloody thoughts with violent pace
465 Shall ne'er look back, ne'er ebb to humble love
Till that a capable and wide revenge
Swallow them up. Now, by yon marble heaven,
In the due reverence of a sacred vow
I here engage my words. *(he kneels)*

**IAGO**

Do not rise yet.
470 Witness, you ever-burning lights above,
You elements that clip us round about,
Witness that here Iago doth give up
The execution of his wit, hands, heart,
To wronged Othello's service. Let him command,
475 And to obey shall be in me remorse,
What bloody business ever.

OTHELLO

Oh, I'd kill that bastard Cassio forty thousand times if I could! Killing him once is not enough revenge. Now I see it's true. Oh, Iago, all the love I felt is gone, vanished in the wind. Welcome, hatred and vengeance! Get out of my heart, love! My heart feels like it's full of poisonous snakes!

IAGO

Calm down—

OTHELLO

I want blood!

IAGO

Be patient, I'm telling you. You may change your mind later.

OTHELLO

Never, Iago. My thoughts of revenge are flowing through me like a violent river, never turning back to love, only flowing toward full revenge that'll swallow them up. I swear to God I'll get revenge. *(he kneels)*

IAGO

Don't get up yet. Let heaven be my witness—I'm putting my mind, my heart, and my hands in Othello's control. Let him command me, and I'll do whatever he asks, no matter how violent.

**OTHELLO**
                              I greet thy love
Not with vain thanks but with acceptance bounteous,
And will upon the instant put thee to 't.
Within these three days let me hear thee say
480   That Cassio's not alive.

**IAGO**
                              My friend is dead,
'Tis done at your request. But let her live.

**OTHELLO**
Damn her, lewd minx! Oh, damn her, damn her!
Come, go with me apart. I will withdraw
To furnish me with some swift means of death
485   For the fair devil. Now art thou my lieutenant.

**IAGO**
I am your own for ever.

*Exeunt*

OTHELLO

I accept your devotion with my deepest love. I'll put you to the test right away. Within the next three days I want to hear you tell me that Cassio's dead.

IAGO

My friend Cassio is dead. It's done, because you request it. But let her live.

OTHELLO

Damn her, the wicked whore! Oh, damn her, damn her! Come away with me. I'm going inside to think up some way to kill that beautiful devil. You're my lieu-tenant now.

IAGO

I'm yours forever.

*They exit.*

## ACT THREE, Scene 4

*Enter* DESDEMONA, EMILIA, *and* CLOWN

**DESDEMONA**
Do you know, sirrah, where Lieutenant Cassio lies?

**CLOWN**
I dare not say he lies anywhere.

**DESDEMONA**
Why, man?

**CLOWN**
He's a soldier, and for one to say a soldier lies, 'tis
5    stabbing.

**DESDEMONA**
Go to. Where lodges he?

**CLOWN**
To tell you where he lodges is to tell you where I lie.

**DESDEMONA**
Can anything be made of this?

**CLOWN**
I know not where he lodges, and for me to devise a lodging
10    and say he lies here, or he lies there, were to lie in mine own
throat.

**DESDEMONA**
Can you inquire him out and be edified by report?

**CLOWN**
I will catechize the world for him, that is, make questions,
and by them answer.

**DESDEMONA**
15    Seek him, bid him come hither. Tell him I have moved my
lord on his behalf, and hope all will be well.

**CLOWN**
To do this is within the compass of man's wit, and
therefore I will attempt the doing it.

*Exit*

# ACT THREE, Scene 4

DESDEMONA, EMILIA *and the* CLOWN *enter.*

**DESDEMONA**

*lies in = sleeps in*

Excuse me, do you know which room Lieutenant Cassio lies in?

**CLOWN**

I wouldn't dare say he lies anywhere.

**DESDEMONA**

Why do you say that?

**CLOWN**

He's a soldier. If I accused a soldier of lying, he'd stab me.

**DESDEMONA**

Oh, come on. Where does he sleep?

**CLOWN**

Telling you where he's sleeping is like telling you where I'm lying.

**DESDEMONA**

What on earth does that mean?

**CLOWN**

I don't know where he's staying, so if I told you he's sleeping here or there, I'd be lying.

**DESDEMONA**

Can you ask around and find out?

**CLOWN**

I'll go ask questions everywhere.

**DESDEMONA**

Find him and tell him to come here. Tell him I've spoken to my husband on his behalf, and I think everything will be all right.

**CLOWN**

I think I can do that. It's not too much to ask.

CLOWN *exits.*

**DESDEMONA**
Where should I lose that handkerchief, Emilia?

**EMILIA**
20 I know not, madam.

**DESDEMONA**
Believe me, I had rather have lost my purse
Full of crusadoes. And but my noble Moor
Is true of mind and made of no such baseness
As jealous creatures are, it were enough
25 To put him to ill thinking.

**EMILIA**
Is he not jealous?

**DESDEMONA**
Who, he? I think the sun where he was born
Drew all such humors from him.

**EMILIA**
Look where he comes.

*Enter* OTHELLO

**DESDEMONA**
30 I will not leave him now till Cassio
Be called to him.—How is 't with you, my lord?

**OTHELLO**
Well, my good lady.—*(aside)* Oh, hardness to dissemble!—
How do you, Desdemona?

**DESDEMONA**
Well, my good lord.

**OTHELLO**
Give me your hand. This hand is moist, my lady.

**DESDEMONA**
35 It hath felt no age nor known no sorrow.

**OTHELLO**
This argues fruitfulness and liberal heart.
Hot, hot, and moist. This hand of yours requires
A sequester from liberty, fasting, and prayer,

**DESDEMONA**

Where could I have lost that handkerchief, Emilia?

**EMILIA**

I don't know, madam.

**DESDEMONA**

Believe me, I'd rather have lost a purse full of gold coins. This would be enough to make my husband suspect me, if he wasn't so free of jealousy.

**EMILIA**

He's not jealous?

**DESDEMONA**

Who, him? I think all tendencies to jealousy were burned out of him by the sun of his native land.

**EMILIA**

Look, here he comes.

*OTHELLO enters.*

**DESDEMONA**

I won't leave him alone until he gives Cassio his job back.—How are you, my lord?

**OTHELLO**

I'm fine, my lady.—*(to himself)* Oh, it's so hard to pretend!—How are you, Desdemona?

**DESDEMONA**

I'm fine, my lord.

**OTHELLO**

*Moist hands were supposed to indicate a tendency toward love.* Give me your hand. Your hand's moist, my lady.

**DESDEMONA**

It's moist because it's still young and inexperienced.

**OTHELLO**

It says you're fertile, and you've got a giving heart. Hot, hot and moist. With a hand like this you need to

Much castigation, exercise devout,
For here's a young and sweating devil here,
That commonly rebels. 'Tis a good hand,
A frank one.

DESDEMONA
                                You may indeed say so,
For 'twas that hand that gave away my heart.

OTHELLO
A liberal hand. The hearts of old gave hands,
But our new heraldry is hands, not hearts.

DESDEMONA
I cannot speak of this. Come now, your promise.

OTHELLO
What promise, chuck?

DESDEMONA
I have sent to bid Cassio come speak with you.

OTHELLO
I have a salt and sorry rheum offends me.
Lend me thy handkerchief.

DESDEMONA
                                          Here, my lord.

OTHELLO
That which I gave you.

DESDEMONA
                                    I have it not about me.

OTHELLO
Not?

DESDEMONA
          No, indeed, my lord.

OTHELLO
                                  That's a fault. That handkerchief
Did an Egyptian to my mother give,
She was a charmer and could almost read

fast and pray to stave off temptations. Someone with
a young sweating hand like this one is bound to act up
sooner or later. It's a nice hand, an open one.

**DESDEMONA**

You're right to say that. This was the hand that gave
you my heart.

**OTHELLO**

This hand gives itself away very freely. In the old days,
people used to give their hearts to each other when they
joined their hands in marriage. But these days, people
give each other their hands without their hearts.

**DESDEMONA**

I don't know about that. Now, don't forget, you
promised me something.

**OTHELLO**

What did I promise, my dear?

**DESDEMONA**

I sent for Cassio to come talk with you.

**OTHELLO**

I have a bad cold that's bothering me. Lend me your
handkerchief.

**DESDEMONA**

Here, my lord.

**OTHELLO**

No, the one I gave you.

**DESDEMONA**

I don't have it with me.

**OTHELLO**

You don't?

**DESDEMONA**

No, my lord.

**OTHELLO**

That's not good. An Egyptian woman gave that handkerchief to my mother. She was a witch, and she could

55  The thoughts of people. She told her, while she kept it
    'Twould make her amiable and subdue my father
    Entirely to her love, but if she lost it
    Or made gift of it, my father's eye
    Should hold her loathèd and his spirits should hunt
60  After new fancies. She, dying, gave it me
    And bid me, when my fate would have me wived,
    To give it her. I did so, and take heed on 't,
    Make it a darling like your precious eye.
    To lose 't or give 't away were such perdition
65  As nothing else could match.

**DESDEMONA**
                              Is 't possible?

**OTHELLO**
    'Tis true. There's magic in the web of it.
    A sibyl, that had numbered in the world
    The sun to course two hundred compasses,
    In her prophetic fury sewed the work.
70  The worms were hallowed that did breed the silk,
    And it was dyed in mummy which the skillful
    Conserved of maidens' hearts.

**DESDEMONA**
                              Indeed? Is 't true?

**OTHELLO**
    Most veritable, therefore look to 't well.

**DESDEMONA**
    Then would to Heaven that I had never seen 't!

**OTHELLO**
75  Ha! Wherefore?

**DESDEMONA**
    Why do you speak so startingly and rash?

**OTHELLO**
    Is 't lost? Is 't gone? Speak, is 't out o' th' way?

**DESDEMONA**
    Bless us!

almost read people's thoughts. She told my mother that as long as she kept it with her, my father would love and desire her. But if she lost it or gave it away, my father would start hating her and looking at other women. When she was dying she gave it to me and told me to give it to my wife when I got married. I did. So pay attention. Treat it as something precious. Losing it or giving it away would be an unspeakable loss, a loss like none other.

**DESDEMONA**

Is that possible?

**OTHELLO**

Yes, it's true. There's magic in its fabric. A two-hun-dred-year-old witch sewed it while she was in a fevered trance. The silk came from sacred silkworms, and it was dyed with fluid made from embalmed vir-gins' hearts.

**DESDEMONA**

Really? Is that true?

**OTHELLO**

It's absolutely true, so take good care of it.

**DESDEMONA**

I wish I had never seen it!

**OTHELLO**

Ha! Why?

**DESDEMONA**

Why are you yelling at me so angrily?

**OTHELLO**

Is it lost? Is it gone? Tell me, is it missing?

**DESDEMONA**

God help me!

ACT THREE

**OTHELLO**
Say you?

**DESDEMONA**
80    It is not lost, but what if it were?

**OTHELLO**
How!

**DESDEMONA**
I say, it is not lost.

**OTHELLO**
                    Fetch 't, let me see 't.

**DESDEMONA**
Why, so I can, sir, but I will not now.
This is a trick to put me from my suit.
85    Pray you, let Cassio be received again.

**OTHELLO**
Fetch me the handkerchief—my mind misgives.

**DESDEMONA**
Come, come,
You'll never meet a more sufficient man.

**OTHELLO**
The handkerchief!

**DESDEMONA**
                    A man that all his time
90    Hath founded his good fortunes on your love,
Shared dangers with you—

**OTHELLO**
The handkerchief!

**DESDEMONA**
In sooth, you are to blame.

**OTHELLO**
Away!

                                        *Exit*

**EMILIA**
95    Is not this man jealous?

**OTHELLO**

What do you have to say for yourself?

**DESDEMONA**

It's not lost, but what if it were?

**OTHELLO**

What do you mean?

**DESDEMONA**

I'm telling you, it's not lost.

**OTHELLO**

Then bring it here. Let me see it.

**DESDEMONA**

I could, sir. But I don't want to now. This is just a trick to take my mind off what I'm asking you for. Please hire Cassio again.

**OTHELLO**

Bring me the handkerchief—My mind is full of doubt.

**DESDEMONA**

Come on. You know you'll never find a more capable man.

**OTHELLO**

The handkerchief!

**DESDEMONA**

He's counted on your friendship for his success. He's shared dangers with you—

**OTHELLO**

The handkerchief!

**DESDEMONA**

Really, I don't think you're behaving very well.

**OTHELLO**

Damn it!

*OTHELLO exits.*

**EMILIA**

And you say he's not jealous?

**DESDEMONA**
I ne'er saw this before.
Sure, there's some wonder in this handkerchief,
I am most unhappy in the loss of it.

**EMILIA**
'Tis not a year or two shows us a man.

They are all but stomachs, and we all but food.
100     To eat us hungerly, and when they are full,
They belch us. Look you, Cassio and my husband!

*Enter* CASSIO *and* IAGO

**IAGO**
There is no other way. 'Tis she must do 't,
And, lo, the happiness! Go and importune her.

**DESDEMONA**
How now, good Cassio, what's the news with you?

**CASSIO**
105     Madam, my former suit. I do beseech you
That by your virtuous means I may again
Exist, and be a member of his love
Whom I, with all the office of my heart
Entirely honor. I would not be delayed.
110     If my offence be of such mortal kind
That nor my service past, nor present sorrows,
Nor purposed merit in futurity,
Can ransom me into his love again,
But to know so must be my benefit.
115     So shall I clothe me in a forced content,
And shut myself up in some other course,
To fortune's alms.

**DESDEMONA**

I never saw him like this before. There must be some magic in that handkerchief. I'm miserable that I lost it.

**EMILIA**

Men are all the same, but it takes longer than a year or two to see how bad they are. They're like stomachs and we're just the food. They eat us up hungrily, and when they're full, they vomit us up. Look, here comes Cassio and my husband.

IAGO *and* CASSIO *enter.*

**IAGO**

There's no other way. She's the one who's got to do it. And what luck, she's here! Go ahead and ask her.

**DESDEMONA**

Hello, Cassio. How are you?

**CASSIO**

Nothing, madam. Just my earlier request. I'm begging you to help me get back on his good side. I'm devoted to him with all my heart. I can't wait any longer. If my wrongdoing was so serious that I can't get back into his good graces either by my past service, or my present situation, or the promise of devoted service in the future, just knowing that would help me. Then I could stop wondering, and find some other career.

**DESDEMONA**
                    Alas, thrice-gentle Cassio,
My advocation is not now in tune.
My lord is not my lord, nor should I know him

120     Were he in favor as in humor altered.
So help me every spirit sanctified
As I have spoken for you all my best
And stood within the blank of his displeasure
For my free speech. You must awhile be patient.

125     What I can do I will, and more I will
Than for myself I dare. Let that suffice you.

**IAGO**
Is my lord angry?

**EMILIA**
                    He went hence but now,
And certainly in strange unquietness.

**IAGO**
Can he be angry? I have seen the cannon

130     When it hath blown his ranks into the air
And, like the devil, from his very arm
Puffed his own brother—and is he angry?
Something of moment then, I will go meet him.
There's matter in 't indeed, if he be angry.

**DESDEMONA**
135     I prithee, do so.

                                  *Exit* IAGO

                    Something, sure, of state,
Either from Venice, or some unhatched practice
Made demonstrable here in Cyprus to him,
Hath puddled his clear spirit, and in such cases
Men's natures wrangle with inferior things,

140     Though great ones are their object. 'Tis even so,
For let our finger ache and it endues
Our other healthful members even to that sense
Of pain. Nay, we must think men are not gods,

**DESDEMONA**

I'm sorry, dear Cassio, but now is not the right time to bring up your case. My husband's not himself. If his face changed as much as his personality has, I wouldn't recognize him. God knows I have done my best to argue for you, and made him angry at me for being so aggressive. You'll just have to be patient for a little while. I'll do what I can, more than I'd do for myself. Let that be enough for you.

**IAGO**

Is Othello angry?

**EMILIA**

He just left, clearly upset about something.

**IAGO**

Can he even get angry? It's hard to believe. I've seen him stay calm when cannons were blowing his soldiers to bits, even killing his own brother without him batting an eyelid—is he really upset? It must be about something important. I'll go talk to him. If he's angry, there must be something seriously wrong.

**DESDEMONA**

Please, do so.

*IAGO exits.*

There must be some political news from Venice, or some dangerous plot here in Cyprus has ruined his good mood. Men always get angry about little things when they're really worried about bigger ones. That's the way it goes. When our finger hurts, it makes the rest of the body hurt too. We shouldn't expect men to

Nor of them look for such observances
145        As fit the bridal. Beshrew me much, Emilia,
I was, unhandsome warrior as I am,
Arraigning his unkindness with my soul,
But now I find I had suborned the witness,
And he's indicted falsely.

**EMILIA**
                                        Pray heaven it be
150        State matters, as you think, and no conception
Nor no jealous toy concerning you.

**DESDEMONA**
Alas the day! I never gave him cause.

**EMILIA**
But jealous souls will not be answered so.
They are not ever jealous for the cause,
155        But jealous for they're jealous. It is a monster
Begot upon itself, born on itself.

**DESDEMONA**
Heaven keep the monster from Othello's mind!

**EMILIA**
Lady, amen.

**DESDEMONA**
I will go seek him.—Cassio, walk hereabout.
160        If I do find him fit, I'll move your suit
And seek to effect it to my uttermost.

**CASSIO**
I humbly thank your ladyship.

                          *Exeunt* DESDEMONA *and* EMILIA
*Enter* BIANCA

**BIANCA**
Save you, friend Cassio!

be perfect, or for them to be as polite as on the wedding-day. Oh, Emilia, I'm so inexperienced that I thought he was being unkind, but actually I was judging him harshly.

EMILIA

I hope to God it's something political, like you think, and not jealousy involving you.

DESDEMONA

Oh no! I never gave him reason to be jealous.

EMILIA

But jealous people don't think like that. They're never jealous for a reason; they're just jealous. It's like a monster that just grows and grows, out of nothing.

DESDEMONA

I hope God keeps that monster from growing in Othello's mind!

EMILIA

Amen to that, lady.

DESDEMONA

I'll go look for him—Cassio, stay around here. If he's in a good mood I'll mention you again, and do everything I can.

CASSIO

I thank you, lady.

DESDEMONA *and* EMILIA *exit.*

BIANCA *enters.*

BIANCA

Hello, Cassio!

ACT THREE

**CASSIO**
What make you from home?
How is 't with you, my most fair Bianca?
165 Indeed, sweet love, I was coming to your house.

**BIANCA**
And I was going to your lodging, Cassio.
What, keep a week away? Seven days and nights?
Eight score eight hours? And lovers' absent hours
More tedious than the dial eightscore times!
170 Oh weary reckoning!

**CASSIO**
Pardon me, Bianca,
I have this while with leaden thoughts been pressed,
But I shall, in a more continuate time,
Strike off this score of absence. Sweet Bianca,
*(giving her* DESDEMONA*'s handkerchief)*
Take me this work out.

**BIANCA**
O Cassio, whence came this?
175 This is some token from a newer friend!
To the felt absence now I feel a cause.
Is 't come to this? Well, well.

**CASSIO**
Go to, woman,
Throw your vile guesses in the devil's teeth
From whence you have them. You are jealous now
180 That this is from some mistress, some remembrance.
No, in good troth, Bianca.

**BIANCA**
Why, whose is it?

**CASSIO**
I know not neither, I found it in my chamber.
I like the work well. Ere it be demanded,
As like enough it will, I would have it copied.
185 Take it and do 't, and leave me for this time.

**BIANCA**
Leave you! Wherefore?

CASSIO

Why are you so far from home? How are you, my pretty Bianca? To tell you the truth, I was just going to your house.

BIANCA

And I was just going to yours. You've kept away from me for a week? Seven days and seven nights? A hundred and sixty-eight hours? And lovers' hours are a hundred and sixty times longer than normal ones! What a tedious wait!

CASSIO

I'm sorry, Bianca. All this time I've been depressed and had problems on my mind. When I get some free time I'll make it up to you. *(he gives her* DESDEMONA*'s handkerchief)* Sweet Bianca, would you copy this embroidery pattern for me?

BIANCA

Oh, Cassio, where did you get this? This is a gift from another woman, a new lover! Now I know why you've been staying away from me. Has it come to this? Well, well.

CASSIO

Oh, come on, woman. Stop jumping to silly conclusions. Now you're jealous, thinking that this is from some mistress of mine, but I swear it's not, Bianca.

BIANCA

Well, whose is it?

CASSIO

I don't even know. I found it in my room. It's pretty. Someone is certainly looking for it, and I'll have to give it back. So I'd like it copied. Take it and do that for me, and leave me alone for a while.

BIANCA

Leave you alone! Why?

**CASSIO**
> I do attend here on the general
> And think it no addition, nor my wish,
> To have him see me womaned.

**BIANCA**
> Why, I pray you?

**CASSIO**
190 Not that I love you not.

**BIANCA**
> But that you do not love me.
> I pray you bring me on the way a little
> And say if I shall see you soon at night.

**CASSIO**
> 'Tis but a little way that I can bring you,
> For I attend here. But I'll see you soon.

**BIANCA**
195 'Tis very good. I must be circumstanced.

*Exeunt*

CASSIO

I'm waiting here for the general, and I don't want him to see me with a woman.

BIANCA

And why's that?

CASSIO

It's not because I don't love you.

BIANCA

But you don't love me. Please, just walk with me a little ways, and tell me if I'll see you later tonight.

CASSIO

I can only walk a little way with you, since I'm waiting here. But I'll see you soon.

BIANCA

All right, have it your way. I have to make do.

*They exit.*

# ACT FOUR

## Scene 1

*Enter* OTHELLO *and* IAGO

IAGO
Will you think so?

OTHELLO
     Think so, Iago?

IAGO
          What,
To kiss in private?

OTHELLO
     An unauthorized kiss!

IAGO
Or to be naked with her friend in bed
An hour or more, not meaning any harm?

OTHELLO
5 Naked in bed, Iago, and not mean harm!
It is hypocrisy against the devil.
They that mean virtuously, and yet do so,
The devil their virtue tempts, and they tempt heaven.

IAGO
So they do nothing, 'tis a venial slip.
10 But if I give my wife a handkerchief—

OTHELLO
What then?

IAGO
Why then 'tis hers, my lord, and, being hers,
She may, I think, bestow 't on any man.

OTHELLO
She is protectress of her honor too.
15 May she give that?

# ACT FOUR

## Scene 1

OTHELLO *and* IAGO *enter.*

**IAGO**

Do you really think so?

**OTHELLO**

What do you mean, do I think so?

**IAGO**

What, just because they kissed in private?

**OTHELLO**

An illicit kiss!

**IAGO**

Maybe she was just naked in bed with him for an hour or so, but they didn't do anything.

**OTHELLO**

Naked in bed together, but without doing anything? Come on, Iago. That would be like playing a trick on the devil: they'd make him think they're going to commit adultery, but then back off. Anyone who acted like that would be letting the devil tempt them, and tempting God to condemn them.

**IAGO**

As long as they didn't do anything, it would only be a minor sin. But if I gave my wife a handkerchief—

**OTHELLO**

Then what?

**IAGO**

Then it's hers. And if it's hers, I guess she can give it to any man she wants.

**OTHELLO**

Her reputation is also her own. Can she give that away too?

**IAGO**
Her honor is an essence that's not seen,
They have it very oft that have it not.
But for the handkerchief—

**OTHELLO**
By heaven, I would most gladly have forgot it.
20  Thou saidst—Oh, it comes o'er my memory,
As doth the raven o'er the infectious house,
Boding to all—he had my handkerchief.

**IAGO**
Ay, what of that?

**OTHELLO**
That's not so good now.

**IAGO**
What if I had said I had seen him do you wrong?
25  Or heard him say—as knaves be such abroad,
Who having, by their own importunate suit,
Or voluntary dotage of some mistress,
Convincèd or supplied them, cannot choose
But they must blab—

**OTHELLO**
Hath he said any thing?

**IAGO**
30  He hath, my lord, but be you well assured
No more than he'll unswear.

**OTHELLO**
What hath he said?

**IAGO**
Why, that he did—I know not what he did.

**OTHELLO**
What? what?

**IAGO**
Lie—

**OTHELLO**
With her?

IAGO

You can't see a reputation. A lot of people don't even deserve the reputations they have. But a handkerchief—

OTHELLO

God, I wish I could forget about the handkerchief! What you told me it haunts me like a nightmare—he's got my handkerchief!

IAGO

Yes, what about it?

OTHELLO

That's not good.

IAGO

What if I'd said I saw him do something to hurt you? Or heard him say something about it. You know there are jerks out there who have to brag about bedding some woman.—

OTHELLO

Has he said anything?

IAGO

Yes, but he'd deny it all.

OTHELLO

What did he say?

IAGO

He said he did—I don't know.

OTHELLO

He what?

IAGO

He was in bed with—

OTHELLO

With her?

IAGO

        With her, on her, what you will.

OTHELLO

Lie with her? lie on her? We say "lie on her" when they
belie her! Lie with her—that's fulsome. Handkerchief—
confessions—handkerchief! To confess, and be hanged
for his labor. First to be hanged, and then to confess—I
tremble at it. Nature would not invest herself in such
shadowing passion without some instruction. It is not
words that shake me thus. Pish! Noses, ears, and lips. Is 't
possible? Confess!—Handkerchief!—Oh, devil!—
*(falls in a trance)*

IAGO

Work on, My medicine, work! Thus credulous fools are
  caught,
And many worthy and chaste dames even thus,
All guiltless, meet reproach.—What, ho! My lord!
My lord, I say! Othello!

*Enter* CASSIO

       How now, Cassio!

CASSIO

What's the matter?

IAGO

My lord is fall'n into an epilepsy.
This is his second fit. He had one yesterday.

CASSIO

Rub him about the temples.

IAGO

        No, forbear.
The lethargy must have his quiet course.
If not, he foams at mouth and by and by
Breaks out to savage madness. Look, he stirs.
Do you withdraw yourself a little while,

**IAGO**

With her, on top of her—however you want to say it.

**OTHELLO**

In bed with her? On top of her? I would have thought people were telling lies about her rather than believe he was lying on her. My God, it's nauseating! Handkerchief—confessions—handkerchief! I'll kill him first, and then let him confess—I'm trembling with rage. I wouldn't be trembling like this if I didn't know deep down this was all true. Noses, ears, lips. Is it possible? Tell me the truth—Handkerchief—Damn it! *(he falls into a trance)*

**IAGO**

Keep working, poison! This is the way to trick gullible fools. Many good and innocent women are punished for reasons like this.—My lord? My lord, Othello!

CASSIO *enters.*

Hey, Cassio!

**CASSIO**

What's the matter?

**IAGO**

Othello's having some kind of epileptic fit. This is his second fit like this. He had one yesterday.

**CASSIO**

Rub his temples.

**IAGO**

No, don't. This fit has to run its course. If you interrupt it, he'll foam at the mouth and go crazy. Look, he's moving. Why don't you go away for a bit? He'll

He will recover straight. When he is gone
55    I would on great occasion speak with you.

*Exit* CASSIO

How is it, general? Have you not hurt your head?

OTHELLO
Dost thou mock me?

IAGO
I mock you not, by heaven.
Would you would bear your fortune like a man!

OTHELLO
A hornèd man's a monster and a beast.

IAGO
60    There's many a beast then in a populous city,
And many a civil monster.

OTHELLO
Did he confess it?

IAGO
Good sir, be a man,
Think every bearded fellow that's but yoked
May draw with you. There's millions now alive
65    That nightly lie in those unproper beds
Which they dare swear peculiar. Your case is better.
Oh, 'tis the spite of hell, the fiend's arch-mock,
To lip a wanton in a secure couch,
And to suppose her chaste. No, let me know,
70    And knowing what I am, I know what she shall be.

OTHELLO
Oh, thou art wise! 'Tis certain.

IAGO
Stand you awhile apart,
Confine yourself but in a patient list.
Whilst you were here o'erwhelmèd with your grief—
A passion most resulting such a man—
75    Cassio came hither. I shifted him away
And laid good 'scuses upon your ecstasy,

get better right away. When he leaves, it's very important that I talk to you.

<small>CASSIO exits.</small>

What happened, general? Did you hit your head?

**OTHELLO**

Are you making fun of me?

**IAGO**

Making fun of you? No, I swear! I wish you could face your bad news like a man!

**OTHELLO**

A man who's been cheated on isn't a real man. He's subhuman, like an animal.

**IAGO**

In that case there are a lot of animals on the loose in this city.

**OTHELLO**

Did he confess?

**IAGO**

Sir, be a man. Every married man has been cheated on. Millions of men sleep with wives who cheat on them, wrongly believing they belong to them alone. Your case is better than that. At least you're not ignorant. The worst thing of all is to kiss your wife thinking she's innocent, when in fact she's a whore. No, I'd rather know the truth. Then I'll know exactly what she is, just as I know what I am.

**OTHELLO**

You're wise! That's for sure.

**IAGO**

Go somewhere else for a while. Calm down. While you were dazed by grief—which isn't appropriate for a man like you—Cassio showed up here. I got him to leave, and made up an excuse for your trance. I told him to come back and talk to me in a bit, and he promised he would. So hide here and watch how he sneers

Bade him anon return and here speak with me,
The which he promised. Do but encave yourself,
And mark the fleers, the gibes, and notable scorns
80    That dwell in every region of his face.
For I will make him tell the tale anew
Where, how, how oft, how long ago, and when
He hath, and is again to cope your wife.
I say, but mark his gesture. Marry, patience,
85    Or I shall say you are all in all in spleen,
And nothing of a man.

**OTHELLO**
                              Dost thou hear, Iago?
I will be found most cunning in my patience,
But—dost thou hear?—most bloody.

**IAGO**
                                          That's not amiss,
But yet keep time in all. Will you withdraw?
                              OTHELLO *withdraws*


90    Now will I question Cassio of Bianca,
A huswife that by selling her desires
Buys herself bread and clothes. It is a creature
That dotes on Cassio, as 'tis the strumpet's plague
To beguile many and be beguiled by one.
95    He, when he hears of her, cannot refrain
From the excess of laughter. Here he comes.

*Enter* CASSIO

As he shall smile, Othello shall go mad.
And his unbookish jealousy must construe
Poor Cassio's smiles, gestures, and light behavior
100    Quite in the wrong.—How do you now, lieutenant?

at you. I'll make him tell me the whole story again—where, how often, how long ago—and when he plans to sleep with your wife in the future. I'm telling you, just watch his face. But stay calm, and don't get carried away by rage, or I'll think you're not a man.

OTHELLO

Do you hear what I'm saying, Iago? I'll be very patient, but—do you hear me?—I'm not done with him yet.

IAGO

That's fine, but for now keep your cool. Will you go hide?

OTHELLO *hides.*

Now I'll ask Cassio about Bianca, a prostitute who sells her body for food and clothes. She's crazy about Cassio. That's the whore's curse, to seduce many men, but to be seduced by one. Whenever he talks about her he can't stop laughing.

CASSIO *enters.*

And when he laughs, Othello will go crazy. In his ignorant jealousy, he'll totally misunderstand Cassio's smiles, gestures, and jokes.—How are you, lieutenant?

CASSIO
> The worser that you give me the addition
> Whose want even kills me.

IAGO
> Ply Desdemona well, and you are sure on 't.
> Now if this suit lay in Bianca's power
105 > How quickly should you speed!

CASSIO
>                                       Alas, poor caitiff!

OTHELLO
> Look how he laughs already!

IAGO
> I never knew woman love man so.

CASSIO
> Alas, poor rogue, I think indeed she loves me.

OTHELLO
> Now he denies it faintly, and laughs it out.

IAGO
110 > Do you hear, Cassio?

OTHELLO
>                             Now he importunes him
> To tell it o'er. Go to, well said, well said.

IAGO
> She gives it out that you shall marry her.
> Do you intend it?

CASSIO
> Ha, ha, ha!

OTHELLO
115 > Do ye triumph, Roman? Do you triumph?

CASSIO
> I marry her! What? A customer? Prithee bear some
> charity to my wit. Do not think it so unwholesome. Ha,
> ha, ha!

OTHELLO
> So, so, so, so! They laugh that win!

CASSIO

It doesn't make me feel any better when you call me lieutenant. I'm dying to have that title back again.

IAGO

Just keep asking Desdemona, and it'll be yours. If it was up to Bianca to get you your job back, you'd have had it already!

CASSIO

The poor thing!

OTHELLO

He's laughing already!

IAGO

I never knew a woman who loved a man so much.

CASSIO

The poor thing, I really think she loves me.

OTHELLO

Now he denies it a bit, and tries to laugh it off.

IAGO

Have you heard this, Cassio?

OTHELLO

He's asking him to tell the story again. Go on, tell it.

IAGO

She says you're going to marry her. Are you?

CASSIO

Ha, ha, ha!

OTHELLO

Are you laughing because you've won? Do you think you've won?

CASSIO

Me, marry her? That whore? Please give me a little credit! I'm not that stupid. Ha, ha, ha!

OTHELLO

So, so, so, so! The winner's always got the last laugh, hasn't he?

**IAGO**

120     Why the cry goes that you shall marry her.

**CASSIO**

Prithee say true!

**IAGO**

I am a very villain else.

**OTHELLO**

Have you scored me? Well.

**CASSIO**

This is the monkey's own giving out. She is persuaded I
125     will marry her, out of her own love and flattery, not out of
my promise.

**OTHELLO**

Iago beckons me. Now he begins the story.

**CASSIO**

She was here even now. She haunts me in every place. I
was the other day talking on the sea-bank with certain
130     Venetians, and thither comes the bauble and, by this
hand, she falls me thus about my neck—

**OTHELLO**

Crying "O dear Cassio!" as it were. His gesture imports it.

**CASSIO**

So hangs and lolls and weeps upon me, so shakes, and
pulls me! Ha, ha, ha!

**OTHELLO**

135     Now he tells how she plucked him to my chamber. Oh, I
see that nose of yours, but not that dog I shall throw it to.

**CASSIO**

Well, I must leave her company.

**IAGO**

Before me! Look, where she comes.

*Enter* BIANCA

**IAGO**

I swear, there's a rumor going around that you'll marry her.

**CASSIO**

You're kidding!

**IAGO**

If it's not true, you can call me a villain.

**OTHELLO**

Have you given me bastard children to raise? All right, then.

**CASSIO**

The little monkey must have started that rumor herself. She thinks I'll marry her because she loves me. She's just flattering herself. I never promised her anything.

**OTHELLO**

Iago is gesturing for me to come closer. Now he's telling the story.

**CASSIO**

She was here just now. She hangs around me all the time. I was talking to some Venetians down by the shore, and the fool showed up. I swear to you, she put her arms around me like this—

**OTHELLO**

Saying "Oh, Cassio," it seems, judging by his gestures.

**CASSIO**

She hangs around me and dangles from my neck and cries, shaking me and pulling at me. Ha, ha, ha!

**OTHELLO**

Now he's saying how she took him into our bedroom. Oh, I can see your nose now. But I can't see the dog I'm going to throw it to.

**CASSIO**

I have to get rid of her.

**IAGO**

Look out, here she comes.

BIANCA *enters.*

**CASSIO**

'Tis such another fitchew. Marry, a perfumed one.—
140   What do you mean by this haunting of me?

**BIANCA**

Let the devil and his dam haunt you! What did you
mean by that same handkerchief you gave me even now?
I was a fine fool to take it. I must take out the
work? A likely piece of work, that you should find
145   it in your chamber, and not know who left it there!
This is some minx's token, and I must take out the
work? There, give it your hobby-horse. Wheresoever
you had it, I'll take out no work on 't.

**CASSIO**

How now, my sweet Bianca! How now, how now?

**OTHELLO**

150   By heaven, that should be my handkerchief!

**BIANCA**

If you'll come to supper tonight, you may. If you will not,
come when you are next prepared for.

*Exit*

**IAGO**

After her, after her.

**CASSIO**

I must, she'll rail in the street else.

**IAGO**

155   Will you sup there?

**CASSIO**

Yes, I intend so.

**IAGO**

Well, I may chance to see you, for I would very fain
speak with you.

**CASSIO**

Prithee come, will you?

**IAGO**

160   Go to! Say no more.

*Exit* CASSIO

**CASSIO**

It's a whore like all the others, stinking of cheap perfume.—Why are you always hanging around me?

**BIANCA**

Damn you! What did you mean by giving me this handkerchief? I was an idiot to take it! You want me to copy the embroidery pattern? That was a likely story, that you found it in your room and didn't know who it belonged to. This is a love token from some other slut, and you want me to copy its pattern for you? Give it back to her, I won't do anything with it.

**CASSIO**

What is it, my dear Bianca? What's wrong?

**OTHELLO**

My God, that's my handkerchief!

**BIANCA**

If you want to come have dinner with me, you can. If you don't want to, then good riddance.

BIANCA *exits.*

**IAGO**

Go after her, go.

**CASSIO**

Actually, I should. She'll scream in the streets if I don't.

**IAGO**

Will you be having dinner with her tonight?

**CASSIO**

Yes, I will.

**IAGO**

Well, maybe I'll see you there. I'd really like to speak with you.

**CASSIO**

Please come. Will you?

**IAGO**

Don't talk anymore, go after her.

CASSIO *exits.*

**OTHELLO**
*(advancing)* How shall I murder him, Iago?

**IAGO**
Did you perceive how he laughed at his vice?

**OTHELLO**
O Iago!

**IAGO**
And did you see the handkerchief?

**OTHELLO**
165  Was that mine?

**IAGO**
Yours by this hand. And to see how he prizes the foolish
woman your wife! She gave it him, and he hath given it his
whore.

**OTHELLO**
I would have him nine years a-killing. A fine woman! A
170  fair woman! A sweet woman!

**IAGO**
Nay, you must forget that.

**OTHELLO**
Ay, let her rot and perish and be damned tonight, for she
shall not live. No, my heart is turned to stone. I strike it
and it hurts my hand. Oh, the world hath not a sweeter
175  creature, she might lie by an emperor's side and command
him tasks.

**IAGO**
Nay, that's not your way.

**OTHELLO**
Hang her! I do but say what she is. So delicate with her
needle, an admirable musician. Oh, she will sing the
180  savageness out of a bear! Of so high and plenteous wit and
invention!

**IAGO**
She's the worse for all this.

**OTHELLO**

*(coming forward)* How should I murder him, Iago?

**IAGO**

Did you see how he laughed about sleeping with her?

**OTHELLO**

Oh Iago!

**IAGO**

And did you see the handkerchief?

**OTHELLO**

Was it mine?

**IAGO**

It was yours, I swear. And do you see how much your foolish wife means to him? She gave it to him, and he gave it to his whore.

**OTHELLO**

I wish I could keep killing him for nine years straight. Oh, she's a fine woman! A fair woman! A sweet woman!

**IAGO**

No, you have to forget all that now.

**OTHELLO**

Yes, let her die and rot and go to hell tonight. She won't stay alive for long. No, my heart's turned to stone—when I hit it, it hurts my hand. Oh, the world never saw a sweeter creature. She could be married to an emperor, and he'd be like her slave!

**IAGO**

But that's not how you're going to be.

**OTHELLO**

Damn her, I'm just describing her truthfully! She's so good at sewing, and a wonderful musician. Oh, she could sing a wild bear to sleep! Oh, she's so witty and creative!

**IAGO**

All the worse that she stooped this low, then.

**OTHELLO**
Oh, a thousand thousand times—and then of so gentle a
condition!

**IAGO**
185     Ay, too gentle.

**OTHELLO**
Nay, that's certain. But yet the pity of it, Iago! O Iago, the
pity of it, Iago!

**IAGO**
If you are so fond over her iniquity, give her patent to
offend, for if it touch not you it comes near nobody.

**OTHELLO**
190     I will chop her into messes! Cuckold me?

**IAGO**
Oh, 'tis foul in her.

**OTHELLO**
With mine officer!

**IAGO**
That's fouler.

**OTHELLO**
Get me some poison, Iago, this night. I'll not expostulate
195     with her, lest her body and beauty unprovide my mind
again—This night, Iago!

**IAGO**
Do it not with poison. Strangle her in her bed, even the
bed she hath contaminated.

**OTHELLO**
Good, good, the justice of it pleases! Very good!

**IAGO**
200     And for Cassio, let me be his undertaker. You shall hear
more by midnight.

**OTHELLO**
Excellent good.

*A trumpet within*

**OTHELLO**

Oh, a thousand times worse, a thousand times—and what a sweet personality she has!

**IAGO**

Yes, a little too sweet.

**OTHELLO**

Yes, that's for sure. Oh, it's dreadful, dreadful, Iago!

**IAGO**

If you still feel so affectionate toward her, then why not give her permission to cheat on you? If it doesn't bother you, it won't bother anyone else.

**OTHELLO**

I'll chop her into pieces. How could she cheat on me?

**IAGO**

Oh, it's horrible of her.

**OTHELLO**

And with my own officer!

**IAGO**

That's worse.

**OTHELLO**

Get me some poison tonight, Iago. I won't argue with her, so her beautiful body won't disarm me.— Tonight, Iago.

**IAGO**

Don't do it with poison. Strangle her in her bed, the same bed she's contaminated.

**OTHELLO**

Good, good, I like that—it's only fair! Very good!

**IAGO**

And let me kill Cassio. You'll hear more from me by midnight.

**OTHELLO**

Excellent, good.

*A trumpet sounds offstage.*

What trumpet is that same?

IAGO

I warrant something from Venice. 'Tis Lodovico, this,
205     comes from the duke. See, your wife's with him.

*Enter* LODOVICO, DESDEMONA, *and attendants*

LODOVICO

Save you, worthy general!

OTHELLO

With all my heart, sir.

LODOVICO

The duke and senators of Venice greet you.
*(gives him a letter)*

OTHELLO

I kiss the instrument of their pleasures.

DESDEMONA

210     And what's the news, good cousin Lodovico?

IAGO

I am very glad to see you, signior. Welcome to Cyprus.

LODOVICO

I thank you. How does lieutenant Cassio?

IAGO

Lives, sir.

DESDEMONA

Cousin, there's fall'n between him and my lord
215     An unkind breach, but you shall make all well.

OTHELLO

Are you sure of that?

DESDEMONA

My lord?

OTHELLO

*(reads)* "This fail you not to do, as you will—"

What's that trumpet for?

IAGO

I think someone's coming from Venice. It's Lodovico. He must be coming from the duke. Look, your wife is with him.

LODOVICO, DESDEMONA *and attendants enter.*

LODOVICO

Greetings, good general!

OTHELLO

Greetings, sir.

LODOVICO

The duke and senators of Venice greet you.
*(he hands* OTHELLO *a piece of paper)*

OTHELLO

I'll do whatever they order me to do in this letter.

DESDEMONA

What's new, cousin Lodovico?

IAGO

Very nice to see you, sir. Welcome to Cyprus.

LODOVICO

Thank you. How is lieutenant Cassio?

IAGO

Well, he's alive.

DESDEMONA

Cousin, there's been a falling out between him and Othello. An unfortunate rift, but you can fix it.

OTHELLO

Are you sure of that?

DESDEMONA

Excuse me?

OTHELLO

*(reading)* "Don't fail to do this, since you'll—"

**LODOVICO**
> He did not call, he's busy in the paper.
220  > Is there division 'twixt my lord and Cassio?

**DESDEMONA**
> A most unhappy one. I would do much
> T' atone them, for the love I bear to Cassio.

**OTHELLO**
> Fire and brimstone!

**DESDEMONA**
>                           My lord?

**OTHELLO**
>                                   Are you wise?

**DESDEMONA**
> What, is he angry?

**LODOVICO**
>                           Maybe the letter moved him,
225  > For, as I think, they do command him home,
> Deputing Cassio in his government.

**DESDEMONA**
> Trust me, I am glad on 't.

**OTHELLO**
> Indeed!

**DESDEMONA**
> My lord?

**OTHELLO**
230  > I am glad to see you mad.

**DESDEMONA**
> Why, sweet Othello—

**OTHELLO**
> (*striking her*) Devil!

**DESDEMONA**
> I have not deserved this.

**LODOVICO**
He didn't say anything, he's reading. So there's a rift between Othello and Cassio?

**DESDEMONA**
Yes, unfortunately. I'd do anything to bring them back together, since I really care for Cassio.

**OTHELLO**
Damn it all!

**DESDEMONA**
Excuse me, my lord?

**OTHELLO**
Are you in your right mind?

**DESDEMONA**
Is he angry?

**LODOVICO**
Maybe the letter upset him. I think they want him to go home and appoint Cassio governor in his place.

**DESDEMONA**
I'm happy about that.

**OTHELLO**
Oh, are you really!

**DESDEMONA**
My lord?

**OTHELLO**
I'm glad you're insane enough to admit it in front of me.

**DESDEMONA**
Why, sweet Othello—

**OTHELLO**
*(striking her)* You devil!

**DESDEMONA**
I haven't done anything to deserve this!

**LODOVICO**
My lord, this would not be believed in Venice,
235    Though I should swear I saw 't. 'Tis very much.
Make her amends, she weeps.

**OTHELLO**
                                        Oh, devil, devil!
If that the earth could teem with woman's tears,
Each drop she falls would prove a crocodile.
Out of my sight!

**DESDEMONA**
240    I will not stay to offend you.

**LODOVICO**
Truly, an obedient lady.
I do beseech your lordship, call her back.

**OTHELLO**
Mistress!

**DESDEMONA**
My lord?

**OTHELLO**
245    What would you with her, sir?

**LODOVICO**
Who, I, my lord?

**OTHELLO**
Ay, you did wish that I would make her turn.
Sir, she can turn, and turn, and yet go on,
And turn again. And she can weep, sir, weep.
250    And she's obedient, as you say, obedient,
Very obedient.—Proceed you in your tears.—
Concerning this, sir—Oh, well-painted passion!—
I am commanded home.—Get you away,
I'll send for you anon.—Sir, I obey the mandate
255    And will return to Venice.—Hence, avaunt!

*Exit* DESDEMONA

**LODOVICO**

My lord, no one will believe this in Venice, even though I'd swear I saw it with my own eyes. That was too much. You should apologize. She's crying.

**OTHELLO**

Oh, you devil, you devil! You can cry all day and all night, and I still won't believe you're sad. Get out of my sight!

**DESDEMONA**

I wouldn't want to stay here and make you angry.

**LODOVICO**

She's obedient—a fine lady. Please, my lord, call her back.

**OTHELLO**

Madam!

**DESDEMONA**

My lord?

**OTHELLO**

What do you want with her, sir?

**LODOVICO**

Who, me?

**OTHELLO**

Yes, you asked me to call her back. See how well she can turn? She can turn and turn, and then turn on you again. And she can cry, sir—oh, how she can cry! And she's obedient, as you say, obedient. Very obedient— keep crying.—Concerning this—oh, what fake emotion!—I am being ordered home—Get away from me, I'll send for you later.—Sir, I'll obey the order and return to Venice. Get away from me, you witch!

> **DESDEMONA** *exits.*

Cassio shall have my place. And, sir, tonight
I do entreat that we may sup together.
You are welcome, sir, to Cyprus. Goats and monkeys!

*Exit*

LODOVICO
Is this the noble Moor whom our full senate
260    Call all in all sufficient? Is this the nature
Whom passion could not shake? Whose solid virtue
The shot of accident nor dart of chance
Could neither graze nor pierce?

IAGO
                                                    He is much changed.

LODOVICO
Are his wits safe? Is he not light of brain?

IAGO
265    He's that he is. I may not breathe my censure
What he might be. If what he might he is not,
I would to heaven he were!

LODOVICO
                                        What? Strike his wife?

IAGO
'Faith, that was not so well. Yet would I knew
That stroke would prove the worst!

LODOVICO
                                                        Is it his use?
270    Or did the letters work upon his blood
And new-create his fault?

Cassio can have my job. And tonight, sir, I invite you to have dinner with me. Welcome to Cyprus. Horny animals!

OTHELLO *exits.*

LODOVICO

Is this the same Moor whom the senate considers so capable? Is this the guy who's supposed to never get emotional, and who never gets rattled, no matter what disaster happens?

IAGO

He's changed a great deal.

LODVICO

Is he sane? Is he losing his mind?

IAGO

He is what he is. I won't say anything negative about what he might be. If he isn't what he might be, then I wish to God he were!

LODOVICO

Hitting his wife?

IAGO

It's true, that wasn't such a nice thing to do. But I wish I could say that's the last time he'll do it!

LODOVICO

Is it a habit of his? Or did the letter make him emotional somehow, and this is the first time he's done it?

IAGO
                              Alas, alas!
It is not honesty in me to speak
What I have seen and known. You shall observe him,
And his own courses will denote him so
275    That I may save my speech. Do but go after
And mark how he continues.

LODOVICO
I am sorry that I am deceived in him.

*Exeunt*

IAGO

> Oh, it's too bad! It wouldn't be right for me to tell you everything I've seen and heard. You'll see what he's like. His own actions will show you what kind of person he is, so I won't have to bother telling you. Just go after him and watch what he does next.

LODOVICO

> I'm sorry I was so wrong about him.

*They exit.*

# ACT FOUR, Scene 2

*Enter* OTHELLO *and* EMILIA

**OTHELLO**
You have seen nothing then?

**EMILIA**
Nor ever heard, nor ever did suspect.

**OTHELLO**
Yes, you have seen Cassio and she together.

**EMILIA**
But then I saw no harm, and then I heard
5    Each syllable that breath made up between them.

**OTHELLO**
What, did they never whisper?

**EMILIA**
Never, my lord.

**OTHELLO**
Nor send you out o' th' way?

**EMILIA**
Never.

**OTHELLO**
10    To fetch her fan, her gloves, her mask, nor nothing?

**EMILIA**
Never, my lord.

**OTHELLO**
That's strange.

**EMILIA**
I durst, my lord, to wager she is honest,
Lay down my soul at stake. If you think other
15    Remove your thought, it doth abuse your bosom.
If any wretch have put this in your head
Let heaven requite it with the serpent's curse
For if she be not honest, chaste, and true
There's no man happy. The purest of their wives
20    Is foul as slander.

## ACT FOUR, Scene 2

OTHELLO *and* EMILIA *enter.*

**OTHELLO**

You haven't seen anything, then?

**EMILIA**

No, and I didn't hear anything either, or suspect anything at all.

**OTHELLO**

But you've seen her and Cassio together.

**EMILIA**

Yes, but I didn't see anything wrong, and I heard every syllable they said.

**OTHELLO**

Didn't they ever whisper?

**EMILIA**

Never, my lord.

**OTHELLO**

Or ask you to leave the room?

**EMILIA**

Never.

**OTHELLO**

Not even to get her fan, or her gloves, or her mask, or anything?

**EMILIA**

No, my lord.

**OTHELLO**

That's strange.

**EMILIA**

I'd swear to you on my soul that she's a good, honest person, sir. If you suspect otherwise, stop thinking that right now because you're wrong. If any jerk has tried to convince you she's bad, I hope God curses him. If she's not honest, faithful, and true, then there's no such thing as a faithful wife or a happy husband.

**OTHELLO**
Bid her come hither. Go.

*Exit* EMILIA

She says enough, yet she's a simple bawd
That cannot say as much. This is a subtle whore,
A closet, lock and key, of villainous secrets.
25 And yet she'll kneel and pray, I have seen her do 't.

*Enter* DESDEMONA *with* EMILIA

**DESDEMONA**
My lord, what is your will?

**OTHELLO**
Pray, chuck, come hither.

**DESDEMONA**
What is your pleasure?

**OTHELLO**
Let me see your eyes.
Look in my face.

**DESDEMONA**
What horrible fancy's this?

**OTHELLO**
30 *(to* EMILIA*)* Some of your function, mistress,
Leave procreants alone and shut the door.
Cough or cry "hem" if any body come.
Your mystery, your mystery! Nay, dispatch!

*Exit* EMILIA

**DESDEMONA**
Upon my knee, what doth your speech import?
35 I understand a fury in your words,
But not the words.

**OTHELLO**
Why, what art thou?

**OTHELLO**

Tell her to come here. Go.

EMILIA *exits.*

She says all the right things, but the dumbest brothel-keeper would tell the same story. Desdemona's a tricky whore with a closet full of awful secrets, but still she'll kneel and pray like an honest woman. I've seen her do it.

DESDEMONA *and* EMILIA *enter.*

**DESDEMONA**

My lord, what do you want?

**OTHELLO**

Please, dear, come here.

**DESDEMONA**

What can I do for you?

**OTHELLO**

Let me see your eyes. Look at my face.

**DESDEMONA**

What horrible thing are you imagining?

**OTHELLO**

*(to* EMILIA*)* Go do what you do best, madam. Leave us alone for our hanky-panky, and shut the door behind you. If somebody comes, give a shout. That's your job, your job. Go on, hurry!

EMILIA *exits.*

Othello implies that Emilia's job is to help men and women have illicit sex.

**DESDEMONA**

I'm begging you on my knees to tell me what your words mean. I can tell you're furious, but I don't understand what you're saying.

**OTHELLO**

Why? Who are you?

**DESDEMONA**
Your wife, my lord. Your true and loyal wife.

**OTHELLO**
Come, swear it, damn thyself.

Lest, being like one of heaven, the devils themselves
40 Should fear to seize thee. Therefore be double damned,
Swear thou art honest!

**DESDEMONA**
       Heaven doth truly know it.

**OTHELLO**
Heaven truly knows that thou art false as hell.

**DESDEMONA**
To whom, my lord? With whom? How am I false?

**OTHELLO**
Ah, Desdemona, away, away, away!

**DESDEMONA**
45 Alas the heavy day, why do you weep?
Am I the motive of these tears, my lord?
If haply you my father do suspect
An instrument of this your calling back,
Lay not your blame on me. If you have lost him,
50 Why, I have lost him too.

**OTHELLO**
       Had it pleased heaven
To try me with affliction, had they rained
All kinds of sores and shames on my bare head,
Steeped me in poverty to the very lips,
Given to captivity me and my utmost hopes,
55 I should have found in some place of my soul
A drop of patience. But, alas, to make me

**DESDEMONA**

I'm your wife, your true and loyal wife.

**OTHELLO**

Go ahead, swear to that, so you'll be damned to hell for lying. Otherwise the devils will mistake you for an angel and be too scared to grab you. Go ahead, make sure you damn yourself by swearing you've been faithful to me.

**DESDEMONA**

Heaven knows I am.

**OTHELLO**

Heaven knows you're as unfaithful as hell.

**DESDEMONA**

Unfaithful, my lord? With whom? How am I unfaithful?

**OTHELLO**

Leave me alone, Desdemona, go away!

**DESDEMONA**

Oh, what a horrible day! Why are you crying? Because of me? If you've been ordered back to Venice because of my father, don't blame me. You may have lost his respect, but so have I.

**OTHELLO**

If God had decided to treat me like Job, making me sick and covered with sores, reducing me to abject poverty, selling me into slavery and destroying all my hopes, I would have found some way to accept it with patience. But instead He's made me a laughingstock for everyone in our time to point at and scorn! Even that I could put up with. But instead, my wife, who's

The fixèd figure for the time of scorn
To point his slow and moving finger at!
Yet could I bear that too, well, very well.
60  But there where I have garnered up my heart,
Where either I must live or bear no life,
The fountain from the which my current runs
Or else dries up—to be discarded thence!
Or keep it as a cistern for foul toads
65  To knot and gender in! Turn thy complexion there,
Patience, thou young and rose-lipped cherubin,—
Ay, there, look grim as hell!

**DESDEMONA**
I hope my noble lord esteems me honest.

**OTHELLO**
Oh, ay, as summer flies are in the shambles,
70  That quicken even with blowing. O thou weed,
Who art so lovely fair and smell'st so sweet
That the sense aches at thee, would thou hadst ne'er been
born!

**DESDEMONA**
Alas, what ignorant sin have I committed?

**OTHELLO**
75  Was this fair paper, this most goodly book,
Made to write "whore" upon? What committed?
Committed? O thou public commoner!
I should make very forges of my cheeks
That would to cinders burn up modesty
80  Did I but speak thy deeds. What committed?
Heaven stops the nose at it and the moon winks,
The bawdy wind that kisses all it meets
Is hushed within the hollow mine of earth
And will not hear 't. What committed!
85  Impudent strumpet!

**DESDEMONA**
By heaven, you do me wrong!

supposed to be like the fountain that my children and all my descendants flow from, has rejected me! Worse than that, she's polluted herself, so that the fountain is a place where disgusting toads copulate and reproduce! Even the goddess of patience couldn't look at this and be patient—it's too horrifying!

**DESDEMONA**

I hope you think I'm faithful to you.

**OTHELLO**

As faithful as flies in rotting meat, which give birth to maggots every time the wind blows. You're like a weed pretending to be a flower, so beautiful and sweet-smelling that I ache when I look at you. Oh, I wish you'd never been born!

**DESDEMONA**

Have I done something to offend you without knowing it?

**OTHELLO**

Was someone as beautiful as you meant to be a whore? What have you done? What have you done? Oh, you streetwalker! If I said out loud what you've done, you'd burn up with shame. What have you done? Heaven has to hold its nose when it sees you! The pure moon in the sky has to shut its eyes when you go by! Even the wind that blows over everything on earth is ashamed to visit you. You brazen whore!

**DESDEMONA**

I swear to God you're accusing me wrongly!

**OTHELLO**
　　Are you not a strumpet?

**DESDEMONA**
　　No, as I am a Christian.
　　If to preserve this vessel for my lord
90　From any other foul unlawful touch
　　Be not to be a strumpet, I am none.

**OTHELLO**
　　What, not a whore?

**DESDEMONA**
　　　　　　　　　　No, as I shall be saved.

**OTHELLO**
　　Is 't possible?

**DESDEMONA**
　　Oh, heaven forgive us!

**OTHELLO**
95　I cry you mercy, then,
　　I took you for that cunning whore of Venice
　　That married with Othello.—You, mistress,
　　That have the office opposite to Saint Peter
　　And keep the gate of hell!

　　*Enter* EMILIA

　　　　　　　　　　　You, you, ay, you!
100　We have done our course. There's money for your pains.
　　I pray you, turn the key and keep our counsel.
　　　　　　　　　　　　　　　　　　　*Exit*

**EMILIA**
　　Alas, what does this gentleman conceive?
　　How do you, madam? How do you, my good lady?

**DESDEMONA**
　　Faith, half asleep.

**EMILIA**
105　Good madam, what's the matter with my lord?

**OTHELLO**

So you're saying you're not a whore?

**DESDEMONA**

No, I'm as honest as I am Christian. If only letting my husband touch my body means I'm not a whore, I'm not a whore.

**OTHELLO**

What, you're not a whore?

**DESDEMONA**

No, I swear it.

**OTHELLO**

Is that possible?

**DESDEMONA**

Oh, heaven help us!

**OTHELLO**

I beg your pardon then. I must have the wrong woman. I mistook you for that sly Venetian woman who married Othello.—You whorehouse-keeper.

*EMILIA enters.*

You're in charge of this hell! You! We've finished our business. Here's some money for you. Please lock the door and keep quiet.

*OTHELLO exits.*

**EMILIA**

What's he talking about? How are you, madam?

**DESDEMONA**

I'm stunned, to tell you the truth.

**EMILIA**

My lady, what's wrong with your husband?

**DESDEMONA**
With who?

**EMILIA**
Why, with my lord, madam.

**DESDEMONA**
Who is thy lord?

**EMILIA**
He that is yours, sweet lady.

**DESDEMONA**
I have none. Do not talk to me, Emilia.
I cannot weep, nor answers have I none,
110 But what should go by water. Prithee, tonight
Lay on my bed my wedding sheets. Remember,
And call thy husband hither.

**EMILIA**
Here's a change indeed!

*Exit*

**DESDEMONA**
'Tis meet I should be used so, very meet.
How have I been behaved that he might stick
115 The small'st opinion on my least misuse?

*Enter* EMILIA *with* IAGO

**IAGO**
What is your pleasure, madam? How is 't with you?

**DESDEMONA**
I cannot tell. Those that do teach young babes
Do it with gentle means and easy tasks.
He might have chid me so, for, in good faith,
120 I am a child to chiding.

**IAGO**
What is the matter, lady?

**DESDEMONA**

With who?

**EMILIA**

Why, with your husband, madam. My lord.

**DESDEMONA**

Who's your lord?

**EMILIA**

My lord is your lord.

**DESDEMONA**

I don't have a lord. Don't talk to me, Emilia. I can't even cry, though tears are the only answers I could give to all your questions. Tonight put my wedding sheets on my bed, and tell your husband to come to me now.

**EMILIA**

Things have certainly changed!

*EMILIA exits.*

**DESDEMONA**

It's fair for him to treat me like this, very fair. What have I ever done that he has anything to complain about?

*IAGO and EMILIA enter.*

**IAGO**

What can I do for you, madam? How are you?

**DESDEMONA**

I don't know. When grown-ups teach little children, they do it gently and easily. He might have treated me like that, because I'm as unused to abuse as a little child.

**IAGO**

What's the matter, lady?

**EMILIA**
 Alas, Iago, my lord hath so bewhored her,
 Thrown such despite and heavy terms upon her,
 That true hearts cannot bear it.

**DESDEMONA**
 Am I that name, Iago?

**IAGO**
125 What name, fair lady?

**DESDEMONA**
 Such as she says my lord did say I was.

**EMILIA**
 He called her "whore." A beggar in his drink
 Could not have laid such terms upon his callet.

**IAGO**
 Why did he so?

**DESDEMONA**
130 I do not know. I am sure I am none such.

**IAGO**
 Do not weep, do not weep. Alas the day!

**EMILIA**
 Hath she forsook so many noble matches,
 Her father and her country, and her friends,
 To be called "whore"? Would it not make one weep?

**DESDEMONA**
135 It is my wretched fortune.

**IAGO**
         Beshrew him for 't!
 How comes this trick upon him?

**DESDEMONA**
         Nay, heaven doth know.

**EMILIA**
 I will be hanged, if some eternal villain,
 Some busy and insinuating rogue,
 Some cogging, cozening slave, to get some office,
140 Have not devised this slander. I will be hanged else!

**EMILIA**

He called her a whore so many times, and heaped up so much abuse on her that good people can't stand to hear it.

**DESDEMONA**

Am I that name, Iago?

**IAGO**

What name, madam?

**DESDEMONA**

What my lord said I was.

**EMILIA**

He called her a whore. A beggar couldn't have called his slut worse names.

**IAGO**

Why did he do that?

**DESDEMONA**

I don't know. I just know I'm not one.

**IAGO**

Don't cry, don't cry. What a day this is!

**EMILIA**

Did she give up all those chances to marry noblemen, give up her father and country and friends, just to be called a whore? Doesn't that make you want to cry?

**DESDEMONA**

It's just my bad luck.

**IAGO**

Damn him! How did he get such an idea?

**DESDEMONA**

Heaven knows.

**EMILIA**

I bet my life some evil busybody, some meddling, lying jerk made up this rumor to get some position. I bet my life on it.

IAGO
    Fie, there is no such man. It is impossible.

DESDEMONA
    If any such there be, heaven pardon him!

EMILIA
    A halter pardon him and hell gnaw his bones!
    Why should he call her "whore"? Who keeps her company?
145    What place? What time? What form? What likelihood?
    The Moor's abused by some most villainous knave,
    Some base notorious knave, some scurvy fellow.
    O heavens, that such companions thou'dst unfold,
    And put in every honest hand a whip
150    To lash the rascals naked through the world
    Even from the east to th' west!

IAGO
                         Speak within door.

EMILIA
    Oh, fie upon them! Some such squire he was
    That turned your wit the seamy side without
    And made you to suspect me with the Moor.

IAGO
155    You are a fool. Go to.

DESDEMONA
                 Alas Iago,
    What shall I do to win my lord again?
    Good friend, go to him. For, by this light of heaven,
    I know not how I lost him. Here I kneel:
    If e'er my will did trespass 'gainst his love,
160    Either in discourse of thought or actual deed,
    Or that mine eyes, mine ears, or any sense,
    Delighted them, or any other form,
    Or that I do not yet, and ever did,

IAGO

Nobody's that bad. It's impossible.

DESDEMONA

If there is, then heaven help him!

EMILIA

A hangman's noose will help him! Let hell chew him
up! Why should he call her a whore? Who's been with
her? When has she had the time, the place, or the
means to sleep with anyone? How is this at all likely?
The Moor is being tricked by some crook, some terrible villain, some rotten bastard. Oh, I wish we could
unmask scoundrels like that, and give a whip to every
good man to beat them senseless with!

IAGO

Keep your voice down.

EMILIA

Oh, to hell with those people! It's the same kind of guy
who got you upset and made you suspect I'd cheated
on you with the Moor.

IAGO

You're a fool. Shut up.

DESDEMONA

Oh God, Iago, what can I do to win my husband back
again? Please go to him, my friend. I swear I have no
idea why he stopped loving me. Here I'm kneeling to
swear that if I ever did anything to destroy his love for
me, either by thoughts or actions, or if I ever took
pleasure in anyone else, or if I never did love him, or
don't love him now—even though he tries to shake me

And ever will—though he do shake me off
165   To beggarly divorcement—love him dearly,
Comfort forswear me! Unkindness may do much,
And his unkindness may defeat my life,
But never taint my love. I cannot say "whore,"
It does abhor me now I speak the word.
170   To do the act that might the addition earn
Not the world's mass of vanity could make me.

**IAGO**

I pray you, be content, 'tis but his humor.
The business of the state does him offence,
And he does chide with you.

**DESDEMONA**

175   If 'twere no other—

**IAGO**

'Tis but so, I warrant.

*Trumpets sound*

Hark, how these instruments summon to supper.
The messengers of Venice stay the meat.
Go in, and weep not. All things shall be well.

*Exeunt* DESDEMONA *and* EMILIA

*Enter* RODERIGO

180   How now, Roderigo!

**RODERIGO**

I do not find that thou deal'st justly with me.

**IAGO**

What in the contrary?

**RODERIGO**

Every day thou daff'st me with some device, Iago, and
rather, as it seems to me now, keep'st from me all
185.   conveniency than suppliest me with the least advantage of

off—then I hope I have a life of misery! Unkindness is powerful, and his unkindness may kill me, but it'll never destroy my love. I can't say "whore." It makes me sick to say the word even now. I wouldn't do the thing that would make me a whore for all the money in the world.

IAGO

Please calm down. He's just in a bad mood. Political business is bothering him, and he's just taking it out on you.

DESDEMONA

If only that were all it is—

IAGO

It is, I promise.

*Trumpets sound.*

Those trumpets are calling us in to dinner. The Venetians are waiting for their food. Go in, and don't cry. Everything will be all right.

DESDEMONA *and* EMILIA *exit.*
RODERIGO *enters.*

How are you, Roderigo?

RODERIGO

I don't think you're treating me fairly.

IAGO

What makes you say that?

RODERIGO

Every day you put me off with some trick. Instead of finding opportunities for me, you seem to be preventing me from making any progress. Well, I won't take

hope. I will indeed no longer endure it, nor am I yet
persuaded to put up in peace what already I have foolishly
suffered.

IAGO

Will you hear me, Roderigo?

RODERIGO

190     I have heard too much, and your words and performances
are no kin together.

IAGO

You charge me most unjustly.

RODERIGO

With naught but truth. I have wasted myself out of my
means. The jewels you have had from me to deliver
195     Desdemona would half have corrupted a votaress. You
have told me she hath received them and returned me
expectations and comforts of sudden respect and
acquaintance, but I find none.

IAGO

Well, go to. Very well.

RODERIGO

200     "Very well," "go to"! I cannot go to, man, nor 'tis not very
well. Nay, I think it is scurvy, and begin to find myself
fopped in it.

IAGO

Very well.

RODERIGO

I tell you 'tis not very well. I will make myself known to
205     Desdemona. If she will return me my jewels I will give
over my suit and repent my unlawful solicitation. If not,
assure yourself I will seek satisfaction of you.

IAGO

You have said now.

RODERIGO

Ay, and said nothing but what I protest intendment of
210     doing.

it any longer. And I'm not going to sit back and accept what you've done.

IAGO

Will you listen to me, Roderigo?

RODERIGO

I've listened to you too much already. Your words and actions don't match up.

IAGO

That's not fair.

RODERIGO

It's the truth. I've got no money left. The jewels you took from me to deliver to Desdemona would've made even a nun want to sleep with me. You told me she got them, and that she promised to give me a little something in return soon, but nothing like that ever happens.

IAGO

Well, all right then. Fine.

RODERIGO

"Fine!" he says. "All right!" It's not fine, and I'm not all right! It's wrong, and I'm starting to realize I'm being cheated!

IAGO

Okay.

RODERIGO

It's not okay! I'm going to tell Desdemona my feelings. If she returns my jewels, I'll stop pursuing her and apologize to her. If not, I'll challenge you to a duel.

IAGO

You've said what you have to say now.

RODERIGO

Yes, and I'll do everything I just said.

**IAGO**

Why, now I see there's mettle in thee, and even from this
instant to build on thee a better opinion than ever before.
Give me thy hand, Roderigo. Thou hast taken against me
a most just exception, but yet I protest I have dealt most
215   directly in thy affair.

**RODERIGO**

It hath not appeared.

**IAGO**

I grant indeed it hath not appeared, and your suspicion is
not without wit and judgment. But, Roderigo, if thou hast
that in thee indeed, which I have greater reason to believe
220   now than ever—I mean purpose, courage and valor—this
night show it. If thou the next night following enjoy not
Desdemona, take me from this world with treachery and
devise engines for my life.

**RODERIGO**

Well, what is it? Is it within reason and compass?

**IAGO**

225   Sir, there is especial commission come from Venice to
depute Cassio in Othello's place.

**RODERIGO**

Is that true? Why, then Othello and Desdemona return
again to Venice.

**IAGO**

Oh, no, he goes into Mauritania and taketh away with him
230   the fair Desdemona, unless his abode be lingered here by
some accident—wherein none can be so determinate as
the removing of Cassio.

**RODERIGO**

How do you mean, removing of him?

**IAGO**

Why, by making him uncapable of Othello's place:
235   knocking out his brains.

**RODERIGO**

And that you would have me to do!

**IAGO**

Well, all right then. Now I see that you have some guts. From this moment on I have a higher opinion of you than before. Give me your hand, Roderigo. Your complaint against me is perfectly understandable, but I still insist I've done everything I could to help you.

**RODERIGO**

It doesn't look that way to me.

**IAGO**

I admit it doesn't look that way to me, and the fact that you suspect me shows that you're smart. But Roderigo, if you're as courageous and determined as I think you are, then wait just a bit longer. If you're not having sex with Desdemona tomorrow night, then I suggest you find some way to stab me in the back and kill me.

**RODERIGO**

Well, what's your plan? Is it feasible?

**IAGO**

Venice has made Cassio governor here on Cyprus.

**RODERIGO**

Is that true? Then Desdemona and Othello will go back to Venice.

**IAGO**

Oh, no. He'll go to Mauritania and take the beautiful Desdemona with him, unless he gets stuck here for some reason. The best way to extend his stay here is to get rid of Cassio.

**RODERIGO**

What do you mean, get rid of him?

**IAGO**

I mean knock his brains out, so he can't take Othello's place.

**RODERIGO**

And that's what you want me to do!

ACT FOUR

**IAGO**

Ay, if you dare do yourself a profit and a right. He sups
tonight with a harlotry, and thither will I go to him. He
knows not yet of his honorable fortune. If you will watch
240    his going thence (which I will fashion to fall out between
twelve and one) you may take him at your pleasure. I will
be near to second your attempt, and he shall fall between
us. Come, stand not amazed at it, but go along with me. I
will show you such a necessity in his death that you shall
245    think yourself bound to put it on him. It is now high
suppertime, and the night grows to waste. About it!

**RODERIGO**

I will hear further reason for this.

**IAGO**

And you shall be satisfied.

*Exeunt*

**IAGO**

Yes, if you want to help yourself. He's having dinner tonight with a prostitute, and I'll go visit him. He doesn't know he's been appointed governor yet. When you see him walking by here (as I'll make sure he does between twelve and one) you can nab him. I'll be nearby to help you, and between the two of us we can handle him. Come on, don't stand there in a daze. Come along with me. I'll give you such reasons for killing him that you'll feel obliged to snuff him out. It's nearly dinner time, and the night's going to be wasted. Let's go!

**RODERIGO**

I want to hear more about this.

**IAGO**

You will. You'll hear all you want to hear.

*They exit.*

## ACT FOUR, Scene 3

*Enter* OTHELLO, LODOVICO, DESDEMONA, EMILIA *and attendants*

**LODOVICO**
    I do beseech you, sir, trouble yourself no further.

**OTHELLO**
    Oh, pardon me, 'twill do me good to walk.

**LODOVICO**
    Madam, good night. I humbly thank your ladyship.

**DESDEMONA**
    Your honor is most welcome.

**OTHELLO**
5    Will you walk, sir?—O Desdemona—

**DESDEMONA**
    My lord?

**OTHELLO**
    Get you to bed on th' instant, I will be returned
    Forthwith. Dismiss your attendant there, look 't be done.

**DESDEMONA**
    I will, my lord.

*Exeunt* OTHELLO, LODOVICO, *and attendants*

**EMILIA**
10    How goes it now? He looks gentler than he did.

**DESDEMONA**
    He says he will return incontinent,
    And hath commanded me to go to bed
    And bid me to dismiss you.

**EMILIA**
                      Dismiss me?

**DESDEMONA**
    It was his bidding. Therefore, good Emilia,
15    Give me my nightly wearing, and adieu.
    We must not now displease him.

# ACT FOUR, Scene 3

OTHELLO, LODOVICO, DESDEMONA *and* EMILIA *enter, with attendants.*

**LODOVICO**

Please, sir, don't trouble yourself.

**OTHELLO**

I beg your pardon; walking will make me feel better.

**LODOVICO**

Good night, madam. Thank you.

**DESDEMONA**

You're most welcome.

**OTHELLO**

Would you walk out with me, sir?—Oh, Desdemona—

**DESDEMONA**

Yes, my lord?

**OTHELLO**

Go to bed right this minute. I'll be there shortly. Send your maid Emilia away. Make sure you do what I say.

**DESDEMONA**

I will, my lord.

> OTHELLO, LODOVICO, *and attendants exit.*

How are things now? He looks calmer than he did before.

**DESDEMONA**

He says he'll come back right away. He asked me to go to bed and to send you away.

**EMILIA**

Send me away?

**DESDEMONA**

That's what he said. So give me my nightgown, Emilia, and I'll say goodnight. We shouldn't displease him.

**EMILIA**
Ay. Would you had never seen him!

**DESDEMONA**
So would not I. My love doth so approve him
That even his stubbornness, his checks, his frowns—
20      Prithee, unpin me—have grace and favor.

**EMILIA**
I have laid those sheets you bade me on the bed.

**DESDEMONA**
All's one. Good Father, how foolish are our minds!
If I do die before thee, prithee, shroud me
In one of these same sheets.

**EMILIA**
Come, come! You talk!

**DESDEMONA**
25      My mother had a maid called Barbary,
She was in love, and he she loved proved mad
And did forsake her. She had a song of "Willow,"
An old thing 'twas, but it expressed her fortune
And she died singing it. That song tonight
30      Will not go from my mind. I have much to do
But to go hang my head all at one side
And sing it like poor Barbary. Prithee, dispatch.

**EMILIA**
Shall I go fetch your nightgown?

**DESDEMONA**
No, unpin me here.
This Lodovico is a proper man.

**EMILIA**
35      A very handsome man.

**DESDEMONA**
He speaks well.

**EMILIA**
I know a lady in Venice would have walked barefoot
to Palestine for a touch of his nether lip.

**EMILIA**

Yes. I wish you'd never met him.

**DESDEMONA**

That's not what I wish. I love him even when he's harsh and mean—Help me unpin this, would you?—I love even his stubbornness, his frowns, his bad moods.

**EMILIA**

I put those wedding sheets on your bed, as you asked.

**DESDEMONA**

It doesn't matter. Oh, how silly we are! If I die before you do make sure I'm wrapped in those sheets in my coffin.

**EMILIA**

Listen to you! Don't be silly!

**DESDEMONA**

My mother had a maid named Barbary. She was in love, and her lover turned out to be wild and left her. She knew an old song called "Willow" that reminded her of her own story, and she died singing it. I can't get that song out of my head tonight. It's all I can do to keep myself from hanging my head down in despair and singing it like poor Barbary. Please, hurry up.

**EMILIA**

Should I get your nightgown?

**DESDEMONA**

No, just help me unpin this. That Lodovico is a good-looking man.

**EMILIA**

He's very handsome.

**DESDEMONA**

He speaks well.

**EMILIA**

I know a lady in Venice who'd walk all the way to Palestine for a kiss from him.

**DESDEMONA**
*(singing)*
> *The poor soul sat sighing by a sycamore tree,*
> *Sing all a green willow.*
40 > *Her hand on her bosom, her head on her knee,*
> *Sing willow, willow, willow.*
> *The fresh streams ran by her, and murmured her moans,*
> *Sing willow, willow, willow.*
> *Her salt tears fell from her, and softened the stones*
45 > *Sing willow, willow, willow—*
> *Lay by these—*
> > *Willow, willow—*
> *Prithee, hie thee, he'll come anon—*
> *Sing all a green willow must be my garland.*
> *Let nobody blame him, his scorn I approve—*
50 Nay, that's not next—Hark! Who is 't that knocks?

**EMILIA**
It's the wind.

**DESDEMONA**
*(sings)*
> *I called my love false love but what said he then?*
> > *Sing willow, willow, willow.*
> *If I court more women you'll couch with more men—*
So, get thee gone, good night. Mine eyes do itch,
55 Doth that bode weeping?

**EMILIA**
'Tis neither here nor there.

**DESDEMONA**
I have heard it said so. Oh, these men, these men!
Dost thou in conscience think—tell me, Emilia—
That there be women do abuse their husbands
In such gross kind?

**EMILIA**
There be some such, no question.

**DESDEMONA**
60 Wouldst thou do such a deed for all the world?

**DESDEMONA**

*(singing)*
*The poor soul sat singing by the sycamore tree,*
*Everyone sing the green willow,*
*She had her hand on her breast and her head on her knee,*
*Sing willow, willow, willow.*
*The fresh streams ran by her and murmured her moans,*
*Sing willow, willow, willow.*
*Her salt tears fell from her and softened the stones,*
*Sing willow, willow, willow.—*
*Put these things over there.—*
*Please, hurry, he'll come right away.—*
*Everyone sing, a green willow must be my garland.*
*Nobody blame him, he's right to hate me—*
No, that's not how it goes.—Who's knocking?

**EMILIA**

It's the wind.

**DESDEMONA**

*(singing) I told my lover he didn't love me, but what did*
*he say? Sing willow, willow, willow.*
If I chase more women, you'll sleep with more men—
Okay, go away now. Good night. My eyes itch—is
that an omen I'll be crying soon?

**EMILIA**

No, it doesn't mean anything.

**DESDEMONA**

I heard someone say that's what it means. Oh, these
men, these men! Do you honestly think—tell me,
Emilia—there are women who'd cheat on their husbands in such a disgusting manner?

**EMILIA**

There are women like that out there, no question.

**DESDEMONA**

Would you ever do such a thing for all the world?

EMILIA
Why, would not you?

DESDEMONA
                                        No, by this heavenly light!

EMILIA
Nor I neither, by this heavenly light.
I might do 't as well i' th' dark.

DESDEMONA
Wouldst thou do such a deed for all the world?

EMILIA
65    The world's a huge thing. It is a great price for a small vice.

DESDEMONA
In troth, I think thou wouldst not.

EMILIA
In troth, I think I should, and undo 't when I had done.
Marry, I would not do such a thing for a joint-ring, nor for
measures of lawn, nor for gowns, petticoats, nor caps, nor
70    any petty exhibition. But for the whole world? Why, who
would not make her husband a cuckold to make him a
monarch? I should venture purgatory for 't.

DESDEMONA
Beshrew me, if I would do such a wrong
For the whole world.

EMILIA
75    Why the wrong is but a wrong i' th' world, and having the
world for your labor, 'tis a wrong in your own world, and
you might quickly make it right.

DESDEMONA
I do not think there is any such woman.

EMILIA
Yes, a dozen, and as many to th' vantage as would store the
80    world they played for.
But I do think it is their husbands' faults
If wives do fall. Say that they slack their duties
And pour our treasures into foreign laps,
Or else break out in peevish jealousies,

**EMILIA**

Why, wouldn't you?

**DESDEMONA**

By the light of heaven, no, I would not!

**EMILIA**

I wouldn't either, by daylight. It would be easier to do it in the dark.

**DESDEMONA**

Could you really do such a thing, for all the world?

**EMILIA**

The world's huge. It's a big prize for such a small sin.

**DESDEMONA**

I don't think you would.

**EMILIA**

Actually I think I would, and then I'd undo it after I did it. I wouldn't do it for a nice ring, or fine linen, or pretty gowns or petticoats or hats. But for the whole world? Who wouldn't cheat on her husband to make him king? I'd risk my soul for that.

**DESDEMONA**

I'd never do such a bad thing, not for the whole world!

**EMILIA**

Why, a bad action is just a wrong in this world, but when you've won the whole world, it's a wrong in your own world, so you can make it right then.

**DESDEMONA**

I don't think any woman like that exists.

**EMILIA**

Yes, a dozen of them—as many as there are women in the world, in fact. But I do think it's the husband's fault if we wives cheat on them. For instance, our husbands may stop sleeping with us, and give it out to other women instead. Or they may get insanely jeal-

85    Throwing restraint upon us. Or say they strike us,
      Or scant our former having in despite.
      Why, we have galls, and though we have some grace,
      Yet have we some revenge. Let husbands know
      Their wives have sense like them. They see and smell
90    And have their palates both for sweet and sour,
      As husbands have. What is it that they do
      When they change us for others? Is it sport?
      I think it is. And doth affection breed it?
      I think it doth. Is 't frailty that thus errs?
95    It is so too. And have not we affections,
      Desires for sport, and frailty, as men have?
      Then let them use us well, else let them know,
      The ills we do, their ills instruct us so.

**DESDEMONA**
      Good night, good night. Heaven me such uses send,
100   Not to pick bad from bad, but by bad mend!

                                          *Exeunt*

ous, and keep us from going anywhere. Or let's say they hit us, or cut back on the money they give us out of spite. We have feelings. We may be able to forgive them, but we want to get back at them too. Husbands need to know that their wives are human beings too. They see, smell, and taste sweet and sour just like their husbands. Why do they replace us with other women? Do they do it for fun? I think they do. Is it out of lust? I think so. Is it a weakness? It is. And don't we have passions, and a taste for fun, and weaknesses, just like men? Then tell them to treat us well. Or let them figure out that the bad things we do are just what we learned from them.

**DESDEMONA**

Good night, good night. I pray that God will let me learn from women like that—not to follow their bad example, but to avoid it!

*They exit.*

# ACT FIVE

## Scene 1

*Enter* IAGO *and* RODERIGO

IAGO

Here, stand behind this bulk, straight will he come.
Wear thy good rapier bare, and put it home.
Quick, quick! Fear nothing. I'll be at thy elbow.
It makes us, or it mars us. Think on that,
5 And fix most firm thy resolution.

RODERIGO

Be near at hand, I may miscarry in 't.

IAGO

Here, at thy hand. Be bold, and take thy stand.

*Withdraws*

RODERIGO

I have no great devotion to the deed
And yet he hath given me satisfying reasons.
10 'Tis but a man gone. Forth, my sword: he dies.

IAGO

*(aside)* I have rubbed this young quat almost to the sense,
And he grows angry. Now, whether he kill Cassio
Or Cassio him, or each do kill the other,
Every way makes my gain. Live Roderigo,
15 He calls me to a restitution large
Of gold and jewels that I bobbed from him
As gifts to Desdemona.
It must not be. If Cassio do remain
He hath a daily beauty in his life
20 That makes me ugly. And besides, the Moor
May unfold me to him—there stand I in much peril.
No, he must die. But so, I hear him coming.

# ACT FIVE

## Scene 1

IAGO *and* RODERIGO *enter.*

**IAGO**

Here, stand behind this wall; he'll come right away. Keep your sword out, and then stick it in as far as it'll go. Quick, quick. Don't be afraid. I'll be right next to you. This will either make us or break us. Keep that in mind, and be steady.

**RODERIGO**

Stay right near me. I may mess it up.

**IAGO**

I'm right behind you. Be bold, and get ready.

IAGO *moves aside.*

**RODERIGO**

I don't really want to do this, but he's given me good reasons. I guess it's only one man—no big deal. My sword comes out, and he dies.

**IAGO**

*(to himself)* I've rubbed this young pimple until he's ready to pop, and now he's angry. Whether he kills Cassio, or Cassio kills him, or they kill each other, it all works in my favor. If Roderigo survives, though, he'll ask me for all the gold and jewelry that I stole from him and said I gave to Desdemona. I can't let that happen. If Cassio survives, he's so handsome and well-spoken that he makes me look ugly. And besides, the Moor might tell him about my lies about him.—That would be very dangerous for me. No, he's got to die. Let it be so. I hear him coming.

*Enter* CASSIO

RODERIGO
I know his gait, 'tis he.—Villain, thou diest!

*Thrusts at* CASSIO

CASSIO
That thrust had been mine enemy indeed
But that my coat is better than thou know'st
I will make proof of thine.

*Draws, and wounds* RODERIGO

RODERIGO
                                        Oh, I am slain!

                    IAGO *from behind wounds* CASSIO *in the
                                                legs, exits*

CASSIO
I am maimed for ever. Help, ho! Murder! Murder!

*Enter* OTHELLO

OTHELLO
The voice of Cassio. Iago keeps his word.

RODERIGO
Oh, villain that I am!

OTHELLO
It is even so.

CASSIO
Oh, help, ho! Light! A surgeon!

OTHELLO
'Tis he. Oh, brave Iago, honest and just,
That hast such noble sense of thy friend's wrong!

CASSIO *enters.*

**RODERIGO**

I know the sound of his walk.—Die, villain!

**RODERIGO** *thrusts his sword at* CASSIO.

**CASSIO**

That thrust might really have hurt me if I didn't have this armor on under my cloak. Now let's see what you've got on.

CASSIO *draws his sword and stabs* RODERIGO.

**RODERIGO**

Oh, I'm dead!

> *From behind,* IAGO *stabs* CASSIO *in the leg and then exits.*

**CASSIO**

I'll be crippled forever! Help! Murder! murder!

OTHELLO *enters.*

**OTHELLO**

That's Cassio's voice. Iago has kept his word.

**RODERIGO**

Oh, what a villain I am!

**OTHELLO**

That's the truth.

**CASSIO**

Help me! Get some light! Get me a surgeon!

**OTHELLO**

It's him! Brave Iago, how honest and trustworthy you are! You even went as far as murder to help your friend in his misfortune. You teach me how I should act.

Thou teachest me. Minion, your dear lies dead,
35   And your unblest fate hies. Strumpet, I come.
For, of my heart, those charms, thine eyes, are blotted.
Thy bed, lust-stained, shall with lust's blood be spotted.

*Exit*

*Enter* LODOVICO *and* GRATIANO

CASSIO
What, ho! No watch? No passage? Murder! Murder!

GRATIANO
40   'Tis some mischance, the cry is very direful.

CASSIO
Oh, help!

LODOVICO
Hark!

RODERIGO
Oh, wretched villain!

LODOVICO
Two or three groan. 'Tis heavy night,
45   These may be counterfeits. Let's think 't unsafe
To come in to the cry without more help.

RODERIGO
Nobody come? Then shall I bleed to death.

LODOVICO
Hark!

*Enter* IAGO

GRATIANO
Here's one comes in his shirt, with light and weapons.

IAGO
50   Who's there? Whose noise is this that cries on murder?

Whore, your lover's dead now, and you'll be going to hell soon. I'm coming, slut! I've shut the memory of your beautiful eyes out of my heart. You've already stained our sheets with your lust; now I'll stain them with your whore's blood.

OTHELLO *exits.*

LODOVICO *and* GRATIANO *enter.*

CASSIO

Help! Isn't there a guard around? No one passing by? Murder! Murder!

GRATIANO

Something's wrong, the man sounds panicked.

CASSIO

Oh, help!

LODOVICO

Listen!

RODERIGO

I've acted like such a villain!

LODOVICO

Two or three men are groaning. But it's dark out, and it could be a trap. It's not safe to go near them till we get more help.

RODERIGO

Nobody's coming? I'll bleed to death.

LODOVICO

Look!

IAGO *enters.*

GRATIANO

Here's someone coming in his pajamas, with a candle and weapons.

IAGO

Who's there? Who's shouting "murder"?

**LODOVICO**
We do not know.

**IAGO**
                                        Do not you hear a cry?

**CASSIO**
Here, here! For heaven's sake, help me!

**IAGO**
                                            What's the matter?

**GRATIANO**
*(to* LODOVICO*)* This is Othello's ancient, as I take it.

**LODOVICO**
The same indeed, a very valiant fellow.

**IAGO**
55      *(to* CASSIO*)* What are you here that cry so grievously?

**CASSIO**
Iago? Oh, I am spoiled, undone by villains!
Give me some help.

**IAGO**
Oh, me, lieutenant! What villains have done this?

**CASSIO**
I think that one of them is hereabout,
60      And cannot make away.

**IAGO**
                                    Oh, treacherous villains!—
*(to* LODOVICO *and* GRATIANO*)*
What are you there? Come in, and give some help.

**RODERIGO**
Oh, help me there!

**CASSIO**
That's one of them.

**IAGO**
                            O murd'rous slave! O villain!

*Stabs* RODERIGO

**LODOVICO**

We don't know.

**IAGO**

Didn't you hear someone shouting?

**CASSIO**

I'm here, here! For heaven's sake, help me!

**IAGO**

What's the matter?

**GRATIANO**

*(to* LODOVICO*)* That's Othello's ensign, I think.

**LODOVICO**

It is. He's a good man.

**IAGO**

*(to* CASSIO*)* Who's shouting so loudly?

**CASSIO**

Is that you, Iago? I'm here, I've been destroyed by villains! Help me.

**IAGO**

Oh, lieutenant! What villains did this to you?

**CASSIO**

I think one of them is nearby and can't get away.

**IAGO**

The treacherous criminals!—*(to* LODOVICO *and* GRATIANO*)* Who's there? Come here and help!

**RODERIGO**

Somebody help me over here!

**CASSIO**

That's one of them.

**IAGO**

*(to* RODERIGO*)* Murderer! Villain!

IAGO *stabs* RODERIGO.

ACT FIVE

**RODERIGO**
O damned Iago! O inhuman dog!

**IAGO**
65      Kill men i' th' dark! Where be these bloody thieves?
How silent is this town!—Ho! murder! murder!—
What may you be? Are you of good or evil?

**LODOVICO**
As you shall prove us, praise us.

**IAGO**
Signior Lodovico?

**LODOVICO**
70      He, sir.

**IAGO**
I cry you mercy. Here's Cassio hurt by villains.

**GRATIANO**
Cassio!

**IAGO**
How is 't, brother!

**CASSIO**
My leg is cut in two.

**IAGO**
75      Marry, heaven forbid!
Light, gentlemen, I'll bind it with my shirt.

*Enter* BIANCA

**BIANCA**
What is the matter, ho? Who is 't that cried?

**IAGO**
Who is 't that cried?

**BIANCA**
                   Oh, my dear Cassio!
My sweet Cassio! O Cassio, Cassio, Cassio!

**IAGO**
80      O notable strumpet! Cassio, may you suspect
Who they should be that have thus mangled you?

**RODERIGO**

Damned Iago! You inhuman dog!

**IAGO**

Killing men in the dark? Where are these murderers? This is such a quiet, sleepy town!—Murder, murder!—Who's that coming? Are you good or evil?

**LODOVICO**

Judge for yourself.

**IAGO**

Signor Lodovico?

**LODOVICO**

That's me.

**IAGO**

I beg your pardon. Cassio's been wounded.

**GRATIANO**

Cassio!

**IAGO**

How are you doing, brother?

**CASSIO**

My leg's been cut in two.

**IAGO**

God forbid! Bring me some light, gentlemen, I'll bind the wound with my shirt.

**BIANCA** *enters.*

**BIANCA**

What's the matter? Who's shouting?

**IAGO**

Who's shouting?

**BIANCA**

Oh, my dear Cassio! My sweet Cassio! Oh, Cassio, Cassio, Cassio!

**IAGO**

You notorious whore! Cassio, do you know who might have stabbed you like this?

**CASSIO**
    No.

**GRATIANO**
    I am sorry to find you thus. I have been to seek you.

**IAGO**
    Lend me a garter. So.—Oh, for a chair,
85    To bear him easily hence!

**BIANCA**
    Alas, he faints! O Cassio, Cassio, Cassio!

**IAGO**
    Gentlemen all, I do suspect this trash
    To be a party in this injury.—
    Patience awhile, good Cassio.—Come, come,
90    Lend me a light. Know we this face or no?
    Alas, my friend and my dear countryman
    Roderigo! No—yes, sure! Yes, 'tis Roderigo.

**GRATIANO**
    What, of Venice?

**IAGO**
    Even he, sir. Did you know him?

**GRATIANO**
95    Know him? Ay.

**IAGO**
    Signior Gratiano? I cry you gentle pardon,
    These bloody accidents must excuse my manners
    That so neglected you.

**GRATIANO**
                            I am glad to see you.

**IAGO**
    How do you, Cassio?—Oh, a chair, a chair!

**GRATIANO**
100    Roderigo!

**IAGO**
    He, he, 'tis he.

    *A chair is brought in*

CASSIO

No.

GRATIANO

I'm sorry to find you like this. I've been looking all over for you.

IAGO

Lend me your sash—Oh, if we only had a stretcher to carry him out of here!

BIANCA

He's fainted! Oh Cassio, Cassio, Cassio!

IAGO

Sir, I believe this piece of trash, Bianca, has something to do with all this trouble.—Hang in there, Cassio.— Come here, bring the light. Do you recognize this face? Oh, no, it's my friend and countryman, Roderigo.—Yes, it's Roderigo!

GRATIANO

What, Roderigo from Venice?

IAGO

That's the one, sir. Do you know him?

GRATIANO

Know him? Yes.

IAGO

Signor Gratiano, I beg your pardon. I didn't mean to ignore you—it's just because of this bloody uproar.

GRATIANO

I'm glad to see you.

IAGO

How are you doing, Cassio?—Someone bring me a stretcher!

GRATIANO

Roderigo!

IAGO

It's him, it's him.

*A stretcher is brought in.*

Oh, that's well said—the chair!
Some good man bear him carefully from hence.
I'll fetch the general's surgeon.—*(to* BIANCA*)* For you,
    mistress,
Save you your labor.—He that lies slain here, Cassio,
Was my dear friend. What malice was between you?

CASSIO

None in the world, nor do I know the man.

IAGO

*(to* BIANCA*)*
What, look you pale?—Oh, bear him out o' the air.—

CASSIO *and* RODERIGO *are borne off*

Do you perceive the gastness of her eye?—Stay you, good
gentlemen.—Look you pale, mistress?—
Nay, if you stare, we shall hear more anon.—
Behold her well. I pray you, look upon her.
Do you see, gentlemen? Nay, guiltiness
Will speak, though tongues were out of use.

*Enter* EMILIA

EMILIA

Alas, what is the matter? What is the matter, husband?

IAGO

Cassio hath here been set on in the dark
By Roderigo and fellows that are 'scaped.
He's almost slain, and Roderigo dead.

EMILIA

Alas, good gentleman! Alas, good Cassio!

IAGO

This is the fruits of whoring. Prithee, Emilia,
Go know of Cassio where he supped tonight.—
*(to* BIANCA*)* What, do you shake at that?

Good—here's the stretcher. Get somebody strong to carry him out of here. I'll get the general's surgeon. *(to* BIANCA*)* As for you, ma'am, don't bother. The man lying here was my dear friend, Roderigo. —What was the problem between you?

CASSIO

There wasn't any problem. I don't even know him.

IAGO

*(to* BIANCA*)* You're pale?—Get Cassio out of here.— You look awfully pale, Bianca.

CASSIO *and* RODERIGO *are carried away.*

Do you see how afraid she is? Watch her, we'll get the whole story. Keep an eye on her. Do you see? The guilty speak volumes even when they're silent.

EMILIA *enters.*

EMILIA

What's the matter? What's the matter, husband?

IAGO

Cassio was attacked here in the dark by Roderigo and men who escaped. He's near death, and Roderigo's dead already.

EMILIA

Oh, no, good gentleman! Oh no, good Cassio!

IAGO

This is what happens when you visit whores. Please, Emilia, ask Cassio where he was at dinner tonight.— *(to* BIANCA*)* What, does that make you nervous?

**BIANCA**
He supped at my house, but I therefore shake not.

**IAGO**
Oh, did he so? I charge you, go with me.

**EMILIA**
Oh, fie upon thee, strumpet!

**BIANCA**
125    I am no strumpet, but of life as honest
As you that thus abuse me.

**EMILIA**
                  As I! Fie upon thee!

**IAGO**
Kind gentlemen, let's go see poor Cassio dressed.—
Come, mistress, you must tell 's another tale.
Emilia, run you to the citadel
130    And tell my lord and lady what hath happed.—
Will you go on afore?
*(aside)*
                This is the night
That either makes me or fordoes me quite.

*Exeunt*

**BIANCA**

He ate at my house, but that doesn't make me nervous.

**IAGO**

Oh, did he? I order you to come with me.

**EMILIA**

Go to hell, you whore!

**BIANCA**

I'm no whore. I'm as moral as you are.

**EMILIA**

As moral as me! Damn you!

**IAGO**

Gentlemen, let's go make sure Cassio's wounds are properly dressed.—Come on, ma'am, you can tell us another story. Emilia, go to the castle and tell Othello and Desdemona what happened.—Will you please go now? *(to himself)* This is the night that'll either make me or break me.

*They all exit.*

ACT FIVE

## ACT FIVE, Scene 2

DESDEMONA *asleep in bed*
*Enter* OTHELLO *with a light*

OTHELLO
It is the cause, it is the cause, my soul.
Let me not name it to you, you chaste stars,
It is the cause. Yet I'll not shed her blood,
Nor scar that whiter skin of hers than snow
5   And smooth as monumental alabaster.
Yet she must die, else she'll betray more men.
Put out the light, and then put out the light.
If I quench thee, thou flaming minister,
I can again thy former light restore
10   Should I repent me. But once put out thy light,
Thou cunning'st pattern of excelling nature,
I know not where is that Promethean heat
That can thy light relume. When I have plucked thy rose
I cannot give it vital growth again,
15   It must needs wither. I'll smell thee on the tree.
Oh, balmy breath, that dost almost persuade
Justice to break her sword! One more, one more.
Be thus when thou art dead and I will kill thee
And love thee after. *(kissing her)* One more, and that's
the last.
20   So sweet was ne'er so fatal. I must weep,
But they are cruel tears. This sorrow's heavenly,
It strikes where it doth love. She wakes.

DESDEMONA
Who's there? Othello?

OTHELLO
Ay, Desdemona.

# ACT FIVE, Scene 2

DESDEMONA *is asleep in bed.* OTHELLO *enters with a candle.*

OTHELLO

I have to do it, I have to do it. I have to keep my reason in mind. I won't say out loud what my reason is, but I have to do it. But I won't shed any of her blood or scar that beautiful skin, whiter than snow and smooth as the finest marble. But she's got to die, or she'll cheat on other men. Put out the light of the candle, and then put out the light of her heart. If I extinguish the candle, I can light it again if I regret it. But once I kill you, you beautiful, fake woman, I do not know the magic that could bring you back. When I've plucked this rose, I can't make it grow again; it will have no choice but to wither and die. Let me smell you while you're still on the tree. *(he kisses her)* Oh, that sweet breath almost convinces me not to kill you and carry out justice. One more, one more kiss. If you're this beautiful when you're dead, I'll kill you and then love you afterward. *(kissing her)* One more, and this is the last. Such a sweet kiss was never so deadly. I have to cry, but I have to be cruel too. I'm acting like God in the Old Testament—I have to punish the one I love. She's waking up.

DESDEMONA

Who's there? Othello?

OTHELLO

Yes, Desdemona.

**DESDEMONA**
25      Will you come to bed, my lord?

**OTHELLO**
Have you prayed tonight, Desdemon?

**DESDEMONA**
Ay, my lord.

**OTHELLO**
If you bethink yourself of any crime
Unreconciled as yet to heaven and grace,
30      Solicit for it straight.

**DESDEMONA**
Alack, my lord, what do you mean by that?

**OTHELLO**
Well, do it, and be brief. I will walk by.
I would not kill thy unpreparèd spirit.
No, heavens forfend, I would not kill thy soul!

**DESDEMONA**
35      Talk you of killing?

**OTHELLO**
                    Ay, I do.

**DESDEMONA**
                            Then heaven
Have mercy on me!

**OTHELLO**
Amen, with all my heart.

**DESDEMONA**
If you say, I hope you will not kill me.

**OTHELLO**
Humh!

**DESDEMONA**
40      And yet I fear you, for you're fatal then
When your eyes roll so. Why I should fear I know not,
Since guiltiness I know not. But yet I feel I fear.

**OTHELLO**
Think on thy sins.

**DESDEMONA**

Will you come to bed, my lord?

**OTHELLO**

Have you said your prayers tonight, Desdemona?

**DESDEMONA**

Yes, my lord.

**OTHELLO**

If you can think of any crime you haven't confessed, then pray for forgiveness right away.

**DESDEMONA**

Oh, my lord, what do you mean by that?

**OTHELLO**

Well, hurry up and confess. Be quick about it. I'll wait over here. I don't want to kill you before you've readied your soul. No, I don't want to send your soul to hell when I kill you.

**DESDEMONA**

You're talking about killing?

**OTHELLO**

Yes, I am.

**DESDEMONA**

Then heaven have mercy on me.

**OTHELLO**

Amen to that, from the bottom of my heart.

**DESDEMONA**

If you really feel that way, then I hope you won't kill me.

**OTHELLO**

Hmmph!

**DESDEMONA**

You're scaring me. You terrify me when you have that look in your eyes. I don't know why I should be afraid, since I haven't done anything wrong. But I'm still afraid.

**OTHELLO**

Think of your sins.

**DESDEMONA**
They are loves I bear to you.

**OTHELLO**
45      Ay, and for that thou diest.

**DESDEMONA**
That death's unnatural that kills for loving.
Alas, why gnaw you so your nether lip?
Some bloody passion shakes your very frame.
These are portents, but yet I hope, I hope
50      They do not point on me.

**OTHELLO**
                                        Peace, and be still.

**DESDEMONA**
I will so. What's the matter?

**OTHELLO**
That handkerchief
Which I so loved and gave thee, thou gav'st
To Cassio.

**DESDEMONA**
55      No, by my life and soul!
Send for the man and ask him.

**OTHELLO**
Sweet soul, take heed, take heed of perjury.
Thou art on thy deathbed.

**DESDEMONA**
Ay—but not yet to die!

**OTHELLO**
60      Presently.
Therefore confess thee freely of thy sin,
For to deny each article with oath
Cannot remove nor choke the strong conception
That I do groan withal. Thou art to die.

**DESDEMONA**
65      Oh, heaven have mercy on me!

**OTHELLO**
                                        I say "amen."

**DESDEMONA**

My only sin was loving you too much.

**OTHELLO**

Yes, that's why you have to die.

**DESDEMONA**

You're wrong to kill me for loving you. Why are you chewing on your lower lip like that? You're shaking with emotion. These are bad omens, but I hope, I hope, they don't predict my future.

**OTHELLO**

Quiet. Stay still.

**DESDEMONA**

I will. What's this all about?

**OTHELLO**

You gave that handkerchief, the one I loved and gave to you, to Cassio.

**DESDEMONA**

No, I swear by my life and soul! Bring him here and ask him.

**OTHELLO**

My sweet darling, don't lie. You're on your deathbed.

**DESDEMONA**

I am? But I'm not dying yet!

**OTHELLO**

Yes, right now. So confess your sin freely now. Even if you swear you're innocent of every accusation, you won't change my mind or remove the thought that's tormenting me. You're going to die.

**DESDEMONA**

Then heaven have mercy on me!

**OTHELLO**

Amen to that.

ACT FIVE

**DESDEMONA**
 And have you mercy too! I never did
 Offend you in my life, never loved Cassio
 But with such general warranty of heaven
 As I might love. I never gave him token.

**OTHELLO**
70 By heaven, I saw my handkerchief in 's hand.
 O perjured woman, thou dost stone my heart,
 And mak'st me call what I intend to do
 A murder, which I thought a sacrifice!
 I saw the handkerchief.

**DESDEMONA**
 He found it then,
75 I never gave it him. Send for him hither,
 Let him confess a truth.

**OTHELLO**
 He hath confessed.

**DESDEMONA**
 What, my lord?

**OTHELLO**
 That he hath usèd thee.

**DESDEMONA**
 How? Unlawfully?

**OTHELLO**
 Ay.

**DESDEMONA**
80 He will not say so.

**OTHELLO**
 No, his mouth is stopped. Honest Iago
 Hath ta'en order for 't.

**DESDEMONA**
 Oh! My fear interprets. What, is he dead?

**OTHELLO**
 Had all his hairs been lives
85 My great revenge had stomach for them all.

DESDEMONA

> And you have mercy on me too! I never did anything wrong to you in my life. I never loved Cassio, except with the pure love that I feel for humankind. I never gave him any token of romantic love.

OTHELLO

> I saw him holding the handkerchief! You liar, you're turning my heart to stone, and making me call what I'll do murder, when I had been thinking of it as a sacrifice! I saw the handkerchief.

DESDEMONA

> He found it somewhere, then. I never gave it to him. Tell him to come here. He'll tell the truth.

OTHELLO

> He's already done so.

DESDEMONA

> What, my lord?

OTHELLO

> That he had sex with you.

DESDEMONA

> What? Had sex with me?

OTHELLO

> Yes.

DESDEMONA

> He wouldn't say that.

OTHELLO

> No. He won't say anything anymore. Honest Iago's arranged that.

DESDEMONA

> Oh, I'm scared. What, is he dead?

OTHELLO

> If he had as many lives as he's got hairs on his head, I would've killed them all in revenge.

**DESDEMONA**
Alas, he is betrayed and I undone.

**OTHELLO**
Out, strumpet! weep'st thou for him to my face?

**DESDEMONA**
Oh, banish me, my lord, but kill me not!

**OTHELLO**
Down, strumpet!

**DESDEMONA**
90    Kill me tomorrow—let me live tonight!

**OTHELLO**
Nay, if you strive—

**DESDEMONA**
But half an hour!

**OTHELLO**
Being done, there is no pause.

**DESDEMONA**
But while I say one prayer!

**OTHELLO**
95    It is too late. *(he smothers her)*

**EMILIA**
*(within)* My lord , my lord! What, ho! My lord, my lord!

**OTHELLO**
What noise is this?—Not dead? Not yet quite dead?
I that am cruel am yet merciful,
I would not have thee linger in thy pain.
100    So, so.

**EMILIA**
*(within)* What, ho! My lord, my lord!

**OTHELLO**
                                                    Who's there?

**EMILIA**
*(within)* O good my lord, I would speak a word with you!

**DESDEMONA**

Oh, he's been betrayed, and I've been ruined.

**OTHELLO**

What, you whore, are you crying for him right in front of me?

**DESDEMONA**

Send me away, my lord, but don't kill me!

**OTHELLO**

Down, whore!

*Othello probably wrestles her down.*

**DESDEMONA**

Kill me tomorrow—but let me live tonight.

**OTHELLO**

No, if you struggle with me—

**DESDEMONA**

Just half an hour!

**OTHELLO**

While I'm doing this, I can't pause for a moment.

**DESDEMONA**

Just let me say one prayer!

**OTHELLO**

It's too late. *(he smothers her)*

**EMILIA**

*(offstage)* My lord, my lord! Hello! My lord, my lord!

**OTHELLO**

What's that noise? Aren't you dead yet? I know I'm cruel, but I'm merciful too. I don't want you to linger in pain.

**EMILIA**

*(offstage)* Hello! My lord, my lord!

**OTHELLO**

Who's there?

**EMILIA**

*(offstage)* Oh my lord, I need to speak to you!

**OTHELLO**
Yes, 'tis Emilia.—*(to* EMILIA*)* By and by.—She's dead.—
105 'Tis like she comes to speak of Cassio's death,
The noise was high. Ha! No more moving?
Still as the grave. Shall she come in? Were 't good?
I think she stirs again—No. What's best to do?
If she come in, she'll sure speak to my wife—
110 My wife! my wife! what wife? I have no wife.
Oh, insupportable! Oh, heavy hour!
Methinks it should be now a huge eclipse
Of sun and moon, and that th' affrighted globe
Should yawn at alteration.

**EMILIA**
*(within)*
                                              I do beseech you
115 That I may speak with you, O good my lord!

**OTHELLO**
I had forgot thee—Oh, come in, Emilia.
Soft, by and by. Let me the curtains draw.
Where art thou?

*Unlocks the door. Enter* EMILIA

                              What's the matter with thee now?

**EMILIA**
O my good lord, yonder's foul murders done!

**OTHELLO**
120 What, now?

**EMILIA**
But now, my lord.

**OTHELLO**
It is the very error of the moon,
She comes more nearer earth than she was wont
And makes men mad.

**EMILIA**
125 Cassio, my lord, hath killed a young Venetian
Called Roderigo.

OTHELLO

Yes, it's Emilia.*(to* EMILIA*)*—Just a minute!—She's dead now.—Emilia's probably come to tell me that Cassio's been killed. The fight outside was loud. So! You're not moving anymore? No, you're as still as a grave. Should I let her in? Is that a good idea? I think she's moving again—No. What should I do? If she comes in, she'll try to speak to my wife. My wife, my wife! What wife? I don't have a wife. Oh, this is unbearable! Oh, the horror! There should be a huge eclipse of the sun and the moon, now that Desdemona's no longer on this earth.

EMILIA

*(offstage)* Please, my lord. I need to speak with you. Oh, my good lord!

OTHELLO

I'd forgotten about you—Emilia, wait a moment, let me draw the curtains. *(closes the bed curtains)* Where are you? *(unlocks the door)*

EMILIA *enters.*

What's the matter with you now?

EMILIA

Oh, my lord, terrible murders have been committed over there!

OTHELLO

What? Just now?

EMILIA

Yes, just now, my lord.

OTHELLO

It's because of the full moon. It comes too close to the earth and drives men crazy.

EMILIA

Cassio's killed a young Venetian named Roderigo.

OTHELLO

            Roderigo killed? And Cassio killed!

EMILIA

    No, Cassio is not killed.

OTHELLO

    Not Cassio killed! Then murder's out of tune,
    And sweet revenge grows harsh.

DESDEMONA

130    Oh, falsely, falsely murdered!

EMILIA

    Alas, what cry is that?

OTHELLO

    That? What?

EMILIA

    Out and alas, that was my lady's voice.

*Opens the bedcurtains*

    Help! Help, ho, help! O lady, speak again!
135    Sweet Desdemona! O sweet mistress, speak!

DESDEMONA

    A guiltless death I die.

EMILIA

                Oh, who hath done this deed?

DESDEMONA

    Nobody. I myself. Farewell.
    Commend me to my kind lord. Oh, farewell!

*Dies*

OTHELLO

140    Why, how should she be murdered?

EMILIA

                Alas, who knows?

OTHELLO

    You heard her say herself it was not I.

OTHELLO

Roderigo's been killed? And Cassio's killed?

EMILIA

No, Cassio wasn't killed.

OTHELLO

Cassio's not dead? Then the wrong man is dead, and sweet revenge has gone wrong.

DESDEMONA

Oh, I've been murdered unfairly!

EMILIA

Oh Lord, who's that crying?

OTHELLO

That? What?

EMILIA

Oh, no, that was my lady's voice.

EMILIA *opens the bedcurtains.*

Help! Help! Oh, lady, speak again.
Sweet Desdemona! Oh sweet mistress, speak!

DESDEMONA

I'm dying an innocent woman.

EMILIA

Oh, who did this thing?

DESDEMONA

No one. I did it myself. Give my love to my kind hus-band. Oh, goodbye!

DESDEMONA *dies.*

OTHELLO

Why, how could she have been murdered?

EMILIA

My God, who knows?

OTHELLO

You heard her say it wasn't me.

**EMILIA**
She said so. I must needs report the truth.

**OTHELLO**
She's like a liar gone to burning hell.
'Twas I that killed her.

**EMILIA**
145 Oh, the more angel she,
And you the blacker devil!

**OTHELLO**
She turned to folly, and she was a whore.

**EMILIA**
Thou dost belie her, and thou art a devil.

**OTHELLO**
She was false as water.

**EMILIA**
Thou art rash as fire,
150 To say that she was false. Oh, she was heavenly true!

**OTHELLO**
Cassio did top her, ask thy husband else.
Oh, I were damned beneath all depth in hell,
But that I did proceed upon just grounds
To this extremity. Thy husband knew it all.

**EMILIA**
155 My husband!

**OTHELLO**
Thy husband.

**EMILIA**
That she was false to wedlock?

**OTHELLO**
Ay, with Cassio. Had she been true,
If heaven would make me such another world

Of one entire and perfect chrysolite,
I'd not have sold her for it.

**EMILIA**
My husband?

**EMILIA**

Yes, she said that. I must go report what happened.

**OTHELLO**

She was lying even as she was going down to hell. I did kill her.

**EMILIA**

Then she was even more an angel, and you're an even blacker devil!

**OTHELLO**

She cheated on me, and she was a whore.

**EMILIA**

You slander her, you devil.

**OTHELLO**

She was fickle and unfaithful, like water.

**EMILIA**

You've lost your mind to accuse her of cheating. She was utterly true to you!

**OTHELLO**

Cassio had sex with her. Ask your husband if you doubt me. If I didn't have a good reason to do this, damn me to the very bottom of hell. Your husband knew about everything.

**EMILIA**

My husband!

**OTHELLO**

Your husband.

**EMILIA**

He said she was unfaithful?

**OTHELLO**

Yes, with Cassio. If she'd been faithful to me, I never would have given her up, not even if God himself offered me a jewel as big as a planet in exchange for her.

**EMILIA**

My husband.

**OTHELLO**
160     Ay, 'twas he that told me on her first.
    An honest man he is, and hates the slime
    That sticks on filthy deeds.

**EMILIA**
                             My husband!

**OTHELLO**
    What needs this iterance, woman? I say thy husband.

**EMILIA**
    O mistress, villainy hath made mocks with love!
165     My husband say that she was false!

**OTHELLO**
                          He, woman.
    I say "thy husband"—dost understand the word?
    My friend, thy husband, honest, honest Iago.

**EMILIA**
    If he say so, may his pernicious soul
    Rot half a grain a day! He lies to th' heart.
170     She was too fond of her most filthy bargain.

    **OTHELLO** *draws his sword*

**OTHELLO**
    Ha!

**EMILIA**
    Do thy worst.
    This deed of thine is no more worthy heaven
    Than thou wast worthy her.

**OTHELLO**
                    Peace, you were best.

**EMILIA**
175     Thou hast not half that power to do me harm
    As I have to be hurt. O gull! O dolt!
    As ignorant as dirt! Thou hast done a deed—
    I care not for thy sword, I'll make thee known

OTHELLO

Yes, he's the one who first told me about her. He's an honest man who detests evil actions.

EMILIA

My husband?

OTHELLO

Why do you keep repeating that, woman? I'm telling you, your husband.

EMILIA

Oh, my mistress, a villain has made a mockery of your love! My husband said she was unfaithful!

OTHELLO

Yes, him, woman. I said "your husband."—Do you understand that word? My friend, your husband, the honest, honest Iago.

EMILIA

If he said that, then I hope his malicious soul rots in hell forever. He's lying through his teeth! She was too attached to her filthy marriage ever to do a thing like that!

OTHELLO *draws his sword.*

OTHELLO

Ha!

EMILIA

Go ahead, do your worst. Killing me won't send you to heaven. You weren't good enough for her.

OTHELLO

You'd better shut up!

EMILIA

I can endure far more pain than you could ever give me! Oh, you idiot! You stupid fool! As dumb as dirt! You've committed a terrible evil—I'm not afraid of your sword. I'll tell everyone what you did, even if it

Though I lost twenty lives.—Help! Help, ho! Help!
180    The Moor hath killed my mistress! Murder, murder!

*Enter* MONTANO, GRATIANO, *and* IAGO

**MONTANO**
What is the matter? How now, general?

**EMILIA**
Oh, are you come, Iago? You have done well,
That men must lay their murders on your neck.

**GRATIANO**
What is the matter?

**EMILIA**
185    *(to* IAGO*)* Disprove this villain, if thou be'st a man.
He says thou told'st him that his wife was false.
I know thou didst not, thou'rt not such a villain.
Speak, for my heart is full.

**IAGO**
I told him what I thought, and told no more
190    Than what he found himself was apt and true.

**EMILIA**
But did you ever tell him she was false?

**IAGO**
I did.

**EMILIA**
You told a lie, an odious, damnèd lie.
Upon my soul, a lie, a wicked lie.
195    She false with Cassio! Did you say with Cassio?

**IAGO**
With Cassio, mistress. Go to, charm your tongue.

**EMILIA**
I will not charm my tongue, I am bound to speak.
My mistress here lies murdered in her bed—

**ALL**
Oh, heavens forfend!

costs me my life twenty times over.—Help, help, help! The Moor's killed my mistress! Murder, murder!

*MONTANO, GRATIANO, and IAGO enter.*

MONTANO

What's the matter? What's going on here, general?

EMILIA

Oh, are you here, Iago? You've done a good job, that other men can attribute their murders to you!

GRATIANO

What's the matter?

EMILIA

*(to IAGO)* Tell this villain he's wrong, if you're man enough. He says you told him his wife cheated on him. I know you didn't. You're not that much of a villain. Speak, because I'm too emotional to say any more.

IAGO

I told him what I thought. I didn't tell him anything that didn't make sense or ring true to him.

EMILIA

But did you tell him she cheated on him?

IAGO

I did.

EMILIA

Then you told a lie, a sick, wicked lie. I swear on my soul it was a lie. You said she slept with Cassio. Did you say Cassio?

IAGO

Yes, with Cassio. Now be quiet.

EMILIA

I will not be quiet! I have to speak. My mistress here lies murdered in her bed—

ALL

No, heaven forbid!

ACT FIVE

**EMILIA**

200     And your reports have set the murder on.

**OTHELLO**

Nay, stare not, masters, it is true, indeed.

**GRATIANO**

'Tis a strange truth.

**MONTANO**

                              Oh, monstrous act!

**EMILIA**

Villainy, villainy, villainy!
I think upon 't, I think I smell 't, Oh, villainy!
205     I thought so then, I'll kill myself for grief.
Oh, villainy, villainy!

**IAGO**

What, are you mad? I charge you, get you home.

**EMILIA**

Good gentlemen, let me have leave to speak.
'Tis proper I obey him, but not now.
210     Perchance, Iago, I will ne'er go home.

**OTHELLO**

Oh! Oh! Oh!

**EMILIA**

                              Nay, lay thee down and roar,
For thou hast killed the sweetest innocent
That e'er did lift up eye.

**OTHELLO**

                              Oh, she was foul!—
I scarce did know you, uncle. There lies your niece,
215     Whose breath, indeed, these hands have newly stopped.
I know this act shows horrible and grim.

**GRATIANO**

Poor Desdemon! I am glad thy father's dead,
Thy match was mortal to him, and pure grief
Shore his old thread in twain. Did he live now,

**EMILIA**

And your lies caused this murder.

**OTHELLO**

Don't stand there gaping, everyone. It's true.

**GRATIANO**

It may be true, but it's unbelievable.

**MONTANO**

Oh, what a horrible deed!

**EMILIA**

Evil, evil, evil! I can smell it! I suspected it earlier. I'll kill myself out of grief! Oh, evil, evil!

**IAGO**

Are you crazy? I'm ordering you, go home.

**EMILIA**

Good gentlemen, give me permission to speak. I know I ought to obey my husband, but not now. Maybe I'll never go home again, Iago!

**OTHELLO**

Oh! Oh! Oh!

**EMILIA**

Yes, go ahead and moan, because you killed the sweetest, most innocent woman who ever lived!

**OTHELLO**

*Gratiano is Brabantio's brother and Desdemona's uncle.*

She was filthy! I barely knew you, Uncle Gratiano. Here's your niece lying here dead. I killed her with these hands. I know this looks horrible.

**GRATIANO**

Poor Desdemona! I'm glad your father isn't alive to see this. Your marriage made him die of grief before his time. If he was alive now, this sight would hurt him

ACT FIVE

220 This sight would make him do a desperate turn,
Yea, curse his better angel from his side
And fall to reprobation.

**OTHELLO**
'Tis pitiful, but yet Iago knows
That she with Cassio hath the act of shame
225 A thousand times committed. Cassio confessed it,
And she did gratify his amorous works
With that recognizance and pledge of love
Which I first gave her. I saw it in his hand,
It was a handkerchief, an antique token
230 My father gave my mother.

**EMILIA**
                            Oh, heaven! Oh, heavenly powers!

**IAGO**
Zounds, hold your peace.

**EMILIA**
'Twill out, 'twill out.—I peace?
No, I will speak as liberal as the north.
Let heaven and men and devils, let them all,
235 All, all cry shame against me, yet I'll speak.

**IAGO**
Be wise, and get you home.

*Draws his sword*

**EMILIA**
I will not.

**GRATIANO**
Fie! Your sword upon a woman?

**EMILIA**
O thou dull Moor! That handkerchief thou speak'st of
240 I found by fortune and did give my husband.
For often, with a solemn earnestness—
More than indeed belonged to such a trifle—
He begged of me to steal it.

terribly. It would make him curse the heavens and be damned to hell.

OTHELLO

It's sad, but Iago knows she had sex with Cassio a thousand times. Cassio confessed it, and she pledged her love to him by giving him the handkerchief I'd given her. I saw it in his hand.

It was an old memento that my father gave to my mother.

EMILIA

Oh, God! Dear God in heaven!

IAGO

Damn it, shut your mouth.

EMILIA

No, the truth will come out—Me, shut my mouth? Let heaven and men and devils tell me to shut me up. I'll say what I have to say.

IAGO

If you're smart, you'll go home.

IAGO *draws his sword.*

EMILIA

I won't.

GRATIANO

Shame on you! Drawing your sword on a woman?

EMILIA

Oh, you stupid Moor! I found that handkerchief by accident and gave it to my husband. He'd begged me to steal it many times.

**IAGO**

Villainous whore!

**EMILIA**

She give it Cassio? No, alas, I found it
245 And I did give 't my husband.

**IAGO**

Filth, thou liest!

**EMILIA**

By heaven, I do not, I do not, gentlemen.—
(*to* OTHELLO)
O murderous coxcomb! What should such a fool
Do with so good a wife?

**OTHELLO**

Are there no stones in heaven
But what serve for the thunder?—Precious villain!

*He runs at* IAGO
IAGO *stabs* EMILIA

**GRATIANO**

250 The woman falls! Sure he hath killed his wife.

**EMILIA**

Ay, ay. Oh, lay me by my mistress' side.

*Exit* IAGO

**GRATIANO**

He's gone, but his wife's killed.

**MONTANO**

'Tis a notorious villain. Take you this weapon,
Which I have recovered from the Moor.
255 Come, guard the door without. Let him not pass,
But kill him rather. I'll after that same villain,
For 'tis a damnèd slave.

*Exeunt* MONTANO *and* GRATIANO

IAGO

You evil whore!

EMILIA

You think she gave it to Cassio? No, I found it and gave it to my husband.

IAGO

You piece of filth, you're lying!

EMILIA

I swear I'm not lying. *(to* OTHELLO*)* Oh, you murderous fool! How did you ever get such a good wife?

OTHELLO

Won't heaven strike this Iago dead? You absolute villain!

OTHELLO *runs at* IAGO. IAGO *stabs* EMILIA.

GRATIANO

The woman's falling down! He's killed his wife!

EMILIA

Yes, yes! Lay me next to my mistress.

IAGO *exits.*

GRATIANO

He's gone, and his wife's dead.

MONTANO

He's a wicked, horrible criminal. Take the Moor's sword and guard the door from the outside. Kill him rather than let him leave this room. I'm going after Iago. He's a horrid criminal.

MONTANO *and* GRATIANO *exit.*

**OTHELLO**
I am not valiant neither,
But ever puny whipster gets my sword.
But why should honor outlive honesty?
260 Let it go all.

**EMILIA**
What did thy song bode, lady?
Hark, canst thou hear me? I will play the swan.
And die in music.
*(singing)* *Willow, willow, willow—*

Moor, she was chaste, she loved thee, cruel Moor.
So come my soul to bliss, as I speak true.
265 So speaking as I think, alas, I die.

*Dies*

**OTHELLO**
I have another weapon in this chamber,
It was a sword of Spain, the ice-brook's temper.
Oh, here it is. Uncle, I must come forth.

**GRATIANO**
*(within)* If thou attempt it, it will cost thee dear.
270 Thou hast no weapon, and perforce must suffer.

**OTHELLO**
Look in upon me then and speak with me,
Or, naked as I am, I will assault thee.

*Enter* GRATIANO

**GRATIANO**
What is the matter?

**OTHELLO**
Behold, I have a weapon.
A better never did itself sustain
275 Upon a soldier's thigh. I have seen the day

**OTHELLO**

I'm not that strong, if a puny nobody can grab my sword. But why should my reputation for honor last longer than my honor did? Let it all go.

**EMILIA**

What did your song mean, lady? Can you hear me? I'll die like a swan. They sing when they die.
*(singing) Willow, willow, willow.—*
Moor, she never cheated on you. She loved you, you cruel man. I swear on my soul I'm telling the truth, and as I say this, I die.

EMILIA *dies.*

**OTHELLO**

I've got another weapon in the room. It's a Spanish sword, hardened in ice cold water and razor sharp. Here it is. Uncle, I'm coming out!

**GRATIANO**

*(offstage)* If you try that, you'll pay for it. You've got no weapon, so you'll have to suffer.

**OTHELLO**

Look in on me, and talk with me, or I'll attack even without a weapon.

GRATIANO *enters.*

**GRATIANO**

What's the matter?

**OTHELLO**

Look, I have a weapon, the best sword a soldier could have. I've fought my way through obstacles twenty times more terrifying than you with this weapon. But

That with this little arm and this good sword
I have made my way through more impediments
Than twenty times your stop. But, oh, vain boast!
Who can control his fate? 'tis not so now.
280    Be not afraid, though you do see me weaponed.
Here is my journey's end, here is my butt,
And very sea-mark of my utmost sail.
Do you go back dismayed? 'tis a lost fear.
Man but a rush against Othello's breast,
285    And he retires. Where should Othello go?—
Now, how dost thou look now? O ill-starred wench,
Pale as thy smock! When we shall meet at compt
This look of thine will hurl my soul from heaven
And fiends will snatch at it. Cold, cold, my girl,
290    Even like thy chastity. O cursed, cursed slave!
Whip me, ye devils,
From the possession of this heavenly sight!
Blow me about in winds, roast me in sulfur,
Wash me in steep-down gulfs of liquid fire!—
295    Oh, Desdemona! Desdemona! dead! Oh! Oh!

*Enter* LODOVICO, MONTANO, CASSIO *carried in a chair,
and officers with* IAGO, *prisoner*

**LODOVICO**
Where is this rash and most unfortunate man?

**OTHELLO**
That's he that was Othello. Here I am.

**LODOVICO**
Where is that viper? Bring the villain forth.

IAGO *is brought forward*

who can control his fate? I'm not like that now. Don't be afraid, even though you see me with a weapon. This is the end of my journey, the end of my life. Are you backing away in fear? There's no reason to be afraid. You could tap me with a feather and I'd back away. Where would Othello go?—Oh, look at you! Such cruel luck! You're as pale as your nightgown! When we meet on Judgment Day, that look of yours will send me from heaven to hell, where devils will grab me. You're cold, cold, and you were never hot with lust. Oh you damned villain! Whip me, you devils, so I don't have to look at this heavenly sight! Blow on me with hot winds, roast me in lava, drown me in liquid fire! Oh, Desdemona! Dead Desdemona! Oh, oh!

LODOVICO *and* MONTANO *enter, followed by* CASSIO *on a stretcher, and officers with* IAGO, *prisoner.*

**LODOVICO**

Where is that poor rash man?

**OTHELLO**

You mean the man who used to be Othello? Here I am.

**LODOVICO**

Where's that snake? Bring the villain forward.

IAGO *is brought forward.*

ACT FIVE

**OTHELLO**
I look down towards his feet, but that's a fable.
300    If that thou be'st a devil, I cannot kill thee.

*Stabs* IAGO

**LODOVICO**
Wrench his sword from him.

*They take* OTHELLO*'s sword*

**IAGO**
                                                            I bleed, sir, but not killed.

**OTHELLO**
I am not sorry neither. I'd have thee live,
For in my sense 'tis happiness to die.

**LODOVICO**
O thou Othello, thou was once so good,
305    Fall'n in the practice of a cursèd slave,
What shall be said to thee?

**OTHELLO**
                                            Why, anything.
An honorable murderer, if you will,
For naught I did in hate, but all in honor.

**LODOVICO**
This wretch hath part confessed his villainy.
310    Did you and he consent in Cassio's death?

**OTHELLO**
Ay.

**CASSIO**
Dear general, I never gave you cause.

**OTHELLO**
I do believe it, and I ask your pardon.
Will you, I pray, demand that demi-devil
315    Why he hath thus ensnared my soul and body?

**OTHELLO**

I'm looking to see if you have cloven hooves like the devil. But that's just a fairy tale. If you are a devil, I won't be able to kill you.

*OTHELLO stabs IAGO.*

**LODOVICO**

Take his sword away from him.

*They take OTHELLO's sword away.*

**IAGO**

I'm bleeding, but you didn't kill me.

**OTHELLO**

I'm not sorry, either. I want you to live, since to me, death is happiness.

**LODOVICO**

Oh Othello, you were once so good, then you were tricked by this villain. What can I say to you?

**OTHELLO**

Say anything. Call me an honorable murderer if you like. I did nothing out of hate, only out of honor.

**LODOVICO**

This poor guy's partly confessed his plan. Did you plan Cassio's death with him?

**OTHELLO**

Yes.

**CASSIO**

Dear general, I never gave you any reason to hate me.

**OTHELLO**

I believe you; and I ask you to forgive me. Will you please make this half-devil say why he tricked me and damned my soul?

**IAGO**
>Demand me nothing. What you know, you know.
>From this time forth I never will speak word.

**LODOVICO**
>What, not to pray?

**GRATIANO**
>Torments will ope your lips.

**OTHELLO**
320
>Well, thou dost best.

**LODOVICO**
>Sir, you shall understand what hath befall'n,
>Which, as I think, you know not. Here is a letter
>Found in the pocket of the slain Roderigo,
>And here another. The one of them imports
325
>The death of Cassio to be undertook
>By Roderigo.

**OTHELLO**
>Oh, villain!

**CASSIO**
>Most heathenish and most gross!

**LODOVICO**
>Now here's another discontented paper
330
>Found in his pocket too, and this, it seems,
>Roderigo meant to have sent this damnèd villain
>But that, belike, Iago in the interim
>Came in and satisfied him.

**OTHELLO**
>O thou pernicious caitiff!
335
>How came you, Cassio, by that handkerchief
>That was my wife's?

**CASSIO**
>                    I found it in my chamber,
>And he himself confessed but even now
>That there he dropped it for a special purpose
>Which wrought to his desire.

**IAGO**

Don't ask me anything. You know what you know. From this moment on, I'll never say another word.

**LODOVICO**

What, not even to pray?

**GRATIANO**

Torture will make you talk.

**OTHELLO**

Well, do your best.

**LODOVICO**

Sir, you'll understand everything that has happened. I don't think you know now. Here is a letter we found in Roderigo's pocket. And here's another. This one talks about how Roderigo should kill Cassio.

**OTHELLO**

Oh, you villain!

**CASSIO**

Ungodly and monstrous!

**LODOVICO**

Here's another letter from his pocket, addressed to Iago and full of complaints. We think he was going to send it to Iago, but then Iago stepped in and answered his complaints by killing him.

**OTHELLO**

Oh, you wicked scoundrel! Cassio, how did you get my wife's handkerchief?

**CASSIO**

I found it in my room, and Iago just confessed that he put it there for his own purposes.

ACT FIVE

**OTHELLO**
                                        O fool! fool! fool!

**CASSIO**
340     There is besides in Roderigo's letter
        How he upbraids Iago, that he made him
        Brave me upon the watch, whereon it came
        That I was cast. And even but now he spake,
        After long seeming dead—Iago hurt him,
345     Iago set him on.

**LODOVICO**
        (to OTHELLO) You must forsake this room and go with us.
        Your power and your command is taken off
        And Cassio rules in Cyprus. For this slave,
        If there be any cunning cruelty
350     That can torment him much and hold him long,
        It shall be his. You shall close prisoner rest
        Till that the nature of your fault be known
        To the Venetian state.—Come, bring him away.

**OTHELLO**
        Soft you, a word or two before you go.
355     I have done the state some service, and they know 't.
        No more of that. I pray you, in your letters,
        When you shall these unlucky deeds relate,
        Speak of me as I am. Nothing extenuate,
        Nor set down aught in malice. Then must you speak
360     Of one that loved not wisely, but too well.
        Of one not easily jealous, but being wrought,
        Perplexed in the extreme. Of one whose hand,
        Like the base Indian, threw a pearl away
        Richer than all his tribe. Of one whose subdued eyes,
365     Albeit unused to the melting mood,
        Drop tears as fast as the Arabian trees
        Their medicinal gum. Set you down this,

**OTHELLO**

Oh, what a fool I am!

**CASSIO**

Also, in his letter to Iago, Roderigo criticizes Iago for telling him to get me angry while I was on guard duty, and get me demoted. And just now he admitted it, even though he'd seemed to be dead for a long while— Iago tricked him, Iago urged him to do it.

**LODOVICO**

*(to OTHELLO)* You'll have to leave this room and come with us. You're stripped of your power and your command, and Cassio will govern Cyprus. As for this slave, Iago, if we can think of any torture that will hurt him a lot but keep him alive a long time, he'll have it. You'll remain a prisoner until we bring your crimes to the Venetian government.—Okay, take him away.

**OTHELLO**

Wait. A word or two before you go. I've given the state of Venice a bit of help in the past, and they know it. But enough about that. When you record these sad events in your letters, please describe me exactly as I am. Don't tone things down or exaggerate them out of hostility. If you're being fair, you'll have to describe me as someone who loved too much, but who wasn't wise about it. I was not easily made jealous, but once I was tricked and manipulated, I worked myself into a frenzy. Describe me as a fool who threw away a precious pearl with his own hands, like a silly Indian who didn't know what it was worth. As someone who was not emotional, but who then cried a lot. Write all this

ACT FIVE

And say besides that in Aleppo once,
Where a malignant and a turbaned Turk
370  Beat a Venetian and traduced the state,
I took by the throat the circumcisèd dog,
And smote him, thus.

*Stabs himself*

**LODOVICO**
Oh, bloody period!

**GRATIANO**
All that is spoke is marred.

**OTHELLO**
(*to* **DESDEMONA**)
375  I kissed thee ere I killed thee. No way but this,
Killing myself, to die upon a kiss.

*Kisses* **DESDEMONA**, *dies*

**CASSIO**
This did I fear, but thought he had no weapon,
For he was great of heart.

**LODOVICO**
(*to* **IAGO**)
                              O Spartan dog,
More fell than anguish, hunger, or the sea,
380  Look on the tragic loading of this bed.
This is thy work. The object poisons sight,
Let it be hid.—Gratiano, keep the house
And seize upon the fortunes of the Moor,
For they succeed on you.—To you, lord governor,
385  Remains the censure of this hellish villain:
The time, the place, the torture. Oh, enforce it!
Myself will straight aboard, and to the state
This heavy act with heavy heart relate.

*Exeunt*

down, and then say also that in Aleppo I once saw a Turk beating a Venetian, so I grabbed the Turk by the throat and hit him like this.

OTHELLO *stabs himself.*

**LODOVICO**

Oh, what a bloody end to all this!

**GRATIANO**

Everything we've heard is bad.

**OTHELLO**

*(to* DESDEMONA*)* I kissed you before I killed you. Now, killing myself, I'm dying while I kiss you again.

OTHELLO *kisses* DESDEMONA *and dies.*

**CASSIO**

I was afraid this would happen, because he was a noble, brave man, but I didn't think he had a weapon.

**LODOVICO**

*(to* IAGO*)* You bloodthirsty dog, you're crueler than sadness or hunger, crueler than the sea. Look at these dead people on this bed. You did all this. He makes me sick. Take him away. Gratiano, take care of the house, and take the Moor's property. You've inherited every-thing.—*(to* CASSIO*)* Governor, I leave it in your hands to punish this evil villain: just decide the time, the place and the means of torture. And then carry it out! I have to go back to Venice, and tell them about these sad events.

*They all exit.*

# PART III

---

# STUDY
# GUIDE

# 6

# THEMATIC QUESTIONS

**1.** To what extent does Othello's final speech affect our assessment of him? What is the effect of his final anecdote about the Turk?

Certainly, Othello's final speech is not all that one might wish for—his claim to be "one not easily jealous" is open to question, and his claim that he "loved not wisely, but too well" seems both an understatement and an exaggeration (5.2.). Further, Othello's invocation of his own military triumphs might be seen as another example of Othello dangerously misordering his priorities. He seems to position his political reputation as his biggest concern, as he did in Act 3, scene 3, when, having decided that Desdemona does not love him, he exclaims, "Farewell the tranquil mind! Farewell content! / Farewell the plumèd troops and the big wars / That makes ambition virtue!"

At the same time, however, Othello's final speech does seem to restore to him somewhat the nobility that characterized him at the beginning of the play. From almost the first time he opens his mouth, Othello demonstrates—and the other characters confirm—his hypnotic eloquence when he speaks about his exploits in battle. Othello's final speech puts us in mind of his long speech in Act 1, scene 3, so that we see him, even if only for a moment, as we saw him then. This process of conflating two different times and views of Othello is similar to the rhetorical effect achieved by Othello's dying words, where he makes his suicide seem like a noble and heroic deed by conflating it with the killing of a Turk in service of the state.

**2.** What role does incoherent language play in Othello? How does Othello's language change over the course of the play? Pay particular attention to the handkerchief scene in Act 3, scene 3, and Othello's fit in Act 4, scene 1.

At the beginning of the play, Othello has such confidence in his skill with language that he can claim that he is "rude" in speech, knowing that no one will possibly believe him (1.3.). He then dazzles his audience with a forty-line speech that effortlessly weaves words such as "hair-breadth" and "Anthropophagi" into blank verse lines. But in the moments when the pressure applied by Iago is particularly extreme, Othello's language deteriorates into fragmented, hesitant, and incoherent syntax. Throughout Act 3, scene 3, Othello speaks in short, clipped exclamations and half-sentences such as "Ha!" (3.3.), "Oh misery!" (3.3.), and "Dost thou say so?" (3.3.). There is also notable repetition, as in "Not a jot, not a jot" (3.3.), "Oh, monstrous! Monstrous!" (3.3.), "Oh, blood, blood, blood!" (3.3.), and "Damn her, lewd minx! Oh, damn her, damn her!" (3.3.).

Such moments, when Othello shifts from his typical, seemingly effortless verse to near inarticulateness, demonstrate the extent to which Othello's passion has broken down his self-control. In Act 3, scene 3, he is still speaking in mostly coherent sentences or phrases; but this is no longer the case in Act 4, scene 1. This scene begins with Iago saying, "Do you really think so?" and Othello can only helplessly and automatically echo, "What do you mean, do I think so?" (4.1.). Iago then introduces the word "lie" into the conversation, which sends Othello into a frenzy as he attempts to sort out the semantic differences between Cassio "lying on" (that is, lying about) Desdemona and "lying with" (that is, having sex with) her (4.1.). The various words and images Iago has planted in Othello's mind over the course of the play are transformed into impressionistic, sporadic eruptions out of Othello's mouth: "Lie with her? . . . . that's fulsome! Handkerchief—confessions—handkerchief" (4.1.). These eruptions culminate in the nonsense of "Pish! Noses, ears, and lips." (4.1.). Ultimately, Othello's inability to articulate his thoughts coherently seems to overcome him physically, as he collapses "in a trance" (4.1.).

**3.** Analyze Desdemona's character. To what extent is she merely a passive victim of Othello's brutality? How does her character change when she is not with Othello?

At the end of *Othello*, Desdemona seems to be the most passive kind of victim. Smothered, deprived of breath and of words by her husband, she is totally overwhelmed by Othello's insane jealousy and physical strength. But before her murder, Desdemona is remarkable for showing more passivity when her husband is not around and more assertiveness when he is.

Desdemona's first speech, in which she defends her recent marriage, is confident and forthright. When she gives it, she is the only female character onstage, surrounded by powerful men who include the duke, her husband, and her father, but she is not ashamed to assert her belief in the validity of her desires and actions. Unfortunately, Iago recognizes Desdemona's forthrightness and uses it against her. He exploits her willingness to demand and justify what she wants by making Cassio her cause and, simultaneously, Othello's enemy. In Act 3, scene 3, Desdemona asks Othello to forgive Cassio and persists, in spite of Othello's rising consternation, until her husband declares, "I will deny thee nothing" (3.3). Her courage is apparent in her refusal to search for the missing handkerchief in Act 3, scene 4; in her willingness to shout back at Othello as he abuses her in Act 4, scene 1; and in her insistence upon her innocence in Act 5, scene 2. Her audacity seems to infuriate Othello all the more, as what he takes to be shameless lies convince him that she is unremorseful for what he believes to be her sin.

The terrible effect of Othello's brutality is most obvious in Desdemona's scenes with Emilia. Emilia is cynical and bawdy, and she gives Desdemona every possible opportunity to bad-mouth Othello. Men, she says in Act 3, scene 4, "are all but stomachs, and we all but food. / They eat us hungerly, and when they are full, / They belch us" (3.4.). Later, she insults Othello: "He called her "whore." A beggar in his drink / Could not have laid such terms upon his callet [whore]" (4.2.). And, at the end of Act 4, scene 3, she gives a lengthy discourse about the virtues of infidelity. Desdemona, however, never says anything worse than "Heaven keep the monster [jealousy] from Othello's mind" (3.4.). With her closest confidante, Desdemona does not speak ill of her husband, even as she shows the strain of his terrible abuse.

# 7

# KEY QUESTIONS
# AND ANSWERS

## 1. Why does Iago hate Othello?

The main reason Iago gives for plotting to destroy Othello is a suspicion that Othello may have had an affair with Iago's wife Emilia. However, Iago himself admits that he doesn't know whether or not these rumors are true, explaining that "I know not if't be true, / But I, for mere suspicion in that kind, / Will do as if for surety" (1.3.). Iago also mentions that he is attracted to Desdemona himself: "I do love her too" (2.1.). Neither of these reasons seems totally sufficient for just how much Iago hates Othello, and, notably, he declines to answer when Othello asks him his motivation at the end of the play, saying only, "Demand me nothing. What you know, you know" (5.2.). The lack of a clear reason for Iago's destructive hatred is part of what makes him such a chilling and effective villain, since, in part, he seems to take pleasure in destruction for destruction's sake.

## 2. How does Emilia help Iago?

Emilia gives Desdemona's handkerchief to Iago, explaining that after Desdemona dropped it, she "being here, took't up" (3.3.). Because Emilia steals the handkerchief, Desdemona is unable to produce it when Othello asks her to show it to him, leading him to become even more convinced that she is guilty of adultery. Because this belief, and his resulting jealous rage, lead him to kill Desdemona, Emilia does have some connection to the murder. However, Emilia is clearly horrified and distraught when she learns that her mistress is dead, lamenting that "thou hast killed the sweetest innocent / That e're did lift up eye" (5.2.). She also insists on uncovering the story of what really happened and demonstrating Iago's guilt, even when this endangers her, explaining that "Let heaven and men and devils, let them all, / All, all cry shame against me, yet I'll speak" (5.2.).

### 3. Why does Othello care about Desdemona's handkerchief?

Othello first explains that he has a sentimental attachment to Desdemona's handkerchief because it was the first gift he ever gave her: "I gave her such a one, 'twas my first gift" (3.3.). He later elaborates on the family history of the handkerchief, telling Desdemona that it was a gift from his mother, who had used it as a charm to maintain his father's love. He explains, "There's magic in the web of it" (3.4.), leaving Desdemona unsure of whether or not to believe him. Because of Othello's strong attachment to the handkerchief, he is particularly upset that Desdemona cannot find it, and horrified that she might have given it away to another man. Iago's scheme to make it appear as though Cassio then gave the handkerchief to Bianca further disrespects the family heirloom, making it appear as something that can simply be passed around in a cycle of sexual exchange.

## 4. How does Iago manipulate Desdemona?

After Cassio falls from Othello's favor, Iago exploits Desdemona's eagerness to bring the two men back together: "So will I turn her virtue into pitch / And out of her own goodness make the net" (2.3.). Iago plants the idea in Othello's mind that something inappropriate may be happening between Cassio and Desdemona, and encourages Othello to pay attention to whether "your lady strain his entertainment / With any strong or vehement importunity" (3.3.). As a result, when Desdemona does intercede on Cassio's behalf, Othello becomes very jealous and suspicious. Her innocent hopes that "let Cassio be received again" (3.4.) combine with other fears Iago has planted, and drive Othello almost mad with jealousy.

## 5. How does Iago use Bianca to trick Othello?

Iago tricks Cassio into speaking about Bianca, a woman he is having an affair with, while leading Othello to believe that Cassio is describing Desdemona. As a result, Cassio's comments, such as "She is persuaded I will marry her, / Out of her own love and flattery, not out of my promise" (4.1.) sound to Othello like Cassio is admitting to sleeping with Desdemona. The confusion between Desdemona and Bianca is significant because Bianca's status as a prostitute means Cassio does not respect her. Iago points out that "He, when he hears of her, cannot refrain / From the excess of laughter" (4.1.). Othello is enraged because he believes he is hearing his wife being joked about and described like a prostitute, but he also can't help seeing her in that light. Othello goes on to refer to Desdemona as a whore a number of times, presumably because of the way he believes she has been treated by other men.

# 8

# THEMES, MOTIFS, AND SYMBOLS

## Themes

**Themes are the fundamental and often universal ideas explored in a literary work.**

### THE INCOMPABILITY OF MILITARY HEROISM & LOVE

Before and above all else, Othello is a soldier. From the earliest moments in the play, his career affects his married life. Asking "fit disposition" for his wife after being ordered to Cyprus (1.3.), Othello notes that "the tyrant custom . . . / Hath made the flinty and steel couch of war / My thrice-driven bed of down" (1.3.). While Desdemona is used to better "accommodation," she nevertheless accompanies her husband to Cyprus (1.3.). Moreover, she is unperturbed by the tempest or Turks that threatened their crossing, and genuinely curious rather than irate when she is roused from bed by the drunken brawl in Act 2, scene 3. She is, indeed, Othello's "fair warrior," and he is happiest when he has her by his side in the midst of military conflict or business dealings (2.1.). The military also provides Othello with a means to gain acceptance in Venetian society. While the Venetians in the play are generally fearful of the prospect of Othello's social entrance into white society through his marriage to Desdemona, all Venetians respect and honor him as a soldier. Mercenary Moors were, in fact, commonplace at the time.

Othello predicates his success in love on his success as a soldier, wooing Desdemona with tales of his military travels and battles. Once the Turks are drowned—by natural rather than military might—Othello is left without anything to do: The last act of military administration we see him perform is the viewing of fortifications in the extremely short second scene of Act 3. No longer having a means of proving his manhood or honor in a public setting, such as the court or the battlefield, Othello begins to feel uneasy with his footing in a private setting, the bedroom. Iago capitalizes on this uneasiness, calling Othello's epileptic fit in Act 4, scene 1, "[a] passion most resulting such a man." In other words, Iago is calling Othello unsoldierly. Iago also takes care to mention that Cassio, whom Othello believes to be his competitor, saw him in his emasculating trance (4.1.).

Desperate to cling to the security of his former identity as a soldier while his current identity as a lover crumbles, Othello begins to confuse the one with the other. His expression of his jealousy quickly devolves from the conventional—"Farewell the tranquil mind"—to the absurd:

> Farewell the plumèd troops and the big wars
>
> That make ambition virtue! Oh, farewell,
>
> Farewell the neighing steed and the shrill trump,
>
> The spirit-stirring drum, th' ear-piercing fife,
>
> The royal banner, and all quality,
>
> Pride, pomp, and circumstance of glorious war! (3.3.)

One might contend that Othello is saying farewell to the wrong things—he is entirely preoccupied with his identity as a soldier. But his way of thinking is somewhat justified by its seductiveness to the audience as well. Critics and audiences alike find comfort and nobility in Othello's final speech and the anecdote of the "malignant and . . . turbaned Turk" (5.2.), even though in that speech, as in his speech in Act 3, scene 3, Othello depends on his identity as a soldier to glorify himself in the public's memory, and to try to make his audience forget his and Desdemona's disastrous marital experiment.

## THE DANGER OF ISOLATION

The action of *Othello* moves from the metropolis of Venice to the island of Cyprus. Protected by military fortifications as well as by the forces of nature, Cyprus faces little threat from external forces. Once Othello, Iago, Desdemona, Emilia, and Roderigo have come to Cyprus, they have nothing to do but prey upon one another. Isolation enables many of the play's most important effects: Iago frequently speaks in soliloquies; Othello stands apart while Iago talks with Cassio in Act 4, scene 1, and is left alone onstage with the bodies of Emilia and Desdemona for a few moments in Act 5, scene 2; Roderigo seems attached to no one in the play except Iago. And, most prominently, Othello is visibly isolated from the other characters by his physical stature and the color of his skin. Iago is an expert at manipulating the distance between characters, isolating his victims so that they fall prey to their own obsessions. At the same time, Iago, of necessity always standing apart, falls prey to his own obsession with revenge. The characters *cannot* be islands, the play seems to say: Self-isolation as an act of self-preservation ultimately leads to self-destruction. Such self-isolation leads to the deaths of Roderigo, Iago, Othello, and even Emilia.

## Motifs

**Motifs are recurring structures, contrasts, and literary devices that can help to develop and inform the text's major themes.**

### SIGHT AND BLINDNESS

When Desdemona asks to be allowed to accompany Othello to Cyprus, she says that she "saw Othello's visage in his mind, / And to his honors and his valiant parts / Did I my soul and fortunes consecrate" (1.3.). Othello's blackness, his visible difference from everyone around him, is of little importance to Desdemona: She has the power to see him for what he is in a way that even Othello himself cannot. Desdemona's line is one of many references to different kinds of sight in the play. Earlier in Act 1, scene 3, a senator suggests that the Turkish retreat to Rhodes is "a pageant, / To keep us in false gaze" (1.3.). The beginning of Act 2 consists entirely of people staring out to sea, waiting to see the arrival of ships, friendly or otherwise. Othello, though he demands "ocular proof" (3.3.), is frequently convinced by things he does not see: He strips Cassio of his position as lieutenant based on the story Iago tells; he relies on Iago's story of seeing Cassio wipe his beard with Desdemona's handkerchief (3.3.); and he believes Cassio to be dead simply because he hears him scream. After Othello has killed himself in the final scene, Lodovico says to Iago, "Look on the tragic loading of this bed. / This is thy work. The object poisons sight, / Let it be hid" (5.2.). The action of the play depends heavily on characters *not* seeing things: Othello accuses his wife, although he never sees her infidelity, and Emilia, although she watches Othello erupt into a rage about the missing handkerchief, does not figuratively "see" what her husband has done.

## PLANTS

Iago is strangely preoccupied with plants. His speeches to Roderigo, in particular, make extensive and elaborate use of vegetable metaphors and conceits. Some examples are: "Our bodies are our gardens, to the which our wills are gardeners. So that if we will plant nettles or sow lettuce, set hyssop and weed up thyme . . . the power and corrigible authority of this lies in our wills" (1.3.); "Though other things grow fair against the sun, / Yet fruits that blossom first will first be ripe" (2.3.); "And then, sir, would he gripe and wring my hand, / Cry 'O sweet creature!' and then kiss me hard, / As if he plucked kisses up by the roots / That grew upon my lips" (3.3.). The first of these examples best explains Iago's preoccupation with the plant metaphor and how it functions within the play. Characters in this play seem to be the product of certain inevitable, natural forces, which, if left unchecked, will grow wild. Iago understands these natural forces particularly well: He is, according to his own metaphor, a good "gardener," both of himself and of others.

Many of Iago's botanical references concern poison: "I'll pour this pestilence into his ear" (2.3.); "The Moor already changes with my poison. / Dangerous conceits are in their natures poisons / . . . / . . . Not poppy nor mandragora / Nor all the drowsy syrups of the world / Shall ever medicine thee to that sweet sleep" (3.3.). Iago cultivates his "conceits" so that they become lethal poisons and then plants their seeds in the minds of others. The organic way in which Iago's plots consume the other characters and determine their behavior makes his conniving, human evil seem like a force of nature. That organic growth also indicates that the minds of the other characters are fertile ground for Iago's efforts.

## ANIMALS

Iago calls Othello a "Barbary horse," an "old black ram," and also tells Brabanzio that his daughter and Othello are "making the beast with two backs" (1.1.). In Act 1, scene 3, Iago tells Roderigo, "Ere I would say I would drown myself for the love of a guinea hen, I would change my humanity with a baboon" (1.3.). He then remarks that drowning is for "cats and blind puppies" (1.3.). Cassio laments that, when drunk, he is "by and by a fool, and presently a beast!" (2.3.). Othello tells Iago, "Exchange me for a goat / When I shall turn the business of my soul / To such exsufflicate and blowed surmises" (3.3.). He later says that "[a] hornèd man's a monster and a beast" (4.1.). Even Emilia, in the final scene, says that she will "play the swan, / And die in music" (5.2.). Like the repeated references to plants, these references to animals convey a sense that the laws of nature, rather than those of society, are the primary forces governing the characters in this play. When animal references are used with regard to Othello, as they frequently are, they reflect the racism both of characters in the play and of Shakespeare's contemporary audience. "Barbary horse" is a vulgarity particularly appropriate in the mouth of Iago, but even without having seen Othello, the Jacobean audience would have known from Iago's metaphor that he meant to connote a savage Moor.

## HELL, DEMONS, AND MONSTERS

Iago tells Othello to beware of jealousy, the "green-eyed monster which doth mock / The meat it feeds on" (3.3.). Likewise, Emilia describes jealousy as dangerously and uncannily self-generating, a "monster / Begot upon itself, born on itself" (3.4.). Imagery of hell and damnation also recurs throughout Othello, especially toward the end of the play, when Othello becomes preoccupied with the religious and moral judgment of Desdemona and himself. After he has learned the truth about Iago, Othello calls Iago a devil and a demon several times in Act 5, scene 2. Othello's earlier allusion to "some monster in [his] thought" ironically refers to Iago (3.3.). Likewise, his vision of Desdemona's betrayal is "monstrous! Monstrous!" (3.3.). Shortly before he kills himself, Othello wishes for eternal spiritual and physical torture in hell, crying out, "Whip me, ye devils, / . . . / . . . roast me in sulfur, / Wash me in steep-down gulfs of liquid fire!" (5.2.). The imagery of the monstrous and diabolical takes over where the imagery of animals can go no further, presenting the jealousy-crazed characters not simply as brutish, but as grotesque, deformed, and demonic.

## Symbols

**Symbols are objects, characters, figures, and colors used to represent abstract ideas or concepts.**

### THE HANDKERCHIEF

The handkerchief symbolizes different things to different characters. Since the handkerchief was the first gift Desdemona received from Othello, she keeps it with her constantly as a symbol of his love. Iago manipulates the handkerchief so that Othello comes to see it as a symbol of Desdemona herself—her faith and chastity. By taking possession of it, he is able to convert it into evidence of her infidelity. But the handkerchief's importance to Iago and Desdemona derives from its importance to Othello himself. He tells Desdemona that it was woven by a two-hundred-year-old sibyl, or female prophet, using silk from sacred worms and dye extracted from the hearts of mummified virgins. Othello claims that his mother used it to keep his father faithful to her, so, to him, the handkerchief represents marital fidelity. The pattern of strawberries (dyed with virgins' blood) on a white background strongly suggests the bloodstains left on the sheets on a virgin's wedding night, so the handkerchief implicitly suggests a guarantee of virginity as well as fidelity.

## THE SONG "WILLOW"

As she prepares for bed in Act 5, Desdemona sings a song about a woman who is betrayed by her lover. She was taught the song by her mother's maid, Barbary, who suffered a misfortune similar to that of the woman in the song; she even died singing "Willow." The song's lyrics suggest that both men and women are unfaithful to one another. To Desdemona, the song seems to represent a melancholy and resigned acceptance of her alienation from Othello's affections, and singing it leads her to question Emilia about the nature and practice of infidelity.

# 9

# QUOTES AND ANALYSIS
# BY THEME

## APPEARANCE VERSUS REALITY

*I am not what I am. (1.1.)*

Iago utters these words in conversation with Roderigo, thereby signaling that he is not all that he appears to be. However, Iago's words also contain a deeper, more subversive message. The phrase "I am not what I am" serves as a parodic allusion to a well-known biblical quote from Exodus 3:14, in which Moses asks God his name and God offers an enigmatic response: "I am that I am." By transforming God's words into a negative formulation, Iago indicates his identity as a diabolical figure.

*The Moor is of a free and open nature*

*That thinks men honest that but seem to be so,*

*And will as tenderly be led by th' nose*

*As asses are. (1.3.)*

Iago delivers these lines in his soliloquy at the end of Act 1. He begins his speech by declaring his intention to manipulate Roderigo for his own gain. Iago then turns his attention to Othello and his hatred for the man. Much like Roderigo, who believes too readily in Iago's friendship, Othello "thinks men honest that but seem to be so." Thus, Iago intends to use Othello just as he will use Roderigo, exploiting the man's naïve belief in the reality of appearances to lead him (like a trusting donkey) to his own destruction.

*Men should be what they seem,*

*Or those that be not, would they might seem none! (3.3.)*

Iago says these words to Othello during a discussion of Cassio's trustworthiness. Given Iago's previous claims about his own deviousness, these words have an ironic ring. Iago's words are doubly ironic, in fact, since he espouses the truism not just to cover up his own treachery, but also to cause Othello to doubt Cassio's honesty. The kind of duplicity Iago demonstrates here points to his deep-rooted cynicism about the world. It also serves as a warning to the audience to remain wary of appearances.

## DECEPTION AND TREACHERY

> *Thus do I ever make my fool my purse,*
>
> *For I mine own gained knowledge should profane*
>
> *If I would time expend with such a snipe*
>
> *But for my sport and profit. (1.3.)*

Iago makes this confession to the audience immediately after he sends Roderigo off to sell his land. Although he ostensibly persuades Roderigo to amass a small fortune for his own personal advancement, Iago makes it clear here that he intends to manipulate Roderigo in such a way that he will essentially function as Iago's "purse." Iago's confession is the first moment in the play where he indicates the depth of his treachery. No one—even those apparently on his side—will be spared from his plot.

> *And, good*
>
> *lieutenant, I think you think I love you. (2.3.)*

Iago speaks to Cassio in these lines. As implied by his use of the phrase "good lieutenant," the surface meaning of these words has a positive ring. Essentially, Iago tells him, "I think you know I am your friend." However, Iago's recursive use of "think" also conceals a deceptive second meaning. To say "I think you think I love you" implies love without actually expressing it. In a single move, then, Iago both comforts Cassio and undermines his trust.

*So will I turn her virtue into pitch*

*And out of her own goodness make the net*

*That shall enmesh them all. (2.3.)*

Iago utters these lines at the end of a soliloquy in which he further develops his treacherous plot against Othello. Here, he speaks specifically of Desdemona and how he plans to turn her goodness against her. Iago uses two ill-matched metaphors. He initially wants to "turn her virtue into pitch," which is a sticky, black, tar-like substance. But in mid-sentence Iago shifts from sticky pitch to the image of a web in which he can ensnare all his enemies. Iago's treachery runs so deep that he cannot even commit to a single metaphor!

## TIMING

*How poor are they that have not patience!*

*What wound did ever heal but by degrees?*

*Thou know'st we work by wit and not by witchcraft,*

*And wit depends on dilatory time. (2.3.)*

In response to Roderigo's frustration with how slowly Iago's plot is unfolding, Iago stresses the importance of patience. Iago knows that in order for any plan to work, one must be willing to wait for the right opportunities. Being able to spot the right opportunity depends on one's wit, and wit, Iago emphasizes, "depends on dilatory time"—that is, time that moves slowly. Much like Roderigo, the audience is also subject to Iago's dilatory time. We, too, must patiently watch as his treacherous plot plays out, and the slowness of its unfolding only increases the dramatic tension.

*In happy time, Iago. (3.1.)*

Cassio utters these words upon Iago's entrance. Cassio has just asked the Clown to notify Emilia, Iago's wife, that he would like to speak with her. When Iago appears immediately after the Clown exits, Cassio tells him that he's come "in happy time"—that is, at just the right moment. Although apparently unimportant, the temporal expression Cassio uses in this line has an ironic significance, particularly given Iago's previous discussion of the importance of waiting for the right moment to act. It would seem that Iago's timing is, as always, impeccable, and his impeccable timing proves crucial to his success.

> My lord, I would I might entreat your honor
> To scan this thing no farther. Leave it to time. (3.2.)

With Othello fretting over the idea of Desdemona's betrayal and deception, Iago tells him that he should try to take his mind off the subject. As always, Iago speaks with a concealed sense of irony. He knows that telling Othello to stop thinking about Desdemona will only make him dwell on the matter with even more anxiety. Furthermore, Iago's suggestion that Othello leave the matter "to time" has a deeply sinister ring to it. Since Iago has a specific vision of how events will play out if they go according to plan, he knows precisely what crisis "time" will bring.

## JEALOUSY

> Oh, beware, my lord, of jealousy!
> It is the green-eyed monster which doth mock
> The meat it feeds on. (3.3.)

As Iago makes insinuations about Desdemona's alleged adultery and Othello pressures him to reveal what he knows, Iago warns Othello against succumbing to jealousy. Of course, Iago issues this warning with a false earnestness. That is, he knows that saying the word "jealousy" and conjuring an offensive visual image will intensify Othello's concern. Iago's anthropomorphizing of jealousy as a "green-eyed monster" is famous, and his use of the color green stems from a Renaissance belief that green was a "bilious hue," linked to an imbalance of the humors that caused fear and jealousy.

*Trifles light as air*

*Are to the jealous confirmations strong*

*As proofs of holy writ. (3.3.)*

Iago delivers these lines in a short soliloquy where he informs the audience of his plan to plant Desdemona's handkerchief in Cassio's room. Here, the handkerchief is the "trifle light as air." In itself the handkerchief signifies nothing. However, knowing that Othello's jealousy has already been ramped up, Iago predicts that he will overestimate the handkerchief's significance, taking it as a "proof of holy writ"—that is, as evidence direct from the Bible.

*But jealous souls will not be answered so.*

*They are not ever jealous for the cause,*

*But jealous for they're jealous. It is a monster*

*Begot upon itself, born on itself. (3.4.)*

Emilia says these words to Desdemona in an attempt to explain the irrational nature of jealousy. Even though jealous individuals may state specific reasons for their jealousy, jealousy has no cause but itself. In other words, jealous people are inherently jealous. Emilia signals the circularity of this logic with the confounding image of jealousy as a monster that gives birth to itself. Emilia's image recalls Iago's "green-eyed monster." It also recalls the ancient symbol of the ouroboros, which depicts a snake swallowing its own tail and therefore stuck in a self-perpetuating loop.

## JUSTICE

*Villain, be sure thou prove my love a whore;*

*Be sure of it. Give me the ocular proof,*

*Or, by the worth of mine eternal soul*

*Thou hadst been better have been born a dog*

*Than answer my waked wrath! (3.3.)*

In response to Iago's insinuations about Desdemona's infidelity, Othello demands "ocular proof"—that is, evidence that will visually confirm the allegation against his wife. Othello's emphasis on the need for Iago to "prove [his] love a whore" demonstrates his commitment to justice. However, Othello's commitment to law and reason also comes into direct conflict with his emotional and irrational response to Iago's rumormongering. This conflict disrupts Othello's otherwise black-and-white understanding of the world and leads to disastrous consequences.

> It is the cause, it is the cause, my soul.
>
> Let me not name it to you, you chaste stars,
>
> It is the cause. (5.2.)

Othello utters these words as he enters Desdemona's chambers with the intent to kill her. His refrain of "the cause, . . . the cause" indicates his need to convince himself of the justness of his planned actions. However, this refrain also recalls Emilia's words earlier in the play, where she claimed that jealous individuals "are not ever jealous for the [stated] cause." In this light, Othello's insistence on "the cause" may serve to conceal his innate jealousy and thereby subvert his commitment to legal procedure.

> O perjured woman, thou dost stone my heart,
>
> And mak'st me call what I intend to do
>
> A murder, which I thought a sacrifice. (5.2.)

Othello addresses these lines to Desdemona. His word choice here once again signals his commitment to the law. Calling Desdemona a "perjured woman," he implies that by denying the allegations against her she has lied under oath. Desdemona's supposed false testimony has dire consequences for Othello's interpretation of her death. Whereas he sees her execution as lawfully necessary and therefore "a sacrifice," if she is actually speaking the truth it would make him a murderer. The uncertainty she causes in him turns his heart to stone.

# 10

## QUOTES AND ANALYSIS
## BY CHARACTER

### OTHELLO

> *She loved me for the dangers I had passed,*
> *And I loved her that she did pity them (1.3.)*

Othello speaks these lines while explaining how Desdemona came to fall in love with him. While the other Venetians are shocked that Desdemona could love a man from a different race and background, Othello's explanation shows that he and Desdemona fell in love out of mutual admiration and respect. The quote also reveals that Othello is a charismatic and impressively articulate individual, who can charm someone with the power of his words.

> *I know, Iago,*
> *Thy honesty and love doth mince this matter (2.3.)*

Othello says this to Iago after Iago has explained to him about Cassio's involvement in a drunken brawl. Ironically, Othello assumes that Iago is being tactful and trying not to blame Cassio for what happened, whereas Iago has actually engineered the entire situation in order to get Cassio in trouble. The quote reveals Othello's blind spot where Iago is concerned, and sets the stage for how Othello's belief in Iago's integrity and honesty will lead to disaster.

> *I prithee speak to me as to thy thinkings (3.3.)*

Othello says this to Iago after starting to become suspicious about what might be happening between Desdemona and Cassio. A master manipulator, Iago plants a seed of suspicion, but then seemingly hesitates to make any direct accusations. As a result, Othello actually has to beg Iago to reveal the very suspicions that Iago is eager to pass along. The quote also shows that once Othello has begun to think about the possibility of his wife being unfaithful, he is unable to leave the idea alone.

*No, Iago, I'll see before I doubt (3.3.)*

Here, Othello asserts his faith in Desdemona and his refusal to be suspicious of her without due cause. The quote shows that Othello does love his wife and does not want to think ill of her. However, Othello's faith in Desdemona also opens the door for Iago to give Othello seeming "proof" of Desdemona's infidelity. Because Othello resists believing in Desdemona's guilt, Iago has more fuel to persuade him.

*I saw 't not, thought it not, it harmed not me (3.3.)*

Othello says this line as he rages about the torment he is experiencing now that he is suspicious of his wife's fidelity. Othello recalls the time when he was blissfully unaware of Desdemona's alleged betrayal, and, as a result, he lived in happy ignorance. Now that Iago has awakened jealousy and suspicion in him, he cannot think about anything else.

*Even so my bloody thoughts with violent pace*
*Shall ne'er look back, ne'er ebb to humble love (3.3.)*

Finally convinced that Desdemona has betrayed him, Othello vows revenge against her and Cassio. The quote shows how fully Othello's feelings toward Desdemona have changed: He now hates her as passionately as he previously loved her. The quote darkly foreshadows how Othello will be unmoved by Desdemona's insistence on her innocence and pleas for her life to be spared.

*Therefore be double damned: Swear thou art honest! (4.2.)*

Here, Othello prepares to kill Desdemona. He believes that her soul is damned because of her adultery, and the more she protests her innocence, the more enraged he becomes. The quote shows the terrible bind Desdemona is trapped in: Her attempts to speak the truth and tell her husband that she is faithful to him only make him more angry at her because he believes she is lying.

> Then must you speak
>
> Of one that loved not wisely but too well. (5.2.)

Othello says this line at the very end of the play, once he realizes that he has been tricked and deceived. At this point, all he can do is try to explain how he would like his story to be told. He specifies that he sees his downfall as his passion for Desdemona, since it ultimately made him succumb to jealousy. Had he been less in love with his wife, he would not have become as jealous.

## DESDEMONA

> I do perceive here a divided duty. (1.3.)

Desdemona says this line when she realizes that she is torn between her father and her new husband. At that time, a woman was expected to show total obedience to the male authority in her life, but Desdemona is now transitioning from loyalty to her father to loyalty to her new husband. The quote reveals that Desdemona is very much aware of, and eager to honor, social expectations that she show loyalty to her husband. This loyalty will later endanger Desdemona because she refuses to defend herself or challenge Othello's authority over her.

> Do not doubt, Cassio,
>
> But I will have my lord and you again
>
> As friendly as you were. (3.3.)

Here, Desdemona cheerfully reassures Cassio that she will bring about a reconciliation between him and Othello. The quote shows that, at this point, Desdemona feels confident in her marital relationship and sure that she can persuade her husband to share her perspective. The quote is an example of dramatic irony in that Desdemona thinks she is being kind and helpful, but has no idea that she is about to fall victim to the trap Iago has laid.

*I think the sun where he was born*

*Drew all such humors from him. (3.4.)*

Desdemona insists to Emilia that Othello is not a jealous man. She makes a playful reference to Othello's origins, suggesting that the sun in his native land made him impervious to jealousy, and therefore he is an exception to the typical Venetian tendency to be suspicious of women's behavior. The quote shows Desdemona's naïve and trusting nature, since she does not realize just how jealous her husband is capable of being.

*His unkindness may defeat my life*

*But never taint my love. (4.2.)*

Desdemona says this line to Emilia and Iago as she explains how she will remain faithful and loving to Othello, even if he insists on accusing her of infidelity. Desdemona swears she would love him even if his mistreatment were responsible for her death, but we don't know how seriously she takes this possibility. It seems most likely that she still clings to the belief that she can persuade Othello of her innocence, and does not yet understand how much danger she is in.

*Beshrew me if I would do such a wrong*

*For the whole world. (4.3.)*

Desdemona explains to Emilia that she would never consider being unfaithful, no matter what the circumstances. The quote shows that Desdemona is so virtuous that she cannot even understand why a woman would betray her husband. Desdemona's innocence is part of her undoing because she never stops to think about how her behavior might appear to someone who is viewing it with suspicion. Instead, she assumes that everyone will recognize her integrity and purity.

*Kill me tomorrow—let me live tonight! (5.2.)*

Here, Desdemona pleads for her life in the moments before Othello kills her. Desdemona only comes to understand her husband's murderous intentions at the last instant, because she cannot believe he would actually harm her. Even when Desdemona does speak out, she seems to accept that Othello has the right to kill her if he wants to. She doesn't ask that her life be spared, but only that her death be delayed.

## IAGO

*I follow him to serve my turn upon him. (1.1.)*

Iago says this to Roderigo at the start of the play as he explains that he secretly hates Othello and is plotting against him. Although everyone, including Othello, believes that Iago is a loyal and devoted friend, Iago understands the strategic advantage that false friendship gives him. As a trusted confidant, he is able to sway Othello's opinion and manipulate him much more effectively than if he were not so trusted. The quote shows that from the moment the action begins, Iago is already looking for ways to bring about Othello's downfall.

*If thou canst cuckold him, thou dost thyself a pleasure,*

*me a sport. (1.3.)*

Here Iago explains how Roderigo can help him. He knows that Roderigo lusts after Desdemona and is angry to learn that she married Othello. Iago encourages Roderigo to believe that by participating in Iago's plot, he might have the chance to have an affair with Desdemona.

*It is thought abroad that 'twixt my sheets*

*He's done my office. (1.3.)*

This quote is one of the few moments where Iago explains his possible motivation for being obsessed with destroying Othello.

He claims that there are rumors Othello has had an affair with Emilia, which would be a plausible reason for wanting to destroy Othello's trust in his own wife. However, Iago only mentions this motivation very briefly, and it does not seem to fully explain the depth of his hatred toward Othello.

*She did deceive her father, marrying you (3.3.)*

Iago makes this comment to Othello as a way of refuting Othello's insistence that Desdemona is honest and would not lie to him. He points out that Desdemona demonstrably has the capacity to lie and keep secrets, since she hid her courtship with Othello from her disapproving father. This quote shows Iago's skill at psychological manipulation: He subtly plants a seed of doubt in Othello's mind, using the couple's own love as a weapon to increase the distrust between them.

*Strangle her in her bed, even the bed she hath*

*contaminated. (4.1.)*

Here Iago orchestrates even the way in which Desdemona will be killed. The quote shows Iago's desire to control every aspect of how his plan will unfold, and also his sinister sense of poetic justice. He argues that since Desdemona has committed her crimes in bed, by sleeping with other men, she should also die in bed. The quote also reinforces the fact that Iago has complete control over Othello at this point, since Othello immediately agrees to the gruesome plan.

## CASSIO

*'Tis my breeding*

*That gives me this bold show of courtesy. (2.1.)*

Cassio makes this comment to Iago after greeting Emilia with a kiss. He intends to signal that he did not mean any disrespect by kissing another man's wife, but that this sort of behavior is simply part of the good manners he is used to displaying. He might also be commenting on manners in his native Florence being different from what would be expected in Venice. The quote is significant because it shows how Cassio's gallant and possibly even flirtatious behavior could be open to misinterpretation, a weakness Iago will later exploit.

*An inviting eye, and yet methinks right modest. (2.3.)*

Cassio compliments Desdemona to Iago as the two men praise Desdemona's beauty. Iago seems to be trying to get a read on Cassio's feelings about Desdemona by encouraging him to praise her. Cassio certainly acknowledges her beauty, but his comments remain respectful and he notes that Desdemona is a virtuous and loyal woman, who always behaves appropriately. The quote shows that Cassio is not looking to make trouble in anyone's marriage or cause problems for Desdemona.

*I have very poor and unhappy brains for drinking. (2.3.)*

Here Cassio explains to Iago why he needs to carefully moderate how much alcohol he consumes, since he has a weak tolerance and rapidly becomes very inebriated. Cassio thinks Iago is a trusted friend who will look after him and make sure he does not get into trouble. Iago, however, deliberately uses this information against Cassio, getting him very drunk and setting him up to be involved in a fight.

*Oh, I have lost my reputation! I have lost the immortal part of myself, and what remains is bestial. (2.3.)*

Cassio says these lines in shame and sadness after Othello has angrily chastised him and stripped him of his position. Although not physically hurt, Cassio knows that he has lost his good reputation and the respect of Othello, both of which pain him. The quote shows how much value Cassio places on his honor and good name, and how he would never willingly do something shameful.

## EMILIA

> *What he will do with it,*
>
> *Heaven knows, not I. (3.3.)*

Emilia says this line after she picks up the handkerchief Desdemona has dropped, planning to turn it over to Iago. This quote shows that Emilia at this point feels little moral responsibility, and, in fact, might prefer not to know the details of what her husband is plotting. Later in the play, she will be devastated to realize how her action contributed to a chain of events culminating in Desdemona's death.

> *'Tis not a year or two shows us a man. (3.4.)*

Emilia explains to Desdemona that her friend is only newly married and may not yet understand her husband's true nature. The quote suggests that Emilia has only gradually learned who Iago truly is, and that she is trying to encourage her friend to be more cautious and less naïve.

> *They are not ever jealous for the cause,*
>
> *But jealous for they're jealous. (3.4.)*

Here, Emilia and Desdemona argue about whether Othello will ever believe in Desdemona's innocence. Desdemona thinks she can prove her fidelity to her husband, but Emilia is more cynical and contends that now that Othello has become suspicious, he will never be able to fully trust his wife again. Emilia's insight might come from her less-happy relationship, but it turns out to be true.

> *If any wretch have put this in your head*
>
> *Let heaven requite it with the serpent's curse (4.2.)*

Here, Emilia chastises Othello for doubting Desdemona's fidelity. Ironically, Emilia immediately hits upon the truth that Othello's suspicions result from someone else planting these ideas. However, she has no idea that it is actually her own husband who is the person she curses here. The quote reflects the important theme of deception, showing that even married couples may not know all that much about their spouse's true character.

# 11

# WHAT DOES
# THE ENDING MEAN?

THE PLAY ENDS IN A SPECTACLE OF TRAGIC VIOLENCE: Emilia intercepts Othello after he's murdered Desdemona and reveals Iago's treachery. Her revelation is corroborated by information from Cassio and a letter found in Roderigo's pocket. In a vain attempt to prevent his scheme from being revealed, Iago stabs and kills Emilia, and is then taken prisoner while Othello, lamenting the loss of his wife, kills himself next to her. Notably, Iago is left wounded but alive at the end of the play. Cassio is charged with determining Iago's punishment, and urges "the time, the place, the torture. Oh, enforce it" (5.2.). The ending symbolizes the culmination of the violent forces put in motion by Iago at the start of the play. He aimed at "practicing upon [Othello's] peace and quiet / Even to madness" (2.1). Iago has been so successful that Othello feels compelled to kill himself, explaining that "I kissed thee ere I killed thee. No way but this, / Killing myself, to die upon a kiss" (5.2). Not only has Othello murdered his beloved wife, he also has to face the horrible truth that his suspicions about her infidelity were completely unfounded.

Othello's suicide serves as a kind of trial in which he decides on and carries out a punishment for his crime of killing Desdemona. In his final speech, he explains how he hopes to be remembered, saying, "When you shall these unlucky deeds relate, / Speak of me as I am" (5.2.). Perhaps because he knows he has never been fully accepted by Venetian society, and that they will be quick to twist his reputation into that of a barbaric killer, Othello spends his final moments reminding his audience of the ways he has faithfully served Venice. Immediately before he stabs himself, Othello draws a comparison to how he killed "a malignant and a turbaned Turk . . . the circumcisèd dog" (5.2.). The comparison might suggest that Othello, as a result of his crimes, now sees himself as an outcast who deserves to die in the same way, or it might imply that by voluntarily punishing himself for his crimes, he acts in a way that is consistent with his previous military valor. Either way, Othello asserts an autonomy and control over his destiny that contrasts sharply with the way he has been manipulated throughout most of the play.

# 12

## HOW TO WRITE
## LITERARY ANALYSIS

WHEN YOU READ FOR PLEASURE, your only goal is enjoyment. You might find yourself reading to get caught up in an exciting story, to learn about an interesting time or place, or just to pass the time. Maybe you're looking for inspiration, guidance, or a reflection of your own life. There are as many different, valid ways of reading a book as there are books in the world.

When you read a work of literature in an English class, however, you're being asked to read in a special way: you're being asked to perform *literary analysis*. To analyze something means to break it down into smaller parts and then examine how those parts work, both individually and together. Literary analysis involves examining all the parts of a novel, play, short story, or poem—elements such as character, setting, tone, and imagery—and thinking about how the author uses those elements to create certain effects.

## A LITERARY ESSAY IS NOT A BOOK REVIEW

You're not being asked whether or not you liked a book or whether you'd recommend it to another reader. A literary essay also isn't like the kind of book report you wrote when you were younger, where your teacher wanted you to summarize the book's action. A high school- or college-level literary essay asks, "How does this piece of literature actually work?" "How does it do what it does?" and, "Why might the author have made the choices he or she did?"

## The Seven Steps

No one is born knowing how to analyze literature; it's a skill you learn and a process you can master. As you gain more practice with this kind of thinking and writing, you'll be able to craft a method that works best for you. But until then, here are seven basic steps to writing a well-constructed literary essay:

1. Ask questions

2. Collect evidence

3. Construct a thesis

4. Develop and organize arguments

5. Write the introduction

6. Write the body paragraphs

7. Write the conclusion

## 1. ASK QUESTIONS

When you're assigned a literary essay in class, your teacher will often provide you with a list of writing prompts. Lucky you! Now all you have to do is choose one. Do yourself a favor and pick a topic that interests you. You'll have a much better (not to mention easier) time if you start off with something you enjoy thinking about. If you are asked to come up with a topic by yourself, though, you might start to feel a little panicked. Maybe you have too many ideas—or none at all. Don't worry. Take a deep breath and start by asking yourself these questions:

> **What struck you?** Did a particular image, line, or scene linger in your mind for a long time? If it fascinated you, chances are you can draw on it to write a fascinating essay.

**What confused you?** Maybe you were surprised to
see a character act in a certain way, or maybe you didn't
understand why the book ended the way it did. Confusing
moments in a work of literature are like a loose thread in a
sweater: if you pull on it, you can unravel the entire thing.
Ask yourself why the author chose to write about that
character or scene the way he or she did and you might tap
into some important insights about the work as a whole.

**Did you notice any patterns?** Is there a phrase that the
main character uses constantly or an image that repeats
throughout the book? If you can figure out how that pattern
weaves through the work and what the significance of that
pattern is, you've almost got your entire essay mapped out.

**Did you notice any contradictions or ironies?** Great works
of literature are complex; great literary essays recognize and
explain those complexities. Maybe the title totally disagrees
with the book's subject matter. Maybe the main character
acts one way around his family and a completely different
way around his friends and associates. If you can find a way to
explain a work's contradictory elements, you've got the seeds
of a great essay.

At this point, you don't need to know exactly what you're
going to say about your topic; you just need a place to begin your
exploration. You can help direct your reading and brainstorming
by formulating your topic as a *question,* which you'll then try to
answer in your essay. The best questions invite critical debates
and discussions, not just a rehashing of the summary. Remember, you're looking for something you can *prove* or *argue* based on
evidence you find in the text. Finally, remember to keep the scope
of your question in mind. Is this a topic you can adequately address
within the word or page limit you've been given? Conversely, is
this a topic big enough to fill the required length?

### GOOD QUESTIONS

> *"Are Romeo and Juliet's parents responsible for the deaths of their children?"*

> *"Why doesn't Hamlet kill Claudius right away?"*

> *"Is Lady Macbeth a villain or a victim?"*

### BAD QUESTIONS

> *"What happens to Nick Bottom in* A Midsummer Night's Dream*?"*

> *"What do the other characters in* Julius Caesar *think about Caesar?"*

> *"How does Iago remind me of my brother?"*

## 2.   COLLECT EVIDENCE

Once you know what question you want to answer, it's time to scour the book for things that will help you answer it. Don't worry if you don't know what you want to say yet—right now you're just collecting ideas and material and letting it all percolate. Keep track of passages, symbols, images, or scenes that deal with your topic. Eventually, you'll start making connections between these examples, and your thesis will emerge.

Here's a brief summary of the various parts that compose each and every work of literature. These are the elements that you will analyze in your essay, and that you will offer as evidence to support your arguments.

## ELEMENTS OF STORY

These are the *whats* of the work—what happens, where it happens, and to whom it happens.

**Plot:** All of the events and actions of the work.

**Character:** The people who act and are acted upon in a literary work. The main character of a work is known as the *protagonist*.

**Conflict:** The central tension in the work. In most cases, the protagonist wants something, while opposing forces (antagonists) hinder the protagonist's progress.

**Setting:** When and where the work takes place. Elements of setting include location, time period, time of day, weather, social atmosphere, and economic conditions.

**Narrator:** The person telling the story. The narrator may straightforwardly report what happens, convey the subjective opinions and perceptions of one or more characters, or provide commentary and opinion in his or her own voice.

**Themes:** The main idea or message of the work—usually an abstract idea about people, society, or life in general. A work may have many themes, which may be in conflict with one another.

## ELEMENTS OF STYLE

These are the *hows*—how the characters speak, how the story is constructed, and how language is used throughout the work.

**Structure and organization:** *How the parts of the work are assembled.* Some novels are narrated in a linear, chronological fashion, while others skip around in time. Some plays follow a traditional three- or five-act structure, while others are a series of loosely connected scenes. Some authors deliberately leave gaps in their works, leaving readers to puzzle out the missing information. A work's structure and organization can tell you a lot about the kind of message it wants to convey.

**Point of view:** *The perspective from which a story is told.* In *first-person point of view*, the narrator involves him- or herself in the story. ("I went to the store"; "We watched in horror as the bird slammed into the window.") A first-person narrator is usually the protagonist of the work, but not always. In *third-person point of view*, the narrator does not participate in the story. A third-person narrator may closely follow a specific character, recounting that individual character's thoughts or experiences, or it may be what we call an *omniscient* narrator. Omniscient narrators see and know all: they can witness any event in any time or place and are privy to the inner thoughts and feelings of all characters. Remember that the narrator and the author are not the same thing!

**Diction:** *Word choice.* Whether a character uses dry, clinical language or flowery prose with lots of exclamation points can tell you a lot about his or her attitude and personality.

**Syntax:** *Word order and sentence construction.* Syntax is a crucial part of establishing an author's narrative voice. Shakespeare, for example, is known for writing in iambic pentameter, intermingling prose and verse, and scrambling the usual word order of a sentence.

**Tone:** *The mood or feeling of the text.* Diction and syntax often contribute to the tone of a work. A novel written in short, clipped sentences that use small, simple words might feel brusque, cold, or matter-of-fact.

**Imagery:** *Language that appeals to the senses;* representing things that can be seen, smelled, heard, tasted, or touched.

**Figurative language:** *Language that is not meant to be interpreted literally.* The most common types of figurative language are *metaphors* and *similes*, which compare two unlike things in order to suggest a similarity between them —for example, *"All the world's a stage,"* or *"I'll warrant him, as gentle as a lamb."* (Metaphors say one thing is another thing; similes claim that one thing is *like* another thing.)

## 3.   CONSTRUCT A THESIS

When you've examined all the evidence you've collected and know how you want to answer the question, it's time to write your thesis statement. A *thesis* is a claim about a work of literature that needs to be supported by evidence and arguments. The thesis statement is the heart of the literary essay, and the bulk of your essay will be spent trying to prove this claim. A good thesis will be:

> **Arguable.** *"Julius Caesar* describes the political turmoil in Rome after the murder of Julius Caesar" isn't a thesis—it's a fact.

> **Provable through textual evidence.** *"Hamlet* is a confusing but ultimately very well-written play" is a weak thesis because it offers the writer's personal opinion about the book. Yes, it's arguable, but it's not a claim that can be proved or supported with examples taken from the play itself.

> **Surprising.** "Viola changes a great deal in *Twelfth Night"* is a weak thesis because it's obvious. A really strong thesis will argue for a reading of the text that is not immediately apparent.

> **Specific.** "The relationships in *A Midsummer Night's Dream* tell us a lot about the fickle nature of romance" is almost a good thesis statement, but it's still too vague. What does the writer mean by "a lot"? How do the relationships tell us about the fickle nature of romance?

## GOOD THESIS STATEMENTS

**Question:** In *Romeo and Juliet*, which is more powerful in shaping the lovers' story: fate or foolishness?

**Thesis:** "Though Shakespeare defines Romeo and Juliet as 'star-crossed lovers' and images of stars and planets appear throughout the play, a closer examination of that celestial imagery reveals that the stars are merely witnesses to the characters' foolish activities and not the causes themselves."

**Question:** Does Hamlet's misogyny prove his madness?

**Thesis:** "Hamlet's misogynistic behavior toward Gertrude and Ophelia can be seen as evidence that he really is going mad, because these scenes have little to do with his quest for justice, and yet they seem to provoke his strongest feelings. We see little evidence in the play that either Gertrude or Ophelia is guilty of any wrongdoing, yet he treats them both with paranoia and cruelty, suggesting that Hamlet has lost the ability to accurately interpret other people's motivations."

**Question:** How does blood function as a symbol in *Macbeth*?

**Thesis:** "Once Macbeth and Lady Macbeth embark on their murderous journey, blood comes to symbolize their guilt, and they begin to feel that their crimes have stained them in a way that cannot be washed clean. Blood becomes a permanent stain on the consciences of both characters, and it plagues them throughout life."

## 4. DEVELOP AND ORGANIZE ARGUMENTS

The reasons and examples that support your thesis will form the middle paragraphs of your essay. Since you can't really write your thesis statement until you know how you'll structure your argument, you'll probably end up working on steps 3 and 4 at the same time.

There's no single method of argumentation that will work in every context. One essay prompt might ask you to compare and contrast two characters, while another asks you to trace an image through a given work of literature. These questions require different kinds of answers and therefore different kinds of arguments. Below, we'll discuss three common kinds of essay prompts and some strategies for constructing a solid, well-argued case.

## TYPES OF LITERARY ESSAYS
### Compare and contrast

*Compare and contrast the characters of King Lear and Gloucester in* King Lear.

Chances are you've written this kind of essay before. In an academic literary context, you'll organize your arguments the same way you would in any other class. You can either go *subject by subject* or *point by point*. In the former, you'll discuss one character first and then the second. In the latter, you'll choose several traits (attitude toward life, social status, images and metaphors associated with the character) and devote a paragraph to each. You may want to use a mix of these two approaches—for example, you may want to spend a paragraph apiece broadly sketching King Lear's and Gloucester's personalities before transitioning into a paragraph or two describing a few key points of comparison. This can be a highly effective strategy if you want to make a counterintuitive argument—that, despite seeming to be totally different, the two objects being compared are actually similar in a very important way (or vice versa). Remember that your essay should reveal something fresh or unexpected about the text, so think beyond the obvious parallels and differences.

## Trace

*Choose an image—for example, birds, knives, or eyes—and trace that image throughout* Macbeth.

Sounds pretty easy, right? All you need to do is read the play, underline every appearance of a knife in *Macbeth*, and then list them in your essay in the order they appear, right? Well, not exactly. Your teacher doesn't want a simple catalog of examples. He or she wants to see you make *connections* between those examples—that's the difference between summarizing and analyzing. In the *Macbeth* example above, think about the different contexts in which knives appear in the play and to what effect. In *Macbeth*, there are real knives and imagined knives; knives that kill and knives that simply threaten. Categorize and classify your examples to give them some order. Finally, always keep the overall effect in mind. After you choose and analyze your examples, you should come to some greater understanding about the work, as well as your chosen image, symbol, or phrase's role in developing the major themes and stylistic strategies of that work.

## Debate

*Does Iago in* Othello *hate women?*

In this kind of essay, you're being asked to debate a moral, ethical, or aesthetic issue regarding the work. You might be asked to judge a character or group of characters (*Is Caesar responsible for his own demise?*) or the work itself (*Is Romeo and Juliet a feminist play?*). For this kind of essay, there are two important points to keep in mind. First, don't simply base your arguments on your personal feelings and reactions. Every literary essay expects you to read and analyze the work, so search for evidence in the text. What does Iago have to say about women in *Othello*? How does Iago treat women in *Othello*? As in any debate, you also need to make sure that you define all the necessary terms before you begin to argue your case.

What does it mean to hate a whole gender? What makes a play feminist? You should define your terms right up front, in the first paragraph after your introduction.

Second, remember that strong literary essays make contrary and surprising arguments. Try to think outside the box. In the *Othello* example above, it seems like the obvious answer would be yes, Iago hates women. But can you think of any arguments for the opposite side? Even if your final assertion is that the play depicts an angry, misogynistic man who distrusts women, acknowledging and responding to the counterargument will strengthen your overall case.

## 5. WRITE THE INTRODUCTION

*Your introduction sets up the entire essay.* It's where you present your topic and articulate the particular issues and questions you'll be addressing. It's also where you, as the writer, introduce yourself to your readers. A persuasive literary essay immediately establishes its writer as a knowledgeable, authoritative figure.

An introduction can vary in length depending on the overall length of the essay, but in a traditional five-paragraph essay it should be no longer than one paragraph. However long it is, your introduction needs to:

**Provide any necessary context.** Your introduction should situate the reader and let him or her know what to expect. What book are you discussing? Which characters? What topic will you be addressing?

**Answer the "So what?" question.** Why is this topic important, and why is your particular position on the topic noteworthy? Ideally, your introduction should pique the reader's interest by suggesting how your argument is surprising or otherwise counterintuitive. Literary essays make unexpected connections and reveal less-than-obvious truths.

**Present your thesis.** This usually happens at or very near the end of your introduction.

**Indicate the shape of the essay to come.** Your reader should finish reading your introduction with a good sense of the scope of your essay as well as the path you'll take toward proving your thesis. You don't need to spell out every step, but you do need to suggest the organizational pattern you'll be using.

## Your introduction should not:

**Be vague.** Beware of the two killer words in literary analysis: *interesting* and *important*. Of course the work, question, or example is interesting and important—that's why you're writing about it!

**Open with any grandiose assertions.** Many student readers think that beginning their essays with a flamboyant statement such as "Since the dawn of time, writers have been fascinated with the topic of free will" makes them sound important and commanding. You know what? It actually sounds pretty amateurish.

**Wildly praise the work.** Another typical mistake student writers make is extolling the work or author. Your teacher doesn't need to be told that "Shakespeare is perhaps the greatest writer in the English language." You can mention a work's reputation in passing—by referring to *Romeo and Juliet* as "Shakespeare's enduring classic," for example— but don't make a point of bringing it up unless that reputation is key to your argument.

**Go off-topic.** Keep your introduction streamlined and to the point. Don't feel the need to throw in all kinds of bells and whistles in order to impress your reader—just get to the point as quickly as you can without skimping on any of the required steps.

## 6. WRITE THE BODY PARAGRAPHS

Once you've written your introduction, you'll take the arguments you developed in step 4 and turn them into your body paragraphs. The organization of this middle section of your essay will largely be determined by the argumentative strategy you use, but no matter how you arrange your thoughts, your body paragraphs need to do the following:

**Begin with a strong topic sentence.** Topic sentences are like signs on a highway: they tell the readers where they are and where they're going. A good topic sentence not only alerts readers to what issue will be discussed in the following paragraph but also gives them a sense of what argument will be made about that issue. "Jealousy plays an important role in *A Midsummer Night's Dream*" isn't a strong topic sentence because it doesn't tell us very much. "Jealousy plays out most obviously among the quartet of Athenian lovers, who find themselves in an increasingly tangled knot of misaligned desire" is a much stronger topic sentence—it not only tells us what the paragraph will discuss (jealousy) but how the paragraph will discuss the topic (by showing how jealousy creates a set of conditions that leads to the play's climactic action).

**Fully and completely develop a single thought.** Don't skip around in your paragraph or try to stuff in too much material. Body paragraphs are like bricks: each individual one needs to be strong and sturdy or else the entire structure will collapse. Make sure you have really proven your point before moving on to the next one.

**Use transitions effectively.** Good literary essay writers know that each paragraph must be clearly and strongly linked to the material around it. Think of each paragraph as a response to the one that precedes it. Use transition words and phrases such as *however, similarly, on the contrary, therefore,* and *furthermore* to indicate what kind of response you're making.

## 7. WRITE THE CONCLUSION

Just as you used the introduction to ground your readers in the topic before providing your thesis, you'll use the conclusion to quickly summarize the specifics learned thus far and then hint at the broader implications of your topic. A good conclusion will:

**Do more than simply restate the thesis.** If your thesis argued that *The Merchant of Venice* can be read as a study of religious differences, don't simply end your essay by saying, "And that is why *The Merchant of Venice* can be read as a study of religious differences." If you've constructed your arguments well, this kind of statement will just be redundant.

**Synthesize the arguments, not summarize them.** Similarly, don't repeat the details of your body paragraphs in your conclusion. The readers have already read your essay, and chances are it's not so long that they've forgotten all your points by now.

**Revisit the "So what?" question.** In your introduction, you made a case for why your topic and position were important. You should close your essay with the same sort of gesture. What do your readers know now that they didn't know before? How will that knowledge help them better appreciate or understand the work overall?

**Move from the specific to the general.** Your essay has most likely treated a very specific element of the work—a single character, a small set of images, or a particular passage. In your conclusion, try to show how this narrow discussion has wider implications for the work overall. If your essay on *The Tempest* focused on the character of Prospero, for example, you might want to include a bit in your conclusion about how he fits into the play's larger message about power, humanity, or the pursuit of knowledge.

**Stay relevant.** Your conclusion should suggest new directions of thought, but it shouldn't be treated as an opportunity to pad your essay with all the extra, interesting ideas you came up with during your brainstorming sessions but couldn't fit into the essay proper. Don't attempt to stuff in unrelated queries or too many abstract thoughts.

**Avoid making overblown closing statements.** A conclusion should open up your highly specific, focused discussion, but it should do so without drawing a sweeping lesson about life or human nature. Making such observations may be part of the point of reading, but it's almost always a mistake in essays, where these observations tend to sound overly dramatic or simply silly.

## A+ ESSAY CHECKLIST

*Congratulations!* If you've followed all the steps we've outlined above, you should have a solid literary essay to show for all your efforts. What if you've got your sights set on an A+? To write the kind of superlative essay that will be rewarded with a perfect grade, keep the following rubric in mind. These are the qualities that teachers expect to see in a truly A+ essay. How does yours stack up?

- Demonstrates a thorough understanding of the book
- Presents an original, compelling argument
- Thoughtfully analyzes the text's formal elements
- Uses appropriate and insightful examples
- Structures ideas in a logical and progressive order
- Demonstrates a mastery of sentence construction, transitions, grammar, spelling, and word choice

## SUGGESTED ESSAY TOPICS

1. Discuss the importance of setting in the play, noting in particular physical details that differentiate Venice from Cyprus and that define the specific character of each location as it pertains to the plot of the play.

2. Discuss the role of Emilia. How does her character change during the course of the play? Pay particular attention to moments when Emilia decides to be silent and when she decides to speak. What is the effect of her silence about the handkerchief? Do we forgive this silence when she insists on speaking in spite of Iago's threats in the final scene?

3. Do a close reading of one of Iago's soliloquies. Point to moments in the language where Iago most gains sympathy and moments where he most repels it. Examine how Iago develops arguments about what he must and/or will do. To what extent are these arguments convincing? If they are convincing and an audience's perception of Iago is sympathetic, what happens to its perception of Othello?

4. Analyze one or more of the play's bizarre comic scenes: the banter between Iago and Desdemona in Act 2, scene 1; the drinking song in Act 2, scene 3; the clown scenes (Act 3, scenes 1 and 4). How do these scenes echo, reflect, distort, or comment on the more serious matter of the play?

## A+ STUDENT ESSAY

*Discuss the role that race plays in Shakespeare's portrayal of Othello.*

### HOW DO THE OTHER CHARACTERS REACT TO OTHELLO'S SKIN COLOR OR TO THE FACT THAT HE IS A MOOR? HOW DOES OTHELLO SEE HIMSELF?

Othello incurs resentment for many reasons. He is from a land that Venetians consider exotic and mysterious, he has had daring adventures, and his military accomplishments far exceed those of the men around him. The most visible indicator of his outsider status is also the one that provokes the most poisonous responses: Othello is a black man in white Venice. Whenever characters such as Iago feel jealousy, fear, or simple hatred toward Othello, they give vent to their feelings by using racist slurs. For much of the play, Othello resists, ignores, or seems indifferent to the racism that dogs him. But eventually he internalizes Iago's and others' idea that his blackness makes him barbarous. This belief, as much as his conviction of Desdemona's guilt, prompts Othello to kill his wife. When he turns the race weapon against himself, he dooms both himself and Desdemona.

Among Iago's many repulsive qualities, his eagerness to hurl racial epithets is perhaps the most despicable. In an attempt to enlist Brabanzio in his anti-Othello campaign, Iago refers to the general as "the Moor," "the devil," and "a Barbary horse." These terms reduce Othello to a crude stereotype, turning him into a villain and an animal. When Iago tells Brabanzio that "an old black ram / Is tupping your white ewe," he demeans a passionate and loving relationship between two intelligent adults by characterizing Othello as a mindless rutting animal who has soiled the pure Desdemona with his lust. Iago hopes to disgust Brabanzio with this animal imagery and with the contrast between Othello's blackness and Desdemona's whiteness.

Like Iago, other Venetians resort to racial slurs to deal with their own feelings of inferiority or powerlessness.

Roderigo, on the defensive and trying to present himself and Iago as a unified front, casually refers to Othello as "the Thick-lips." This epithet is both an attempt to undermine Othello's military achievements with a cheap stereotype as well as a way to pit Roderigo and Iago's physical similarity against Othello's unfamiliar appearance. Brabanzio, outraged at his daughter's elopement, expresses disbelief that Desdemona could shun the curly-haired young men of Venice in favor of Othello's "sooty bosom." Brabanzio channels his own insecurity about his daughter's loyalty to him by expressing sneering disgust about Othello's race, implying that Othello's blackness is a dirty coating that threatens to soil Desdemona's purity.

While Othello is barraged by racism, he manages to resist its pull for some time. But in Act 4, he crumbles. Othello discusses his race throughout the play—usually in response to something a white Venetian says—but here he makes his first negative reference to it, suggesting that perhaps his blackness is to blame for his lack of conversational ability. It is a quiet moment, but a hugely significant one. It marks a turning point: Othello has fallen victim to the same racist logic (or illogic) that rules the thinking of people such as Iago and Roderigo. Like those men, Othello wants to place the blame for his feelings of inferiority somewhere else and winds up laying that blame not where it belongs (in this case, at Iago's feet), but on his own skin. The floodgates have opened, and now Othello is in danger of believing all of Iago's racist nonsense. In the next lines, Othello compares himself to a toad living in a dungeon, as if he had begun to suspect that his blackness made him a loathsome animal, somehow less than human.

Only when Othello buys into the absurd idea that his race inherently makes him dangerous does he begin to creep toward the possibility of doing violence to his wife. When he sees himself through society's eyes, as a barbaric interloper, Othello begins to despise himself, and it is that self-hatred that allows him to kill what he loves the most.

# GLOSSARY OF LITERARY TERMS

### Antagonist
The entity that acts to frustrate the goals of the protagonist. The antagonist is usually another character but may also be a non-human force.

### Antihero / Antiheroine
A protagonist who is not admirable or who challenges notions of what should be considered admirable.

### Character
A person, animal, or any other thing with a personality that appears in a narrative.

### Climax
The moment of greatest intensity in a text or the major turning point in the plot.

### Conflict
The central struggle that moves the plot forward. The conflict can be the protagonist's struggle against fate, nature, society, or another person.

### First-person point of view
A literary style in which the narrator tells the story from his or her own point of view and refers to himself or herself as "I." The narrator may be an active participant in the story or just an observer.

### Hero / Heroine
The principal character in a literary work or narrative.

### Imagery
Language that brings to mind sense-impressions, representing things that can be seen, smelled, heard, tasted, or touched.

### Motif
A recurring idea, structure, contrast, or device that develops or informs the major themes of a work of literature.

## Narrative
A story.

## Narrator
The person (sometimes a character) who tells a story; the voice assumed by the writer. The narrator and the author of the work of literature are not the same person.

## Plot
The arrangement of the events in a story, including the sequence in which they are told, the relative emphasis they are given, and the causal connections between events.

## Point of View
The perspective that a narrative takes toward the events it describes.

## Protagonist
The main character around whom the story revolves.

## Setting
The location of a narrative in time and space. Setting creates mood or atmosphere.

## Subplot
A secondary plot that is of less importance to the overall story but that may serve as a point of contrast or comparison to the main plot.

## Symbol
An object, character, figure, or color that is used to represent an abstract idea or concept. Unlike an emblem, a symbol may have different meanings in different contexts.

## Syntax
The way the words in a piece of writing are put together to form lines, phrases, or clauses; the basic structure of a piece of writing.

## Theme
A fundamental and universal idea explored in a literary work.

STUDY GUIDE

### Tone

The author's attitude toward the subject or characters of a story or poem or toward the reader.

### Voice

An author's individual way of using language to reflect his or her own personality and attitudes. An author communicates voice through tone, diction, and syntax.

---

## A NOTE ON PLAGIARISM

*Plagiarism*—presenting someone else's work as your own—rears its ugly head in many forms. Many students know that copying text without citing it is unacceptable. But some don't realize that even if you're not quoting directly, but instead are paraphrasing or summarizing, it is plagiarism unless you cite the source.

### HERE ARE THE MOST COMMON FORMS OF PLAGIARISM:

- Using an author's phrases, sentences, or paragraphs without citing the source

- Paraphrasing an author's ideas without citing the source

- Passing off another student's work as your own

### HOW DO YOU STEER CLEAR OF PLAGIARISM?

- You should always acknowledge all words and ideas that aren't your own by using quotation marks around verbatim text or citations like footnotes and end-notes to note another writer's ideas.

- For more information on how to give credit when credit is due, ask your teacher for guidance or visit www.sparknotes.com.

**NOTES**